HENRY V

HENRY V

The Cautious Conqueror

MARGARET
WADE LABARGE

STEIN AND DAY / *Publishers* / New York

To My Children

First published in the United States of America, 1976
Copyright © 1975 by Margaret Wade Labarge
All rights reserved
Printed in the United States of America
Stein and Day/*Publishers*/Scarborough House,
Briarcliff Manor, N.Y. 10510

Library of Congress Cataloging in Publication Data

Labarge, Margaret Wade.
King Henry V.

1.   Henry V, King of England, 1387-1422.
2.   Great Britain—History—Henry V, 1413-1422.
I.   Title.
DA256.L3   942.04′2′0924 [B]   75-15238
ISBN 0-8128-1869-5

Contents

LIST OF ILLUSTRATIONS   vii

ACKNOWLEDGMENTS   viii

INTRODUCTION   ix

CHAPTER I   *Cousin to the King*   I

CHAPTER II   *Prince of Wales*   II

CHAPTER III   *Apprenticeship to Power*   28

CHAPTER IV   *Crowned King : Rebellion and Heresy*   41

CHAPTER V   *Preparations for War : Diplomatic*
                 Manoeuvres   52

CHAPTER VI   *Preparations for War : Military*
                 Organisation   65

CHAPTER VII   *First Expedition to France*   78

CHAPTER VIII   *The King, the English Church, and the*
                 Council of Constance   94

CHAPTER IX   *Once More to France*   108

CHAPTER X   *The Conquest of Lower Normandy*   123

CHAPTER XI   *The Capture of Rouen*   134

CHAPTER XII   *The Road to Troyes*   144

CHAPTER XIII   *Heir and Regent of France*   158

CHAPTER XIV   *The Last Campaign*   172

EPILOGUE   186

THE NARRATIVE SOURCES   191

ABBREVIATIONS USED IN NOTES   195

NOTES   197

BIBLIOGRAPHY   207

INDEX   209

List of Illustrations

Between pp. 96 and 97

Henry V (*By permission of the Provost and Fellows of Eton College; photo-graph: Courtauld Institute*)

Hoccleve presenting the *De Regimine Principum* to Prince Henry (*British Library*)

Christine de Pisan with Minerva (*British Library*)

St George and the Garter King-of-Arms (*British Library*)

Charles of Orléans in the Tower (*British Library*)

The siege of Rouen (*British Library*)

An Arbalétrier and an Estradiot (*Mary Evans Picture Library*)

A fifteenth-century siege catapult (*Mary Evans Picture Library*)

Tournament or tilting helms (*Mary Evans Picture Library*)

The tomb of Henry V (*By kind permission of Westminster Abbey; photo-graph: P. T. O'Rourke*)

Map (p. 80)
Northern France, 1415–1422

Acknowledgments

The writing of a book such as this would not be possible without the help and hospitality of many libraries and librarians, both in Canada and abroad, and the advice, suggestions, and specialised scholarship of those authorities who have kindly answered my queries and shared their knowledge. I am particularly grateful for the generous assistance of Mlle Regine Pernoud of the Archives Nationales, as well as to Colonel Wemarre and Colonel Martel of the Musée de l'Armée, M. Michel Gallet of the Musée Carnavalet, Miss Barter of the library of the Tower of London, and Miss Wimbush of the National Portrait Gallery. Dr Joan Greatrex kindly read and criticised the typescript. Any errors that still remain are all my own. Friends have shared the pleasant task of applying the general statements of chroniclers to specific topographical maps, and have shared in the search for the sites of Henry's battlefields and sieges, as well as the remaining physical traces of his career. I owe special thanks to Clare Pitman for making it possible for me to retrace Henry's expeditions in northern France, as well as to Mary Reevy and Madeleine and Alex Currall for explorations in England.

Margaret Wade Labarge

Introduction

> There cannot be any more suitable or worthy occupation
> than handing down to posterity the grand and magnani-
> mous feats of arms and the inestimable subtleties of war
> which by valiant men have been performed . . . for the in-
> struction and information of those who in a just cause may
> be desirous of honourably exercising their prowess in arms.[1]

Enguerrand de Monstrelet's introduction to his chronicle echoes the beliefs
and preconceptions of the knightly class of his time, which considered the
duty of relating chivalric successes as part of the essential instruction of
those of gentle birth. Like his better-known predecessor, Jean Froissart,
Monstrelet was interested in the glamorous side of the Hundred Years
War – the exploits of the noble and the famous, whose encounters, even
with their enemies, were governed by a formal courtesy and a rigid etiquette. Such chroniclers were not interested in looking beneath the glittering surface. Famine and brigandage among the poor peasants were
necessary concomitants of war, regrettable perhaps, but relatively unimportant. The prosaic details of royal finance and administration which
were needed to build up the medieval war machine; the exact numbers of
"other ranks"; the tortuous diplomatic manoeuvres often concealed
beneath the chivalric formalities – none of these really concerned them,
since their viewpoint on war, and thus their description of it, was formed
by the unquestioning belief that it was the natural and proper occupation
of the privileged of the land, which served as both proof and buttress of
their nobility. Henry V, if we are able to make ourselves look beneath his
magnificent Shakespearean costuming, emerges as a typical, although
unusually competent, representative of the fifteenth-century ruling class.
Much that puzzles or disturbs the present-day observer of Henry's character or actions becomes clear if the king's beliefs and deeds are studied in
the light of contemporary theory and practice.

To understand Henry we must turn away from the remembered sonori-
ties of Shakespeare to the pedestrian and often tedious treatises which were
well known by fourteenth- and fifteenth-century princes and nobles.
Apart from the expected religious and moral summaries, there were other
more practical works of reference, known and used by Henry and his
contemporaries in both England and France. They included military
treatises inherited from the late Romans, medieval texts on how to choose
the best place for a castle and how to conduct a siege; and, by Henry's
time, practical and popular casebooks of military law – the law applied to
all men-at-arms during times of war and dealt with in special courts without regard to nationality or national boundaries. Besides such reference
books, which tended to form part of the practical library of a king, and
often of a noble, there were also the more abstract and didactic works
which contemporary scholars or poets presented to their prince – sometimes in hopes of influencing his behaviour, more often in hopes of
commending themselves for further patronage. It is such works as these
which explain to a considerable degree the frame of reference in which
fifteenth-century monarchs and magnates lived and worked. They
illuminate the descriptions, the choice of topics, and the judgments of the
many contemporary chroniclers and eulogistic biographers, and they help
to give us some insight into the minds and motives, as well as the actions,
of Henry and the men of his time.

The effort to know Henry is aided by a wide range of contemporary and
near-contemporary sources. We get a many-sided view of a king, whom all
agreed was pre-eminent in the Europe of his day, from the sober chronicles
of Thomas Walsingham of St Albans and the lively, somewhat legendary
collection known as the *Brut*, from the opposing views of Orléanist and
Burgundian supporters, from the sweeping classical phrases of Titus
Livius, the Italian humanist commissioned by Henry's younger brother,
and the prosy eulogistic verses of Thomas of Elmham and other nameless
poets. We are also fortunate enough to have letters written in Henry's own
hand, not merely dictated to a clerk. Even in anonymous print these project
some of the energy, cunning and careful passion for detail which character-
ised so many of his actions.

Henry V is an enigmatic and fascinating figure, but he does not represent
any major shift in ideas or ideals. He fits easily into the accepted pattern of
medieval kings of England. Perhaps the most illuminating comparison that
can be made is one with his remote ancestor, Richard the Lionhearted.
Both Henry and Richard ruled for a decade or less. Both kings enjoyed
great prestige abroad and became almost legendary figures in the society
of their own time. Both spent the greater part of their time, energy, and
royal resources in pursuing their rights to territories in what we consider
France, but which they, in line with the accepted theories of their contemporaries, regarded as a rightful part of their personal domains. Both left

to their successors a heritage of domestic upheaval in England and defeat abroad. Yet both, despite their relative lack of interest in England and their short stays there, were among the most popular and idolised of English kings and greatly encouraged the growth of a national and English patriotism. These paradoxes – more noticeable to us than to their own contemporaries – have helped to keep alight an unquenchable interest in both Richard and Henry. However, their popular, and often uncritical, adulation in England has had the unfortunate result of fitting both these kings into a chauvinistic framework which excludes their own aims and motives. Indeed, both are better understood if their French interests, French concerns and French activities are kept firmly in the foreground.

Despite this necessary emphasis on his French policy, Henry was one of the most English of all English kings. Grandson of John of Gaunt, who was the fourth son of Edward III and Philippa of Hainault, both his mother and grandmother were important English heiresses rather than the foreign princesses usually selected by the king or his direct heir. Henry's solidly based English background did not weaken his firmly held belief in his inherited right to the duchy of Normandy, William the Conqueror's lordship lost by King John at the beginning of the thirteenth century. In diplomatic exchanges he vigorously claimed all the lands of the Plantagenet inheritance as well as those lands in France assigned to Edward III by the Treaty of Bretigny in 1360, but his emotional insistence on his rights was surprisingly enough reserved for Normandy not Aquitaine, to which his claim was so much stronger and more legally enforceable. Henry's dream of the union of the English and French thrones was a chimerical one, but this is a truth more easily perceived by hindsight than recognised by an able and ambitious prince who saw an ideal opportunity for the achievement of his dream in a French kingdom racked by faction and civil war. The incredible victory of Agincourt, the conquest of Normandy, the diplomatic achievements of the Treaty of Troyes created a deceptive atmosphere of invincibility around Henry, for its success was completely dependent on the king's own forceful personality and constant campaigning.

It is one of the more fascinating historical riddles to debate what might have happened in European history if Henry had remained strong and vigorous into middle age instead of dying suddenly at thirty-five, leaving an heir of only nine months. That puzzle is insoluble, but perhaps Henry was fortunate in dying with his reputation as a brilliant commander and tactician intact, at a time when his victories still reconciled the people of England to the weight of taxation needed for the war. The subsequent failure of English efforts in France and the decline of English fortunes made later Englishmen, in a more nationalistic era, look back to Henry's reign as a brief golden age, a happy interlude of success and prestige between two periods of weakness and civil war. They glorified the secretive king as a great national hero. The verdict of modern historians on Henry's character and achievements is more sharply divergent. Indeed it is often difficult to be sure they are dealing with the same person since their summing up of the king ranges from "one of the most aggressive and shifty products of an age of violence and duplicity", "slight of build, diseased and unlovable" to "that princely hero who, through the splendour of his achievements, illumined with the rays of his glory the decline of the medieval world" and who inspired loyalty by "his serious and passionate purpose, and . . . irresistible grace and energy".[2] In the light of these contradictory opinions and of the new specialised studies of the period, dealing particularly with military and economic matters, it is tempting to look once more at this enigmatic and fascinating figure who, whatever his virtues and defects, was, like all successful medieval kings, very much the personal ruler. He was a strong and forceful leader who easily compelled consent for his policies from the great magnates who surrounded him and the common people of England who followed him. The history of Henry's reign is the history of Henry's own achievements.

CHAPTER I

Cousin to the King

The medieval lack of interest in the exact birth dates of even princes and nobles is always a source of irritation for the more precisely oriented biographer. It seems that the future Henry V was born in September 1387 at Monmouth, one of the Lancaster castles on the border of Wales. The town of Monmouth still retains some of its medieval features, including its famous bridge over the Monnow, but the castle itself is in picturesque ruins and the statue of Henry V as its most distinguished native son shares the honours in the crowded marketplace with that of Charles Rolls, the designer of the Rolls-Royce engine. At the time of his birth no one would have considered Henry of Monmouth as a future king of England. His father, Henry of Bolingbroke, was the only legitimate son of John of Gaunt, the uncle of the king, and richest and strongest, as well as most loyal, of the great magnates and princes surrounding the throne of Richard II. In 1387 Richard was only twenty and happily married to Anne of Bohemia. There was little reason to believe that he would not rule for many years and be succeeded by legitimate heirs.

John of Gaunt had laid the foundation of his family's great fortune with his marriage to Blanche, daughter and heir of the Duke of Lancaster. He had increased his prestige, if not his wealth, by his investiture with the title of Duke of Aquitaine and by a second marriage to Constance of Castile who brought him a claim to the Castilian throne. Obviously he would see to it that his heir also benefited by a profitable marriage. In 1380 Gaunt purchased from the king the right to the marriage of Mary de Bohun, younger daughter and co-heiress of the Earl of Hereford. It was an extraordinarily good business stroke, although it did not improve family feeling as John's youngest brother, Thomas of Woodstock, had married Mary's older sister and had planned to secure the whole of the inheritance by putting Mary in a convent. John of Gaunt's adroit manoeuvring prevented that and Mary and Henry of Bolingbroke were married before February 1381. The bride and groom were very young – Henry was perhaps fourteen or fifteen and Mary only ten or eleven. The marriage appears to have been consummated very early and a child born in 1382, who died in infancy. However, the young couple lived apart for at least two years and probably only set up a permanent household together after Mary had reached the age of fourteen, at that time considered adult for a girl. Henry of Monmouth was born when his mother was only seventeen and he was followed in the next three years by three brothers: Thomas, John and Humphrey. Two daughters, Blanche (born in 1392) and Philippa completed the family and proved too great a drain on the strength of the young mother. Mary de Bohun died in childbirth in June 1394, when she was still only twenty-three or twenty-four.

It is interesting to speculate on the genetic inheritance that was passed on to the children in these marriages which began when husband and wife were so young and which frequently ended after a few years with the death of the young wife in childbirth. Bolingbroke, although robust and active, seems to have carried the seeds of some constitutional weakness. As early as the first Christmas of his reign he suffered from an unspecified illness, as did his son Henry, and the last years of his reign saw him sink quickly into enfeebled and sickly old age, suffering from an undetermined affliction, which some of the more sensational chroniclers described as leprosy. He died a pathetic physical figure at forty-six. Although the younger Henry, at the age of eight, was sufficiently ill to have messengers sent post-haste from London to Leicester, he and his brothers were eager and able warriors. Nevertheless, both he and Thomas seem to have been particularly susceptible to the fevers and dysentery which were the invariable accompaniments of medieval campaigning and which were to kill Henry by the age of thirty-five.[1]

Henry saw little of his father during his childhood days, for Bolingbroke was frequently abroad. In any case, it was not usual at this period for the children of the great to be paid much direct attention by their parents. They were well provided for financially and left to the direct care of nurses, tutors and servants, though if their grandparents were alive they might well spend time in their households, as Henry seems to have done in that of John of Gaunt.

Although we have little specific information on Henry of Monmouth's childhood, certain general patterns are apparent. One of his more eulogistic clerics underlines his happiness that Henry was born of native English stock, and emphasises the boy's fondness for outdoor sport, describing his interest in hunting and falconry, in fishing and exploring the countryside on foot or on horseback.[2] The fishing and exploring the countryside on foot are somewhat unexpected, but hunting and falconry were serious subjects for the medieval nobility. They were the greatest resource of their idle hours, and their elaborate code and specialised vocabulary provided a convenient social barrier between the upper and the lower classes. This enthusiasm also encouraged a considerable literature on hunting – much of it strictly practical and didactic in nature – and such works formed an important part of the books which the nobles were beginning to accumulate for themselves. While Henry was Prince of Wales, for example, his cousin, Edward Duke of York, dedicated to him an English translation of the best-known and most authoritative book on hunting, the *Livre de Chasse* by Gaston Phébus, Count of Foix. It was obviously a subject in which Henry retained a passionate interest, for less than a year before he died the king had twelve books on hunting specially written for him and delivered to him in France.[3]

But a great noble's education required much more than a knowledge of hunting and falconry, useful and attractive as those subjects were. Its ideal might best be summed up in the guidelines laid down by the king's council for the Earl of Warwick, custodian of the young King Henry VI. The earl was ordered to instruct and inform his charge, or to have him instructed in, "generous habits, cheerful manners, in literature, and liberal and other useful learning".[4] The grandson of John of Gaunt was provided with grammar books and, although his childhood ended early and he was involved in military campaigns from the age of eleven, his literary education seems to have been remarkably good and left him with a continuing taste for reading.* At the sieges of Caen and Meaux Henry took special interest in books as his share of the booty. Such seizures could reap a rich harvest. After the fall of Meaux some 110 books, probably the collection of a religious house, came into his possession. They included many of the church fathers and some law and, although they may have been destined for Henry's monastic foundation of Sheen, they were still in his possession at the time of his death, and were ultimately given to King's Hall, Cambridge. All the incidental references to Henry's reading suggest a serious-minded and careful man. He had kept for himself Archbishop Arundel's copy of the works of Gregory the Great, which the archbishop had bequeathed to Christchurch, Canterbury. In the year of his death the king was having a Bible written for his own use. As well, he had borrowed a chronicle of Jerusalem and the account of the voyage of Godfrey de Bouillon from his aunt, and, on the lighter side, had his own copy of Chaucer's *Troilus*. The books were well taken care of, too, for not long after Henry came to the throne he ordered elegant covers and protective bags for them.[5]

Henry was conversant with both Latin and French, although he encouraged the use of English even in official documents, and he was capable of writing his own letters when he wished to maintain special secrecy in

---

* The whole family was interested in books. Humphrey's legacy of his library to Oxford has been one of the great treasures of the university, and the family accounts show that the two little girls, when only six and three and a half, had alphabet books ordered for them in London.

diplomatic matters. However, his interests were not primarily scholarly, and the pleasant story that suggests his attendance at Oxford is unsubstantiated legend. Nor is it likely that his education would have been as intellectually stringent as the course of study recommended by Jean Gerson, the learned chancellor of the University of Paris, to the sons of Charles VI. The eminent churchman proposed that the young princes should read "studiously" a long list of works, ranging from the Bible, St Augustine, saints' lives and meditations to French chronicles, treatises on warfare, a scientific study of the sphere, and – perhaps for light relief – *Aesop's Fables*. Taking advantage of this magnificent opportunity, Gerson hastened to recommend to the princes a careful reading of all his own latest works.[6] His list seems to have shared the fate of so many carefully designed programmes of great books, and was generally neglected by those for whom it had been drawn up.

Apart from such book learning, Henry, like every other boy of his class, would have received consistent training in the use of weapons. The Lancaster accounts show small sums spent on a new scabbard for Henry's sword, and on black silk for another. The household also had a genuine interest in music, and Henry was already playing the harp – and needing new harp strings – before he was ten. The love and practice of music continued all his life for he "delighted in songe and musicall instruments".[7] He made careful arrangements to be accompanied in France by his minstrels and the musicians of his chapel, and he continued to play the harp himself throughout his adult campaigns.

During these relatively carefree years of Henry's childhood, his father was seldom at home. Henry of Bolingbroke held an anomalous position in the social structure of England. He was eleven months older than his cousin the king, and potentially the richest and most powerful noble in the kingdom. However, while John of Gaunt still lived and was active both in the affairs of the realm and the control of the vast Lancaster estates, Henry of Bolingbroke had little real power or scope for political action. When his father was away pursuing the will-of-the-wisp crown of Castile, Henry became involved in the affair of the Lords Appellant in 1387 in which, for a time, Richard was forced to put aside his favourites and follow the wishes of the great magnates. The confrontation underlined the fact that at best there was a lack of sympathy, at worst outright enmity, between Henry and his royal cousin. Henry was weaned away from his position of opposition, partly by his father, who devoted much of his energy and ability to upholding Richard and stabilising his position on the throne, and partly by Richard's own efforts at conciliation. In any case, once John of Gaunt returned to England it seemed the ideal moment for the active, energetic, insufficiently occupied Henry of Bolingbroke to follow the pattern of so many medieval nobles in the same situation as himself – when there was no convenient war they indulged in crusades and pilgrimages and the incidental tournament. John of Gaunt was willing to finance him generously, and from 1390 to 1393 Henry spent most of his time abroad. In the spring of 1390 he participated in the famous tournament of St Inglevert, so lovingly detailed by Froissart and delightfully illustrated by his illuminator. There he met and became acquainted with many of the most famous of the footloose nobility of Europe, including the renowned Jean de Boucicaut, later leader of the French army. He shared in one of the Teutonic Knights' crusading expeditions against the embattled forest-dwelling Lithuanians and attempted to do so again, but on this occasion foreign volunteers were turned away. He then set off on a pilgrimage to Jerusalem, by way of the pleasant islands of Rhodes and Corfu. When he returned to England in July 1393 his far-flung voyagings were over, although there would still be visits, both ceremonial and enforced, to France.

Bolingbroke thoroughly enjoyed what he later described to a foreign ambassador as his "gadling days". He lived in luxury, even on his crusading expeditions, as his accounts show. For example, he always travelled with six attendant minstrels, even to the Holy Land, although only one trumpeter accompanied him to Jerusalem itself. He had a favourite pet parrot, which made several appearances in the accounts, and he took it back to England with him. His amusements were typical of his class and he spent about six times as much on gambling as he did on the mandatory alms-giving. The impression that he might have left with his young son when he returned from these travels was that of an energetic, decisive, physically competent man, who was personally brave. A more experienced observer might have discovered that he lacked much intellectual power or sensitivity to others, although he was always attractive to women and had commanded the enduring loyalty of the knights and clerks who formed his retinue during those strenuous years.

By the time Henry of Monmouth was ten the situation in England, with its effect on his father's and thus on his own position, meant that the peaceful days of early childhood were left behind. Inevitably young Henry was gradually absorbed into the tangled net of English, and indeed European, affairs. "Cousin to the king" had by 1397 come to mean danger as well as riches and power.

The situation in England was highly inflammable. Richard was extravagant and insistent on proving the limits of his kingly power, but he was also intelligent and not particularly scrupulous in his efforts to undermine any possible opposition. In the summer of 1397 Richard was at last sure enough of his own power to move against the Lords Appellant who had opposed him in 1387. It was not difficult to suspect them of conspiracy and even to provide sufficient proof. In July the king arrested his youngest uncle, the Duke of Gloucester, and the earls of Warwick and Arundel. Arundel was beheaded in September, and his brother, the Archbishop of

Canterbury, was exiled. The Earl of Warwick was imprisoned but saved his life by an abject confession. The Duke of Gloucester was transferred to the castle of Calais and secretly done away with there. Bolingbroke and Mowbray remained as the only survivors of the Lords Appellant and the centres around which any disaffection amongst the magnates could rally. Richard did not trust his cousin and, as the loyal John of Gaunt grew old and declined in health, the king could not look with equanimity on his replacement by a young and vigorous Bolingbroke whose resources in lands and revenues were almost as great as those of the crown itself. The problem of the succession, although not apparently immediate, would contribute to his distrust of Bolingbroke. Richard and Anne of Bohemia had been childless and Richard's second marriage in 1396 was to the six-year-old Isabella of France. The marriage alliance would, he hoped, strengthen the long truce which had been arranged between the two countries but it would provide no heirs for England for some years. The heir presumptive to the throne of England in 1397 was Roger Mortimer, Earl of March and grandson of Lionel, Duke of Clarence, the third son of Edward III. However, Mortimer did not have either the political strength or the wealth which Bolingbroke would enjoy.

The unease of the magnates over Richard's high-handed actions against the leaders of the baronage was mirrored in the disaffection his new financial expedients aroused among the wealthy burgesses and townspeople. A series of forced loans, of heavy fines to obtain the king's pleasure, and the menacing possibilities envisaged by those who were forced to seal blank charters to be filled in at the king's desire, all contributed to a growing sense of insecurity among that relatively small group who were of political importance. By the beginning of 1398 King Richard was willing to take on both Mowbray and Bolingbroke. It is not necessary to unravel here the complicated tangle of their quarrel which was to lead to the stylised farce of a proposed trial by battle, which was never allowed to take place. Both were exiled – Mowbray for life, Bolingbroke for ten years, later commuted to six. For the moment their rights to their estates were safeguarded and they were empowered to receive their revenues through their proctors.

Richard was always a gambler. In his actions after the death of John of Gaunt, barely four months after Bolingbroke had left England for exile, one senses the belief that "winner takes all". In March 1399 Richard declared the confiscation of all the Lancaster estates and the perpetual banishment of Henry of Bolingbroke in contradiction to what had been promised before his cousin's departure. In so doing he struck at the very base of the power and sense of security of all the magnates of the country. If confiscation for no good cause could be declared at the will of the king, then no one's private property was safe – and the security of private property was a very important matter in the fourteenth century. Richard perhaps underestimated the seriousness of the questionings which he had provoked, or preferred to have an army in action and under his control. In any case, he set out in April on his proposed expedition to Ireland. It seemed safe enough. The heir-apparent, Roger Mortimer, had been killed in 1398, and the son who inherited his claim was only eight. As a prudent gesture, King Richard took with him, ostensibly as part of the expedition but in reality as polite hostages, young Henry of Monmouth and Humphrey, son of the dead Duke of Gloucester. On this expedition Henry got his first experience of warfare in the wild country and bogs of Ireland, and he seems to have acquitted himself well enough. During the campaign Richard knighted the youth, along with ten of his companions-at-arms, and the royal accolade was a wry presage of the future of the newly made knight: "My fair cousin, henceforth be gallant and bold, for unless you conquer you will have little name for valour."[8]

While Henry earned his spurs in Ireland his father, deprived by Richard of his rightful inheritance as Duke of Lancaster, debated his future course from the safety of France. Bolingbroke's exile had not taken him too far. After a brief stay in Calais he had moved on to Paris where he stayed in the Hôtel de Clisson which had been put at his disposal by the French king. Bolingbroke was not an ordinary traveller, nor the usual penniless exile. He had two sisters queens – one of Castile, one of Portugal – and he could, with no sense of incongruity, pursue negotiations for a marriage with Marie of Berry, daughter of the enormously wealthy Duke of Berry and cousin to the French king. The marriage negotiations broke down, perhaps through the influence of the English royal messengers who came to the French court to discuss matters concerning the dowry of Richard's young queen. King Richard was certainly not anxious to see his already rich and powerful cousin marry the daughter of one of the wealthiest nobles of France, but such interference could only have inflamed Bolingbroke's already vivid sense of grievance. Meanwhile the English noble was an interested observer of the intrigues for power and influence which racked the French court, for the political situation in France was one of growing difficulty.

The prudent and able Charles V had regained most of the ground and the initiative lost to England during the first part of the Hundred Years War. When Charles VI came to the throne in 1380 as a boy of twelve, the future looked promising and Charles himself appeared the perfect figure of a king. Unfortunately for France, appearances in both cases were deceiving. Despite Charles' robust build and tall good looks, his physical inheritance was not happy, for it included a strain of insanity from his mother's family. In 1392 he suffered his first disastrous attack of madness, during which he killed four men before he could be restrained. From then until his death in 1422 the king suffered bouts of insanity at unpredictable intervals, and, even when rational, was mentally unstable and fatally easily influenced. Since he could in his moments of lucidity be active in affairs and make decisions he continued to act as king, but his instability and frequent periods of total incapacity led to a continuing bitter struggle for power among the different factions at court. At various times power was concentrated in the hands of the queen, the Duke of Orléans or the Duke of Burgundy, but each pillaged the resources of the crown for personal advantage and the maintenance of personal position. Bad feeling between the princes of the blood led to ominous local struggles and ultimately to full-fledged civil war.

The misunderstandings and rivalries between the Duke of Orléans, Charles VI's brother, and Philip the Bold, his uncle and Duke of Burgundy, had been intentionally intensified by Richard's foreign policy in the 1390s. Richard was not interested in waging war in France, but he was intelligently conscious of the need of maintaining English interests. He regarded with alarm the growing hegemony of the Duke of Burgundy in Flanders and the Low Country and did everything he could in a discreet way to support the local opposition to the duke. The cloth-towns of Flanders were essential to English prosperity and since, in turn, their prosperity was dependent on a steady supply of English wool, the Duke of Burgundy, whose riotous Flemish subjects had caused him much trouble, tried to avoid open hostilities with England. The ambitions of the other French princes led them towards interference in Italy, ostensibly to seat the Avignonese pope on the papal throne in Rome, but in reality to carve out for themselves important enclaves of Italian territory. Although an invasion of Italy was planned in 1391, it was called off by King Charles when he was convinced of the genuine menace behind Richard's veiled threat of re-opening the English attack on France in such a case. Naturally the Orléans faction chafed at the blow to their interests in Italy, and tried to discount the possibility of English intervention. By the time of Bolingbroke's exile the dispute between Orléans and Burgundy for control of the ailing king, and of the power which went with that control, had become even more intense. It was a major factor in the growing weakness of France.

The divisions in France were common knowledge to the exiled Bolingbroke when he asserted his claim to his inheritance as Duke of Lancaster. In debating the situation in England and how best to regain his rights and revenues he was certainly aware of the advantages to him of the troubled state of France. He had been brought up to date on the currents of opposition to Richard in England by the Earl of Arundel, son of the earl who had been executed in 1397, and was further advised by his fellow exile, Archbishop Arundel, who had spent some time in Italy before joining the others in Paris. We know very little of the processes by which Bolingbroke came to the decision to seek his inheritance by force, nor do we know whether he originally sought any more than that inheritance. Perhaps as a form of insurance, he made a treaty of alliance in June 1399 with Louis of

Orléans, the king's brother, and after taking his formal farewell of King Charles left for England.

During the crucial period when Bolingbroke was planning his return to England and his resumption of the lands and titles which were his inheritance, he was not in touch with his son. Henry of Monmouth was with Richard's army in Ireland, for the king had landed at Waterford at the beginning of June. During a march to Dublin and back he had had some skirmishes with the Irish, but not the decisive battle which he had hoped to fight and win. The news reached him in Ireland of Bolingbroke's landing at Ravenspur, north of the Humber, and of his cousin's triumphal progress through the northern strongholds of the Lancasters and the Percies, but Richard delayed his own return at the advice of his councillors. He reproached young Henry for his father's treachery, but the youth proudly proclaimed his ignorance of his father's actions or plans. Nevertheless, when Richard sailed from Ireland for Wales at the end of July he left the two cousins, Henry and Humphrey of Gloucester, under polite guard at the castle of Trim. The king's military strength in England, unknown to him, had almost evaporated, but no one yet knew what the outcome would be. The two boys could only watch from a distance to see what the future would bring in an atmosphere where rumour would flourish but there could be little real news.

However, as soon as Bolingbroke felt sufficiently secure, and learned of the whereabouts of his son, he sent a ship for the two boys. The ship, carrying also the valuable furnishings of Richard's chapel which had been left behind in Ireland, brought Henry safely to Chester, but Humphrey died on the way. The boy of twelve confronted a difficult emotional situation when he arrived at Chester. His father was almost a phantom figure, while Richard had gained his affection and loyalty. At first he took his place with those in attendance on Richard and was found there when his father came. He welcomed him in proper form but was upset by the immediate command that he must leave Richard's service the next day for that of his father. The chronicle which tells the story was written by a partisan of Richard and perhaps exaggerates young Henry's dismay and Richard's words of farewell to his "good sonne Henry".[9] Even without exaggeration the situation must have been profoundly disturbing to the youth so recently knighted by the king he was now forced to abandon, who had adjured him to be "gallant and bold".

Events moved rapidly. By 30 September Bolingbroke had moved beyond the regaining of his own rights to claim the throne and had seen his *de facto* acquisition of power agreed to by parliament, though in a form which has kept the constitutional historians arguing ever since. In fact, despite all the Lancastrian propaganda and the careful stage-managing of Richard's "free" hand-over of power to his cousin and his official deposition, Henry of Lancaster had no right to the throne that did not rest ultimately on naked strength. The weakness of his title seems to have worried him at intervals during his reign, but no shadow of such a doubt ever appears to have crossed his son's mind.

For his coronation, Henry of Lancaster carefully followed the accepted pattern. He gathered his sons and other young nobles at the Tower of London on Sunday 12 October when his younger sons and their comrades were knighted. After the ceremony the young knights rode to Westminster, accompanying the king, in readiness for the coronation on the morrow. Henry IV was crowned on Monday 13 October, the feast of the translation of Edward the Confessor and two years exactly from the day he quitted London to go into exile. At this ceremony young Henry carried the sword of justice, filling the same role which his father had played at Richard's coronation twenty-two years before.[10] The solemn ceremonies and the great feast which followed must have impressed the boy so recently come from the uncertainties of being a hostage in Ireland. As the further magnificence of his new position was unrolled before him with its attractive panoply of prestige, power, and riches, one wonders if that favourite medieval symbol, the wheel of fortune, came to his mind. Certainly the turn of the wheel had been exceedingly rapid. Would fortune – and the intelligent use of power – take him to further unforeseeable heights?

CHAPTER II

Prince of Wales

After his coronation Henry IV made swift provision for his oldest son. The titles and honours followed quickly. On 15 October the proposal was made that Henry should be named Prince of Wales, Duke of Cornwall, and Earl of Chester. Parliament assented and the young prince was invested with the gold rod and ring by his father and given a special seat in parliament. A week later the prince was made Duke of Aquitaine and before the middle of November he had also been presented with the liberties and franchises of the duchy of Lancaster and the title of duke. The Lancaster investiture remained something apart, since the Lancaster inheritance never entered into the general estates of the crown but was the personal property of the king. The most immediately important of these grants were the princedom of Wales and the earldom of Chester, and they were to be no sinecure. The county of Chester had been the stronghold of King Richard, the centre from which he drew his military strength and the district which he had most favoured with grants. The creation of a military and administrative staff for the young prince with headquarters set in Chester itself meant a useful measure of control and supervision for a potentially turbulent district. However, although King Henry did not realise it at the time he invested his heir with the title of Prince of Wales and had his right to succession to the throne recognised by parliament, it was with Wales itself that Prince Henry would be most concerned. For nearly ten years the Welsh rebellion and the need to establish royal control in Wales would occupy his time. At first under the governorship of Harry Percy, and then in substantially personal control, Prince Henry would learn the arts of campaigning and the problems of warfare by continuous practice.

There was little time before the boy of twelve discovered that his newly enhanced position meant even more dangerous enemies. The first rude reminder came at Christmas when Henry IV and his sons had retired to Windsor for the celebration of the feast. The king, had been ill, and probably the prince also, and as always in troubled times the rumours were current that there had been attempts to poison them both. Certainly the state of the country was most unquiet, as many of the great men of the kingdom were still supporters of Richard. During December a plot was formed, under the aegis of the abbot of Westminster, to kill Henry and restore Richard to the throne. The plan was simple but could have been effective. One of Richard's former clerks, who very much resembled him, was to impersonate Richard until he could be freed from imprisonment. During a celebration planned for Twelfth Night at Windsor armed men would be introduced into the castle so that Henry and his court could be overpowered and killed. Only a couple of days before the plan was to have been put into effect, the king got wind of it – probably through the Earl of Rutland, perhaps also through court gossip picked up from a prostitute. In any case, on 4 January Henry was galvanised into rapid and effective action. Surrounded by his sons, the king rode quickly to London and called its citizens to his aid. The rebels were quickly dispersed and set upon by the people of the towns to which they fled. Several of the most important, such as the earls of Kent, Salisbury, and Huntington, and the Lord Despenser, were killed by an enraged mob before they could be brought to trial.

The king had survived the first threat to his rule. Rebellion put down meant confiscations, and the prosaic language of the Close Roll details some of the profits which accrued to the young prince. From the forfeited goods of the Earl of Kent, for example, after his father had taken the first choice for his own chapel and wardrobe, Prince Henry received some valuable items for his own chapel as well as a covered salt-cellar and covered cup of silver-gilt, and two red cloths of gold. His supply of plate soon grew large enough to tempt thieves. In 1403 a Welshman was arrested in London while in possession of a silver plate engraved with the prince's arms which had been stolen from Westminster.[1]

But the prince soon had to turn his attention to events in Wales. Henry Percy, the Hotspur of legend, had been appointed Justice of North Wales, Chester, and Flint and acted as governor of the young prince: the control and maintenance of royal rule in the district were thus effectively in Hotspur's hands. Henry Percy, son of the Earl of Northumberland, was at this time an able and admired warrior of about thirty-five, seasoned by many years of border clashes. The Percy lands and strength, and their extensive family ties, gave them great importance in the north of England, and their adherence to Bolingbroke when he landed from France had provided an essential centre of support to the returning exile. It was urgent for Henry IV to retain their good will and the summer of 1400 saw the king make a military expedition to Scotland in an attempt to display English strength and to reinforce the Percy control of the marches of the north.

Meanwhile in Wales another conflict was developing. Despite Edward I's conquest at the end of the thirteenth century and the building of major royal castles to control and, hopefully, to cow the countryside there were endemic difficulties between Welshmen and Englishmen. The English marcher lords, who had been given extensive powers and jurisdiction in order to ensure peace along the borders, often used their privileges to prey on peaceful Welsh neighbours. The Welsh themselves still cherished their own national ideals, their language, and their dream of freedom from the English and rule by their own prince. In September 1400 a minor territorial dispute between Lord Grey of Ruthin and Owen Glendower, a wealthy Welsh landowner, was swept into the larger political maelstrom. Glendower was an interesting leader for the Welsh. Through his mother he was the heir of the old Welsh princes of Powys Fadog, a man of about forty who held lands at Glyndyfrdwy and Cynllaith Owain. In his youth he had studied law at Westminster, had served in the Scottish campaign of 1385 with enough success to have his feats sung by the Welsh bards, and may have served as a squire of Henry IV. He had married the daughter of Sir David Hanmer, a distinguished Welsh judge of Flintshire, and had a sizeable family. His lordship of Glyndyfrdwy was only about twenty miles south of Ruthin. It was a lovely spot – the name in Welsh means "glen of the water of the Dee" – between Corwen and Llangollen where the river Dee is hemmed in by sharply rising wooded hills. The strip of fertile land is narrow along the riverbed but the view from what is popularly known as Glendower's Mount, is extensive along the stretch of the Dee. Glendower was known to have had a fine lodge and park there. Another twenty miles south, over the Berwyn range, was Owen's main lordship of Cynllaith Owain, with its head at Sycharth. This was a fertile and luxurious region and was the family's favourite residence. Glendower's hospitality must have been generous, since a Welsh poet drew a most idyllic picture of the household at Sycharth not long before the rebellion. The manor was surrounded by a moat with a bridge giving access to the gatehouse. On the motte within were timber houses with lofts which rested on pillars and recalled the cloisters of Westminster. The roofs were tiled, the chimneys carried away the smoke, and the richness of the stuffs which filled the wardrobes conjured up a vision of the shops of Cheapside. As well the manor rejoiced in a mill on the Cynllaith, a tall stone pigeon-house, a fish-pond, a rabbit-warren, and a heronry. In the midst of all this splendour the wealthy, respected and generous Owen saw to it that there was no shortage of food and drink, and no lock or porter to bar the way for his guests.[2]

It was in this minor Eden that trouble erupted so vigorously in the autumn of 1400. One chronicler claims that the trouble sprang from Lord Grey's witholding of Owen's summons to service with the king in Scotland – owed by Owen for his lordship of Glyndyfrdwy – until it was too late for Owen to join the contingent, but this seems untrue, or at least much exaggerated. It appears much more probable that the real cause of the trouble was as so often a territorial dispute, as the lands of Grey and Glendower were contiguous. In any case, by September 1400 Glendower had decided on reprisals against Grey. On 16 September in a meeting at Glyndyfrdwy, Owen was proclaimed as Prince of Wales by his leading associates, and two days later they attacked Ruthin and burnt the town. From there they moved on to ravage many of the settlements of the marches until, on the 24th, the attacking Welsh were met by hurriedly gathered levies from the western counties and defeated in battle.

Henry IV had heard of the rebellion at Northampton on 19 September, while he was on his way back from Scotland. He immediately marched towards the west, and was in Shrewsbury before the end of the month. The king took advantage of the presence of his army to make a show of force in North Wales, and spent some ten days at the beginning of October, marching as far as Bangor and Caernarvon, but then quickly returning to Shrewsbury. His expedition set the pattern for those early years of the Welsh campaigns. The Welsh would score successes. The king, having been roused by the news, would call together an army and proceed to lead an expeditionary force into Wales. The Welsh would generally retreat to the cover of the hills: the English troops would ravage the lands through which they passed, and declare forfeit the estates of the rebels. But within a week or two the English army would withdraw, the Welsh would re-emerge, and the whole process would begin again, for the prince and the resident royal officials did not have the money or the men to deal with the continuing threats. Under the unsettled circumstances, there was also much plain thievery. In an undated letter from the constable and receiver of the Earl of Arundel, the officials of his lands in the marches questioned the earl on what they should do. Because of the hostilities much of the lordship was empty and desolate and the officials asked pathetically for instructions as to how they could govern for their lord's profit, since the men of Chester and elsewhere planned to enter the lordship to rob and devastate under cover of the king's proclamation of "havoc" throughout Wales.[3] When the king returned to London pardons were issued for most of the Welsh rebels but Glendower, and Rhys and William ap Tudor, were specifically excepted, as were those who were already captured and detained, or who had continued in rebellion.[4]

The March parliament of 1401 discussed the Welsh situation with alarm and demanded strong measures. Adam of Usk, the chronicler who was specially knowledgeable about Welsh affairs, describes the sentiment against the Welsh. According to his report it was urged that they should not marry with English, nor get wealth, nor live in England, and that the men of the marches might use reprisals against Welshmen who were their debtors, or who had injured them.[5] The terms of the actual statute are relatively mild, at least if seen against the demands of parliament. However, the statute did limit the rights of the Welsh in England, protected

Englishmen from Welsh juries, provided that for three years no English-man should be indicted or accused by a Welshman, and – interesting provision – restricted the passage of Welsh bards and vagabonds. The power of the Welsh poets to raise national feeling was already recognised. However, much onus was also put on the marcher lords to protect and properly garrison their castles, under pain of forfeiting them. As well, the Welsh themselves were to pay murage for the defence of the towns of North Wales, and also to contribute towards the garrisons of the castles there for three years or more.[6]

The royal ordinances and the statutes were handed down from London. In North Wales itself the carrying out of policy was in the hands of the council of the Prince of Wales, already established in Chester and headed by Henry Percy. Attempts were made to pacify the Welsh, but with little success. The dissidents, William and Rhys Tudor, dissatisfied that they had not been pardoned, seized the great castle of Conway by a crafty stratagem on Good Friday (1 April) with a force of some forty men, while the garrison was in church. The success of their scheme was infinitely em-barrassing for the royal forces and the castle was immediately besieged by the Prince of Wales and his troops. The castle was surrendered again within two months. According to Adam of Usk, William and Rhys saved their own skins by binding, as they slept, nine of their own men who were especially hateful to the prince and then delivering them over to the attacking forces for punishment. This followed swiftly and terribly. The nine unfortunates were immediately drawn, disembowelled, beheaded, and quartered.[7]

The recovery of Conway Castle encouraged the royal forces. The spirits of the prince must also have been raised by the letter he received in June from John Charlton, Lord Powys, who hastened to report to the prince his success against Owen's forces. Powys had been riding with his men in the mountains of his land, and, informed previously by spies, had sent some 400 archers into the district where Owen was reputed to be. They found the Welsh leader and approached to do battle, but Owen was not interested in a formal encounter where he and his troops would be at a disadvantage and slipped away again into the mountains. However, the determined chase by Lord Powys and his men broke Owen's force up into small groups and brought in some useful plunder. Owen's armour was taken, a number of horses and lances, and a quantity of cloth painted with Welsh devices. Powys announced he was sending the prince some of the cloth by the bearer of his letter. The rest he proposed to send to the king along with one of Owen's men who had been captured in the skirmish, and from whom they obviously hoped to extract useful information.[8] Powys' victory had a great moral effect and it forced Owen to divert his activities from north to south Wales where he remained for much of 1401.

Despite such minor successes the situation in Wales continued disturbed and Henry IV considered it advisable to make another show of force in

the rebellious principality. In June, Henry Percy had resigned his charge
in North Wales and the concurrent office of governor of the young prince,
and the king appointed Hugh Despenser to take Percy's place. Meanwhile
the king wrote frequently to his young son, supervising, encouraging. and
occasionally sending the money for supplies and wages which the prince
was constantly requesting. On 10 July he encouraged young Henry with
the news that he was sending him £1,000 for the expenses of the siege of
Harlech, which was currently being assaulted by the rebels. Along with
the money came the sage piece of royal advice that every effort should be
made to hold Harlech, as it was much cheaper to keep a castle than to
retake it. By the end of August the forces of the western counties were
again put in array and by the beginning of September Henry IV wrote to
his son that he was leaving Kennington and hoped to be in Worcester by
1 October, as he had heard of a great assembly of Owen's people.[9]

The expedition was one of harassment and destruction. From Worcester
the king went on to Hereford and Llandovery, some forty-five miles west.
There, according to Adam of Usk, who was one of Glendower's apologists,
Llewellyn ap Gryffith of Cayo, one of the rebels, was drawn, hanged,
beheaded and quartered, at the king's command and in his presence and
that of the prince. Adam's sympathies were naturally with the Welsh and
he claimed that the expedition did not spare children or churches, that the
king himself was lodged in the Cistercian monastery of Strata Florida,
where the choir of the church was used as a stable, and the king's forces
"pillaged even the patens". When the army withdrew, it took with it more
than 1,000 Welsh children of both sexes to act as servants.[10]

The end of 1401 marked a considerable extension of Owen's influence.
The king's brutal and rapid raid in October had achieved nothing of lasting
effect for Henry IV was too short of funds to keep his forces in the field
long enough for real victories. Glendower merely transferred his seat of
operations to North Wales once again, making an abortive attack on Caernarvon Castle, where he unfurled for the first time his standard of a golden
dragon on a white field. At the same time he ravaged much of the Ruthin
lordship. The royal officials were in some disarray. Lord Powys was killed
in Owen's attack on Welshpool. As a strong and able royal leader his death
was a blow to Prince Henry's forces. As well, his governor, Lord Despenser, died. The letter which the prince wrote to his father asking for a
new governor shows that there seems to have been considerable affection
between the two, as the prince speaks movingly of the weight on his heart
from the loss, and the very great tenderness which Despenser had had for
his honour and his estate.[11] Two undated letters of this period illustrate
conflicting strains in the prince's character. His concern for the elder men
around him is pleasantly displayed in his letter to an unidentified abbot,
one of whose monks he had heard could alleviate sciatica. The prince's
chancellor suffered painfully from this disease, so he was sending him for

treatment. On the other hand, his insistence on prompt and efficacious punishment is visible even at this early age. The Welsh rebels had murdered one of his officials and fled. The prince ordered that every effort should be made to capture and punish the rebels or "from now on no Englishman will wish to be an officer in Wales".[12] Henry began at a very early age to wrestle with the problem of the maintenance of authority in unsettled territories.

The council meeting in November, after the king had returned to London, discussed several matters concerning Wales – the always important matter of garrisons for castles, and the need of both a governor for the prince and money to pay his high costs. They authorised £1,000 for the prince's expenses and suggested to the king that he choose the prince's guardian from among several distinguished nobles.[13] The Earl of Worcester, Harry Percy's uncle, was finally given the position. They recognised the extension of Glendower's influence but, although fighting was endemic, no full-scale rebellion was in progress. There even appeared at this time the possibility that a peace might be worked out. Owen certainly seems to have put out some tentative initiatives for peace. At least, through intermediaries, he was in touch with the Earl of Northumberland and showed a willingness for discussions, although he claimed to fear any parleys that took place outside of Wales, because he did not feel his safety could be ensured. Nevertheless, it seems unlikely that the marcher lords whose lands and interests were the ones most vitally affected, were interested in anything but a total crushing of any revolt. Northumberland and the Percies, whose holdings were in the north country, were far less intimately involved and much more open to talk of compromise. The king himself was more likely to lean to the side of the marcher lords, since his wife had brought him a marcher inheritance in the earldom of Hereford. Despite his efforts Owen does not seem to have been too optimistic, for at the same time he was sending messengers to the Irish and Scottish lords, seeking help from them against the English. Several were intercepted by the watchful English and, in any case, no real help was sent, although both Irish and Scottish watched Owen's manoeuvres with a sympathetic eye.

But the young prince was not exclusively concerned with Welsh affairs. In January 1402 Prince Henry was specifically summoned to a Great Council for the first time, and took his place there on 29 January. The prince probably spent all winter and the early spring at his manor of Kennington. At the time various marriage negotiations were much in view. Agreement had already been reached for the marriage of Blanche, now ten, to Louis of Bavaria, son of the king of the Romans. Blanche finally sailed from England in the summer of 1402, and her marriage was celebrated at Heidelberg in July. At the same time rather desultory negotiations were going on with the Scandinavian ambassadors, proposing that King Eric of Denmark should marry Philippa, and the Prince of Wales, Eric's sister.

Both the young people duly appointed proctors to represent them in the negotiations, but the matter was not pursued with any great enthusiasm. The most interesting of the marriages of 1402 was the second marriage of the king himself. On 3 April at Eltham, Henry IV married by proxy Joan of Navarre, widow of the Duke of Brittany. She had been regent of the duchy for her young son since the death of his father in 1399. Joan did not come to England until January 1403, but the marriage, although we have little information as to how the two met, or what were the reasons for the match, seems to have had some basis in real choice. Henry made generous provision for his second wife, and showed her great concern and affection. It is she who shares his tomb in Canterbury Cathedral, rather than the young Mary de Bohun, who had been the mother of all his children. There is no evidence to show how Henry and his brothers got on with their stepmother at this time. In fact the boys were now all old enough and independent enough to have only formal and ceremonial dealings with her.

The spring of 1402 brought further trouble in Wales. The attacks by Owen on the lordship of Ruthin continued, and in April Owen had the good fortune to capture Lord Grey himself. He was, of course, a most valuable hostage and rekindled all the Welsh enthusiasm for the revolt. As well, although Hotspur, who had been reappointed to Wales on 31 March, tried to re-establish royal rule, Glendower moved to the attack in northern Radnorshire, on the edge of the Mortimer lands. Edmund Mortimer, uncle of the boy regarded by Richard as his prospective heir, gathered together the forces of Hereford and led them to battle against Glendower. The armies met at Bryn Glas, a hill west of Pilleth, on 22 June and the result was catastrophic for the English. Their own Welsh archers turned against them. Many Englishmen were slain, and Edmund Mortimer was captured. In three months Owen had captured two important English lords and placed himself in a strong position in Wales. The ransoms demanded for both were high, and much of the continuing Welsh revolt arose from the different treatment of the two by the king and his council. Lord Grey was given every assistance to find the necessary ransom and was released within the year. Mortimer, on the other hand, was given no such co-operation. As Walsingham, the St Albans chronicler, puts it: he turned against the king "because of tedium of captivity, or fear of death or some other unknown cause".[14] Any, or all, of these may have been true, but in addition Mortimer had married Glendower's daughter and taken sides against Henry. This new marriage alliance had other more sinister connotations for the king, as Percy's wife was Mortimer's sister, and likely to be sympathetic to his complaints of unfair treatment by the king.

The events of the summer followed the same pattern as before. The Welsh ravaged in Gwent and Glamorgan and by August the king had decided on another expedition into Wales. After much halfhearted crisscrossing of England the king finally entered Wales at the beginning of September only to be greeted by some of the worst weather in man's memory. On 7 September, for example, he pitched his tent in a pleasant place only to have it suddenly swept away by high winds and torrential rains which could well have overwhelmed the king himself if he had not been sleeping armed. The army was plagued with snow, rain and hail and predictably men muttered of the diabolical arts of Glendower and claimed that he was a magician. Once more the king burnt and devastated the country through which he passed but returned to England with nothing really achieved.[15] Meanwhile, on 14 September, Northumberland and his son had won a notable battle against the Scots at Homildon Hill. The contrast between the Percies' success and the king's complete lack of results was striking and, for some, suggestive.

March 1403 marked the appointment of Prince Henry as royal deputy in Wales, a recognition of the growing importance and ability of the rapidly maturing prince, as well as the realisation by Henry IV that the only trust-worthy supporters of a king who has seized the crown by force are the members of his own family. Certainly, King Henry had some suspicion of the dissatisfaction which was widespread among the Percies and their supporters. Prince Henry was active in his new appointment. At the beginning of May he led a raiding party against Glendower and his suppor-ters which burnt Owen's home and his tenants' houses at Cynllaith Owain and then marched on to Glyndyfrdwy where they destroyed a handsome lodge in his park. In the course of their raid the prince's men scoured the countryside and made several captives, including a gentleman who was one of Owen's chieftains. Despite his offer of generous and immediate ransom he was killed at once with the other captives. Henry was a harsh commander, even in his youth. From Edeirnion the prince's army returned to Shrewsbury, having ravaged and burnt the surrounding countryside, and Henry reported proudly to his father what he had achieved. The lack of money made it difficult to mount any continued effort, for a few weeks later the prince was again writing to his father on the constantly pressing problem of money to pay his soldiers, who were threatening to leave if they were not paid. The prince warned that, unless he could keep his men, he would have to withdraw and leave the marches to the malice of the rebels because "without man-power we cannot do more than any other man of lesser estate". The prince goes on to say that he has raised all he can on the security of his "little jewels" in his efforts to sustain the besieged castles of Harlech and Aberystwyth. The king and council agreed to send £1,000 to the prince for his troops, but were not prepared to go any further to put down the Welsh rebels.[16]

The summer of 1403 saw all Henry IV's enemies combine against him as the Percies rose in revolt and searched for help from Glendower's Welsh. The immediate cause of Percy's disenchantment may have indeed been the king's insistence that the Scottish prisoners taken at Homildon Hill be turned over to him and their ransoms surrendered to him. Certainly, this was much against the Percies' will, and they also felt they had a right to claim large sums which they said they were owed for the keeping of the marches of the north. It seems apparent from the tone of the Earl of Northumberland's letter to the king in June that he felt the need of money – for which the king had given them assignments, but which they had not been able to cash – but that he was not the moving spirit in rebellion. That position was filled by his son, the impetuous Hotspur, for by the beginning of July he had decided on revolt. Accompanied by some 200 of his own men he crossed from Northumberland through Lancashire to Chester. There he gathered the magnates of those shires, where strength had always been greatest for King Richard. Percy also asked for help from Glendower who was immersed in his own campaign in the west country of Wales and did not come immediately to Hotspur's aid. From Chester Percy and his army denounced the king, calling him "Henry of Lancaster" while the Earl of Worcester, who had been with the prince at Shrewsbury, abandoned young Henry and went to join the forces of his nephew.

As Percy's forces headed for Shrewsbury and the weakened army of the Prince of Wales, Henry IV displayed once again the bold swiftness which seemed to inspire him in times of emergency. From Burton-on-Trent he marched rapidly through Lichfield to Shrewsbury, covering the fifty-five miles in three days, and arriving at Shrewsbury before Percy's forces could close in on the town. Battle was inevitable but, according to the formulas of medieval combat, discussions had to take place between the leaders in the attempt to avoid it. Nothing came of the negotiations and it seems likely that the Earl of Worcester, who was sent by his nephew as the Percies' negotiator with the king, did not in fact make any attempt to achieve an accord. In any case, there was a heated argument and the military preparations went on. The battle was fought in the fields about three miles north of Shrewsbury, on the road towards Whitchurch, east of the tiny village of Berwick. The legend declares that Percy, just before the start of battle, called for his favourite sword and was told that it had been left behind in the village of Berwick through which they had just passed. Hotspur blanched at this news since a soothsayer had foretold his death at Berwick, which he, naturally enough, had taken for granted meant Berwick-on-Tweed in his own country.*

The king set his army in readiness. He gave the command of the vanguard to the Earl of Stafford, who was killed early in the battle, and one wing was

---

* This kind of riddling forecast was a common feature in medieval chronicles, as in its literature. In another contemporary example, Henry IV himself had been warned that he would die in Jerusalem. In fact, during his last illness he was transferred to those lodgings of the Abbot of Westminster known as the Jerusalem Chamber (see p. 39).

commanded by the Prince of Wales who bore himself manfully. Although wounded in the face by an arrow, he refused to withdraw, saying angrily: "Lead me, thus wounded, to the front line that I may, as a prince should, kindle our fighting men with deeds, not words."[17] The main effort of the rebels was to penetrate the royal lines deeply enough to kill the king, but Henry had devised a stratagem of having several knights arrayed in replicas of his arms. This diverted the would-be attackers and kept the king himself safe. The outcome of the battle was decided when Hotspur was killed by an arrow and his forces, shocked at the loss of their leader, lost the will to carry on. The casualties were heavy: young Henry Percy was dead; the Earl of Worcester was captured, and was executed the following day; the Earl of Northumberland, whether from genuine inability to arrive in time or a more highly developed sense of self-preservation, had not joined his son, and Percy had no real aid from Glendower.

It is hard to try and make any reasonable estimate of the numbers actually involved in the battle, as medieval chroniclers have a fascination for large and impressive round numbers. Perhaps the best estimate is that both armies were almost evenly matched at around 5,000 men, and that probably around 1,500 were killed. Nevertheless it was the most serious battle between Englishman and Englishman since the battle of Evesham, and was an unhappy augury of the series of conflicts which were to stain the history of England during the fifteenth century. Most of the dead were buried in a pit dug on the site of the battlefield and a few years later a chantry chapel was erected there to pray for the king's soul and for the souls of all those who were killed in the battle. Battlefield Church, as it is now called, is a little distance off the main road and serves as parish church for the district. The most obvious reminiscence of the battle is the statue of Henry IV, crowned and under a canopy, on the outside east wall of the church. The statue shows no markedly individual character, and the expressionless king looks over the churchyard and towards the still undeveloped fields where the fighting raged on that July day.

The battle of Shrewsbury, and the later royal manoeuvres in the north which brought the Earl of Northumberland to heel without further fighting, marked the end of another dangerous threat to Henry IV's ability to hold the crown. Speed and quick determination had once again succeeded in consolidating his position. The Prince of Wales, too, who had not yet reached his sixteenth birthday, had been initiated into the full range of medieval military activity, including the honour of personal leadership in a pitched battle. His training in military matters, because of the disturbances in Wales and the recurrent rebellions against his father, was constant and intense and certainly served as a most useful apprenticeship for his campaigns in France. It seems likely that young Henry's almost exclusive concern with military matters and military advantage during these formative years may have been a factor in focusing his energies, when he succeeded to the throne, on invasion and conquest to enforce his claims in France. His ruthlessness towards even his closest associates when they disobeyed any of his orders – so remarked on by his contemporaries – may have been fostered by the emotional shocks of his youth. At Shrewsbury, as in 1399 when he had formed part of Richard's entourage, Henry of Monmouth found himself at his father's side opposing one who had recently been his governor and exemplar. Hotspur had been intimately involved in the early Welsh campaigns and, with his brilliant reputation as a skilful warrior, must have been a redoubtable model for an impressionable youth. The disillusionment which his treachery would inevitably have aroused must have encouraged the emotional isolation and hardness which were such marked characteristics of Henry as king.

The battle of Shrewsbury had settled the Percies' conspiracy, but it had no real effect on the rebellion in Wales. The Patent Rolls still describe the prince's efforts to bring the Welsh to heel and, once again, the king made his yearly sortie into the principality. This time he got as far as Carmarthen, and left a force there, which was soon pleading to be relieved, but again Owen and his men ebbed like the tide before the king's onslaught, only to sweep back in full force as soon as he had passed. In fact, the year 1404 was to see the greatest extent of Glendower's influence. Glendower's men turned to the siege of the great castles that were the cornerstone of royal administration in Wales. Both Harlech and Aberystwyth were captured. The constable of Harlech seems to have been tricked into surrender by being seized when he came out of the castle to treat with the rebels without any hostage having been taken in his place.[18] Caernarvon, too, was attacked, with aid from the French, and the constable of Caernarvon had to send a woman messenger to the constable of Chester warning of the impending attacks since no one else was willing to go. In most of the many letters that pass at this time it seems obvious that the long years of struggle in Wales had resulted in great difficulty in keeping the royal castles adequately garrisoned. Harlech was meant to have a force of ten men-at-arms and thirty archers. According to the constable of Chester, at the time of the seizure of the constable of Harlech its garrison consisted of only five Englishmen, with sixteen Welsh, who were not considered reliable. Caernarvon's proper complement was twenty men-at-arms and eighty archers but the constable of Caernarvon declared that there were only twenty-eight fighting men in both the town and the castle. As well, eleven of the more able men, veterans of the last siege had died, some of wounds and some of the plague.[19]

Owen's hopes must have risen high in the spring of 1404, as his agents successfully treated with France, and a treaty of alliance between the king of France and Glendower against "Henry of Lancaster" was signed in Paris on 14 July 1404.[20] By August there were reports that the Count of La Marche had a sizeable fleet at Harfleur ready to invade Wales. Although nothing came of it, and the French fleet only cruised in the Channel, the report was worrisome. Meanwhile Glendower was intent on consolidating the new power and prestige among the Welsh which he had achieved by his capture of Harlech and Aberystwyth and his alliance with the French. He held his own parliament at Machynlleth, north-east of Aberystwyth.

The summer had seen activity on the English side as well. The prince, now firmly in control of all the efforts against the Welsh rebels, had kept in constant touch with his father and the council, and had even written specially to Archbishop Arundel. The refrain of all the letters was the same. "The rebels menace our people and our territories in the Marches. I will do all I can to repel them, but what I really need is money with which to pay my soldiers. I have used all the avenues open to me, including pawning my plate. What help can I have?" The answers from the king and his council were, as always, tardy and never quite sufficient. In the minutes of a council held at Lichfield at the end of August, the prince was thanked for his safeguarding of Herefordshire and was asked to continue this. Wine, corn and victuals were to be sent to the garrison at Carmarthen, in part payment of their wages – the supplies were to be bought from the proceeds of the customs at Bristol. So far as further action against the rebels was concerned Prince Henry was to make an expedition through Gwent and Netherwent and Glamorgan and was to be provided with money for the wages of 500 men-at-arms and 2,000 archers for three weeks, and 300 men-at-arms and 2,000 archers for another three weeks.[21] Again, it was not a sufficient force to do more than make a show of strength. Henry IV's grinding financial problems made the pacification of Wales a highly spasmodic and unsatisfactory business, and the king himself made no expedition into Wales during 1404.

At the beginning of 1405 the appearance of Welsh power was greater than ever before for the famous Tripartite Indenture probably belonged to February of this year. It divided the realm between Edmund Mortimer, who got the Thames Valley and the south: Northumberland, who got all the north and a large part of the Midlands: and Glendower, who not only was recognised as ruler of Wales, but also of the neighbouring parts of England from the source of the Severn northwards to the source of the Trent, the Mersey and the sea. Nevertheless, the conspirators had overestimated both their power and their effectiveness for early spring had also seen two setbacks for the rebels in Wales. On the night of Wednesday 11 March, Prince Henry wrote hurriedly to his father of the battle waged at Grosmont between some 8,000 Welsh rebels, who had attacked and burnt part of the town, and a much smaller royal force. It was led by Lord Talbot and included the "little meinie" of the prince's own household and killed some 800 to 1,000 of the Welsh. In a phrase which foreshadows Prince Henry's later exploits, and disclaimers, the prince assured his father that "victory was not in a multitude of people, but in the power of God". The letter was obviously written in haste and the messenger was empowered to describe the affair more fully to the king. The prince added rather wistfully, that they had taken only one prisoner, although he was a great chieftain, whom he would have sent to his father but the prisoner was not yet able to ride at his ease.[22] Another skirmish a little while later was equally successful for the royal forces. Griffith, Owen's eldest son, attacked the castle of Usk, which was defended in such sufficient force that its garrison could sally forth. In a battle fought at Pwl-Melyn Mountain, near Usk in the hill country of the Higher Gwent, the English killed Owen's brother Tudor, captured his son Griffith and killed and captured many of their men. Three hundred of the captives were summarily be-headed in front of the castle of Usk and Griffith and the others of nobler rank were sent to the king. Griffith languished in the Tower of London for six years, and then died there of some illness.[23]

The king was distracted from his concern over Wales by the last of the great conspiracies against his throne. The Scrope–Mowbray–Northumber-land rising in the north in the summer of 1405 was put down with dispatch and some trickery. The punishment of the conspirators was rapid and brutal – the king even executed the Archbishop of York for his share in encouraging the rising in York – and the results incalculable. Pious chronic-lers of the time inevitably considered the illness from which Henry suffered more and more over the next years as the result of his impious act.

At the end of August, Henry IV again turned his attention to Wales. He arrived in Worcester and, although no battle took place, as both sides suffered from a lack of men and provisions, the king embarked on his annual expedition for the pacification of Wales. As so often before, the forces of nature conspired against him. Because of unexpected floods the king lost some fifty chariots, carts and wagons with their baggage, including much of his treasure and his crowns.[24] Meanwhile the French promise of aid to the Welsh had finally produced a small naval force. Although it was attacked in the Channel by Lord Berkeley and others, the French retained sufficient strength to join Glendower's men and take the castle of Car-marthen. They were close to Worcester by the time the king arrived there, but the Welsh lack of provisions and the English lack of men meant the avoidance of battle.

An illuminating sidelight on the problems of Welsh pacification and the constant rumbling of alarms and rumours, is provided in the confession of John Oke, tried as a thief at Huntingdon in August 1405. Oke claimed that he had acted as an agent for prominent ecclesiastics in carrying gold and silver to Sir John Scudamore, the alleged receiver of Owen Glendower, which were used to sustain the rebellion. Another confession of the same sort by John Veyse accused English abbots (including the abbot of Bury St Edmunds), priors and other clerks of secretly supporting the Welsh rebels with cash and plate. Veyse claimed that he had been the intermediary between these clerics and John Swineshead, who then dispatched the contributions to Wales. Those implicated were not convicted and the charges seem basically improbable. Scudamore held several castles from Henry IV, despite the fact that he was married to Glendower's daughter, and his loyalty does not seem to have been doubted.[25] However, no matter how baseless the story in fact it illustrates two very strong contemporary attitudes. The clerics, and especially the friars, often exhibited a continuing loyalty to Richard and were in fact frequently involved in conspiracies in his favour. As well, there was a growing anticlericalism among laymen in high places. It is interesting to note that at three separate parliaments a contingent of Lollard-leaning knights had suggested that the goods of the clergy be taken to pay for the king's expenses in Wales. The suggestion appears to have arisen from the combination of a strongly felt emotional reaction against the clergy with the equally strong conviction that it was none of the knights' business to have to contribute to the king's necessities through taxation.

By 1406 the Prince of Wales was generally recognised as being in full and real charge of matters in Wales. Indeed, in the spring parliament the Commons congratulated him on his activities and demanded that he should devote himself to Wales and have the full royal warrant there. By dint of considerable scraping some £3,500 was collected and sent to the prince's receiver at Tutbury, for his expenses in Wales.[26] Nevertheless, although the king's financial difficulties remained acute and he did not come again to campaign in Wales, the situation there grew steadily better. The assistance promised to Glendower from the French proved to be meagre, and not very effective. Also, the expressions of goodwill from both the French and the Scots may have been encouraging but without material help did little to maintain the force of Glendower's drive. Although it is impossible to define the exact moment of the change, the ebbing of the Welsh tide became more evident over the next couple of years. Despite vigorous English attack, the Welsh managed to hang on at Aberystwyth during 1407, but in the following year both Aberystwyth and Harlech were recaptured by the prince's forces and most of Glendower's family – his wife, two daughters, and grandchildren – taken prisoner.

Some of the orders on the Patent Rolls at this time prefigure Henry's interest and detailed concern for the proper conduct of sieges, and the extraordinary mixture of people who accompanied him. The lord of Berkeley was commanded to cut down and provide sufficient timber to make "machines, bastiles, and other engines". The wood was to be shipped by barge along the coast to Aberystwyth and was to be accompanied by twenty carpenters of whom at least one was to be "a good and curious surveyor and scientific designer for the making of the engines".[27] During the siege of Aberystwyth in 1407, Prince Henry had among his retinue Master Richard Courtenay, the chancellor of Oxford, who administered the oath on the sacrament to the garrison by which they swore to surrender if Glendower did not come to their aid within a set period.[28] Glendower's arrival within the term meant that the castle held out till the following year. Richard Courtenay was an interesting figure, representative of many medieval clerics, but certainly not an ivory-tower academic. He had gained his BCL by 1399, and was chancellor of the university by 1406, at the age of twenty-six. His father was Sir Philip Courtenay of Devon and this noble background, in addition to his own abilities, meant that he was frequently used on royal business. He accompanied Philippa, Prince Henry's sister, to Copenhagen in 1406 for her marriage to King Eric, and from then on he frequently served Prince Henry. It would be interesting to know if the *De Officio Militari* by Richard Ullerston,* which was written for the prince at Courtenay's request to describe the moral and spiritual requirements of the knight's office, arose from this association of the chancellor with the prince in Wales. His treatise aimed to reinforce the serious side of Henry's character which, with his passion for careful planning, was already visible and was strengthened by the lessons he learned in Wales.

From 1408 on the Welsh rebellion was continuously losing ground. More and more of the rebels sued for peace and pardon, and got their lands back on the payment of a fine. Owen himself had lost his magic and the aura of success which had rallied the Welsh to his cause. His personal losses were heavy: one son and a brother killed; his son-in-law, Edmund Mortimer, killed at the siege of Harlech; and his wife and daughters captured and held in London. Glendower himself went into hiding with his one remaining son, Meredith. He was never captured or sued for pardon, although it was offered to him, but slipped untraced out of the historical record and into the mists of Welsh legend. Adam of Usk claims that he died in 1415, after having lain hidden for four years, and that he was buried at night by his followers. The first burial place was discovered by his adversaries, so he was secretly buried a second time, "no man knows where". The exact time and place of his death are uncertain though Owen's most reliable biographer states that it was before 30 April 1417. It seems likely that Owen spent his last years, once the flames of rebellion had died down, at Monnington Stradel, a manor belonging to John Scudamore who had married Owen's daughter Alice but had himself remained loyal to the king. Probably he was buried there in secrecy on the borders of the Wales over which he had ranged so widely. After his father's death, Meredith made no effort to carry on the rebellion, but came to the king and requested pardon. In 1421, during the few months that Henry was in England, Meredith's full pardon was enrolled on the Patent Roll.[30]

* Ullerston was a fellow of Queen's College whose interests were mainly theological. He wrote theological tracts, attended the Council of Pisa and preached before it. He was much interested in the reform of the church, writing out a series of petitions at the request of Bishop Hallum of Salisbury.[29]

Long before this time, as early as the end of 1406, the prince's primary interest in Wales was being transferred to wider matters of the whole realm. The man of nineteen had been toughened by six years of hard fighting. Despite his constant correspondence with the king and the frequent presence of trusted royal officials, he had been bearing an ever increasing share of the load for the last three years. The next two years were to see him win the necessary victories in Wales which allowed that agitated land to return gradually to ways of peace and freed the prince to take his place in the councils of the realm.

CHAPTER III

Apprenticeship to Power

The new and wider focus of activity for the Prince of Wales is marked by several official references. At the end of November 1406 he first appears as a witness to one of his father's charters, and at the beginning of December makes his first known attendance at council.[1] From this time on the young Henry was to play a more important role, serving a strenuous apprenticeship to royal power. His increasing responsibility was encouraged by several factors: the constant financial problems, which had repercussions on his ability to pay his soldiers in Wales; the growing physical weakness of the king, whose undiagnosed illness continued to sap more of his strength and energy; and, undoubtedly, the prince's own ambition.

The council had recently become a far more powerful body than it had been earlier in the reign. The long autumn parliament of 1406 had forced on the king a series of articles to be sworn to by his councillors, and these left the balance of power in the hands of the council. Henry IV spent Christmas at Eltham* but by 30 January 1407 Archbishop Arundel, the king's old friend, had been appointed chancellor and took possession of the great seal from Thomas Langley, Bishop of Durham. He swore the oath of office in the presence of the king, Prince Henry and John and Henry Beaufort, the Earl of Somerset and the Bishop of Winchester. The list of witnesses at this ceremony points up the emergence of the Beauforts as a strong force around the throne, and as particularly close companions and advisers to Prince Henry. John and Henry Beaufort were the older sons of John of Gaunt by his mistress, Katherine Swynford, whom he later married as his third wife. All four children of the union had been legitimated,

---

* Eltham, only a few miles southeast of London in the rolling open country, had been one of Richard's favourite royal manors to which he had added a dancing-chamber and a new bathhouse. Henry IV also used it frequently and made extensive alterations for himself, including a study with two desks, one of which served as a bookcase. None of this remains: the present medieval buildings date from the second half of the fifteenth century.[2]

not only by ecclesiastical law which recognised subsequent marriage as wiping out bastardy, but also by a civil act passed by King Richard, who at that time was anxious to conciliate his powerful uncle Gaunt. One of the first acts of this council of 1407 was to renew this act of legitimation, but below the bland surface of the official pronouncement the terms of the act suggest some cross-currents of struggle for power. The entry on the Patent Roll confirms the legitimation of 1397 with the ensuing ability to inherit, hold office, etc., but adds "excepting the royal dignity".[3] This seems an uncalled-for insult, and an unnecessary one. Henry IV had four active and strenuous sons – it did not seem likely that he would lack for heirs, nor specifically need to exclude any heirs sprung from the Beaufort line. If the statement masks, as it may well do, the already lively opposition between Archbishop Arundel and Henry Beaufort, as the most ambitious and able of the Beaufort clan, the battle lines for power near the throne were being drawn.

Archbishop Arundel, who took over the leading position in the council of 1407, was a man of fifty-five. Son of the Earl of Arundel, he had seen his older brother executed by King Richard and he himself had been exiled from his see of Canterbury. Arundel had risen to preferment in the church very young, as was characteristic of a member of such a great magnate's family. He studied at Oxford, although he never became a master, and was appointed Bishop of Ely when he was only twenty-one. By 1388 he had become Archbishop of York and was translated from there to Canterbury in 1396. Banished by King Richard in 1397 he ultimately joined Henry of Bolingbroke in Paris and crossed to Ravenspur with him when Henry made his bid for his own lands, and ultimately for the king-dom. The presence and support of Arundel had helped to ease Henry's relations with the baronage and gave a greater aura of legitimacy to his actions. As soon as Henry was installed on the throne Arundel was re-instated at Canterbury, and he served the king loyally and intelligently during his whole reign. In the ecclesiastical sphere Archbishop Arundel's greatest interest was in combating heresy, especially Lollardy. It was his initiative that pushed the legislation of 1401 which called for the burning of heretics, and he also set up a series of constitutions regulating preaching. In fact, his ill-wishers claimed that his death from a sudden malady of the throat which rendered him speechless for several days was a judgment on him for having stopped the mouths of the preachers.[4]

Archbishop Arundel's three years at the head of the council were not especially notable ones. Although the various problems which beset Henry IV remained, his difficulties became less acute. In Aquitaine, where French successes had brought a siege army to Bourg, just downstream from Bor-deaux, the situation was dramatically altered. In December of 1406 the citizens of Bordeaux hurriedly recruited a flotilla of river boats and suc-ceeded in destroying the French naval forces assisting in the siege of Bourg.

A month later, the Duke of Orléans, dispirited by the naval defeat and constant rain, withdrew his disheartened and diseased army. The duke's murder in November of 1407 spared Bordeaux from further attacks. For the moment the council could afford to ignore Bordeaux's pleas for help. The border war with Scotland had settled down into a truce after the battle of Homildon Hill and both sides had good reason to encourage the maintenance of the status quo. Henry IV had possession of James of Scotland as a prisoner at his court, for the young king had been captured while on his way to the French court for further education. The regent of Scotland was not anxious to see the king released, while the possession of the royal hostage was always a useful card for King Henry. By mutual agreement, the truce continued to be renewed.

Although relations with Scotland were calm, all was not yet quiet in the north of England. The old Earl of Northumberland, whose son had been killed at Shrewsbury and whose brother had been captured and executed there, still chafed against Lancastrian rule. The earl had been involved in the fated conspiracy which had ended in the execution of Archbishop Scrope of York and Mowbray, but Northumberland himself had escaped the king's vengeance by seeking refuge in Scotland. He was, however, unsure of his safety in the north and so made his way to Wales to seek help and encouragement from Glendower. By the end of 1406 Glendower might be willing to lend encouragement, but he had little else to offer. His own strength was being steadily eroded by the relentless pressure of the forces of the Prince of Wales. Northumberland seems to have gone on to seek help unsuccessfully in both France and Flanders and then came back to Scotland by the end of 1407 determined to act. In January 1408, in the midst of one of the coldest and snowiest winters of many years, he and his supporters crossed the Tweed and marched south through the Northumberland country where many of his tenants turned out to aid him. By the middle of February they had come unopposed beyond Thirsk. At Bramham Moor, south of Thirsk, Northumberland and his forces were met by the Sheriff of Yorkshire with a small royal force. Northumberland was killed in the battle; Bardolf, who had also been involved in the 1405 conspiracy, died of his wounds; and the other rebels were captured. With this battle, Henry finally achieved peace in the north, but, as a precaution, the lands of the Earl of Northumberland were not returned to his heir until after Henry V had come to the throne.

Another continuing problem for the king and the council at this time was at Calais, on the other side of France from Aquitaine. The great port and English foothold in France was an expensive investment – it cost the English exchequer some £17,000 a year. Finding the necessary sums inevitably strained the royal resources since Henry IV was always in financial difficulties. These were not always his fault, for the value of the customs on wool, which formed such an essential part of the revenues of the English king, fell heavily and inexplicably during his reign. Where the average revenue from this source had been £46,000 during Richard's reign it fell consistently during that of Henry IV – down to £39,000 during the first three years and then to a catastrophic £26,000 in 1402–3. Although receipts later improved they still only averaged £36,000 a year for the remainder of Henry IV's reign. Any medieval king had to live from hand to mouth, or, in more orthodox financial terms, from receipt of expected revenues to arranged subsidy, and in many cases the money, even when reluctantly granted by parliament, was not forthcoming with any speed or security. Because of these financial difficulties the Calais garrison had not been paid. The soldiers took matters in their own hands and forced action by the king, seizing the wool which was stored in the merchants' warehouses. The Calais situation was finally settled by various loans, including the largest of all from Richard Whittington, to be repaid from the wool subsidies. In this way the garrison received enough to satisfy them.

The three years in which Archbishop Arundel led the council saw a fair measure of success in the handling of the king's business. There were no notable new developments, but the revolt in Wales was finally quashed, the Percy rebellion in the north sputtered to a close and, by good fortune rather than royal assistance, the menace of French acquisition of Bordeaux was temporarily removed. At the same time the king's health worsened. The winter of 1408–9 saw Henry IV so seriously ill that he made his will and prepared for death. Both the prince and his brother, Thomas, were summoned to court in December because of the apprehension over their father's condition. On this particular occasion the king's health improved but from this time on he lacked physical strength and had difficulty clinging to power. The young and vigorous prince was ambitious and impatient, and resentment naturally flared between the exhausted king and his aggressive son, for the constant human urge for the young and strong to push the disabled out of their way is merely more obvious in the sharper light focused upon a throne. New appointments underlined the prince's growing responsibilities. At the end of February 1409 he was appointed constable of Dover and warden of the Cinque Ports, in place of Sir Thomas Erpingham, trusted retainer and friend of the king and an equally trusted servant of his son. The following year Prince Henry was named captain of Calais, after the death of his uncle John Beaufort, Earl of Somerset, but by that time he had already moved into a position of pre-eminence in the council.

The process by which the prince and his party achieved this take-over is cloaked in obscurity. Henry's regular appearance at council meetings during 1409 gave him further insight into the whole range of royal business. For example, in one important meeting in August the council dealt with a number of topics.[5] There were the relations with Prussia and with Spain, as well as various matters which required financial decisions. The king had placed his sons where he needed trustworthy lieutenants. Thomas had been charged with the governing of Ireland and needed money there. John was in command of the Scottish marches, and he too needed supplies. There was also a deputation from Aquitaine, for its steward and the mayor of Bordeaux had come to England to report their difficulties and to explain the necessity of English help. The mayor seems to have argued his case well and overcome the inertia which had marked the council's attitude to Bordeaux's difficulties three years before, for he was given a small force for the defence of the city. Nevertheless, it is remarkable that so little support was given to English interests in Aquitaine during the reigns of both Henry IV and his son. The wine trade from Bordeaux not only supplied England with the great percentage of its wines but was also valuable in import duties. English claims in Gascony were more long standing and much stronger legally than their claims to the French throne and the larger Plantagenet inheritance. It is perhaps suggestive that neither Henry IV or Henry V were acquainted with Aquitaine at first hand. Unlike most previous English kings, they had no personal contact with the duchy, and apparently little interest in it.

In December 1409 Archbishop Arundel and Sir John Tiptoft, the treasurer, both resigned. The reasons for their resignation are nowhere stated and it was several weeks before they were replaced. The undercurrents, and the ultimate choice of the new officials, point to the growing pre-eminence of the prince in the affairs of the council. He had spent most of the autumn and early winter at his manor of Berkhamsted and was not actually at court when the archbishop resigned, but by the time parliament convened at the end of January the prince and his supporters seem to have seized the initiative. Bishop Beaufort gave the sermon at the opening of parliament and four days later his brother Thomas was installed as chancellor. The Commons themselves had picked Thomas Chaucer as their Speaker and he was a cousin of the Beauforts, as well as the son of the poet. A little earlier, Lord Scrope of Masham, a great friend of the prince as well as the nephew of the executed Archbishop of York, had been appointed treasurer.

The mood of parliament was unco-operative. Once again it suggested that the financial problems of the country could be effectively met by the confiscation of the wealth of the clergy, and someone even worked out a detailed table of what the clerical wealth of the realm could provide. It asserted that the wealth of the bishops, abbots, and priors could provide the king with £20,000 annually, and in addition there would be enough to maintain fifteen earls, 1,500 knights, and 6,200 esquires. A further tapping of the resources of all the religious houses would support some 15,000 parish priests and enable every town to maintain its own poor.[6] It is tempting to link this strongly anti-clerical and Lollard document with the presence for the first time among the lords of Sir John Oldcastle, who was now lord of Cobham by right of his wife. Sir John had fought with the prince in Wales and had been one of his trusted commanders there, but his Lollard leanings were already well known and must have encouraged the anti-clerical knights who had been putting forward such proposals, though in less detail, for some years. Despite the financial stringency, such draconian measures did not appeal to either the orthodox king or the prince and nothing came of the suggestion.

During 1410 and 1411 while the prince assumed leadership on the council, Archbishop Arundel devoted much of his time to a dedicated struggle against Lollardy. In March 1410 he presided over the trial of John Badby, the tailor, for his Lollard opinions. Badby had been interrogated a year before and had been declared heretical but had been given a year in prison to rethink his position. At the beginning of March his trial was reopened and despite the archbishop's arguments Badby not only persisted in his heresy but, according to Walsingham, declared that the host was not the body of Christ, but an inanimate object worse than a toad or a spider. Not surprisingly, he was declared a recalcitrant heretic and handed over to the secular arm. His execution followed swiftly. He was enclosed in a barrel at Smithfield and before the fire was set, the prince, who was in attendance, came up and warned him to repent, but the tailor paid no heed. When he was struck by the flames he groaned miserably, which the onlookers interpreted as a desire to recant. The prince had the fire extinguished and the man removed from the flames and he himself comforted the half-dead heretic and promised him, even at that late moment, his life and pardon, and a grant of 3d a day from the royal treasury if he would repent. But Badby, whose spirit had revived somewhat, was firm in his belief and spurned the prince's offer. Thereupon, he was once more given to the flames and died there.[7] The incident is interesting in its light upon the willingness of the prince at this time to go as far, and perhaps even further than the law allowed to save a heretic. But, in the end, where obstinate heresy was involved not only the clerics, but the royal family and the lords could not condone these variations in belief which they felt struck at the very foundations of society. Anticlericalism was general, but orthodox faith was still considered a necessary safeguard for the whole social structure.

The archbishop also attacked the University of Oxford which he regarded with suspicion because of its continued harbouring of professed Wycliffites. The university, on the other hand, was generally less interested in opposing the archbishop on the issue of heresy than in reacting with great force and vigour to any effort, by an archbishop or anyone else, to thrust aside its cherished privileges and exemptions. The resultant quarrel between militant archbishop and rebellious university was inflamed on both sides by these very separate issues.

The archbishop's concern over Lollardy at Oxford had first surfaced at a convocation of the southern province held in Oxford in 1407. This assembly passed a series of constitutions to suppress Wycliffite opinions and set up committees to test theological writings for orthodoxy. Although the university dragged its feet in carrying out the archbishop's demand to have Wycliffe's works searched for errors, it slowly complied with his requirements and the committee reported in March 1411. Armed with their list of some 267 errors, Arundel decided to hold a full-scale visitation of the university with particular attention to matters of heresy. At this, the university balked. The canonical right of visitation was invariably much disputed in all ecclesiastical institutions of the Middle Ages, and Oxford was particularly anxious to insist on its freedom from archiepiscopal jurisdiction. In 1395, under a previous archbishop of Canterbury, it had obtained a papal bull of exemption from such archiepiscopal powers and it flatly refused to recognise the archbishop's right to visit. Recalcitrant proctors forced the chancellor to resign for publishing the archbishop's citation setting the visitation for 7 August. The university then elected as chancellor Richard Courtenay, who had previously filled the office, no doubt hoping that his connections with the court might ease the struggle. King Henry did try to head off the confrontation between the inflexible archbishop and the obstinate university, by urging the archbishop not to extend his visitation beyond matters of heresy and by reminding the university that, though he would protect their rightful liberties, the papal bull had never been confirmed by him or his predecessors and therefore was not in force in England. Both sides refused to give way or to appear conciliatory. Courtenay as chancellor warned the archbishop that he, or any other graduate, who upset university privileges was perjured, and therefore excommunicate. On the day set for the visitation, St Mary's church, the named meeting place, was locked against the archbishop. The angry Arundel had the door forced open and then laid an interdict on the church which a rebellious proctor refused to recognise and celebrated mass there in open defiance. It took the king himself to put an end to the unseemly quarrel. Henry commanded an end of the visitation and cited both sides to appear before him. The chancellor and the proctors were forced to surrender their offices and the proctors were imprisoned, though Courtenay was re-elected chancellor by the middle of November, perhaps with the backing of the Prince of Wales. The pope, under royal pressure, revoked the bull of exemption, and the university formally recognised the archbishop's rights. Both the irate king and the offended archbishop* were finally mollified and the

---

* Whatever the feelings of animosity in the university against Archbishop Arundel they had at least to thank him for the settlement of a long-standing controversy over the ownership of the fifty books, nucleus of the university library, whose possession had been disputed between Oriel and the university for some eighty years. Arundel restored them to the university and Courtenay immediately encouraged statutes for the regulation of the library and the enrolment of its distinguished benefactors. In return, a grateful university accorded Courtenay the special privilege of free lifetime access to the library during the daytime – perhaps the first example of a scholar's special library privileges.[8]

controversy subsided with no desperate results for anyone. It seems likely that Prince Henry had an important part in the final reconciliation. Certainly the university felt that he had pleaded their cause with success. In March 1412 a great congregation of regents and non-regents decreed that a solemn mass should be said for Prince Henry annually on All Hallows Eve, because he had reconciled the king and the archbishop to the university "against which they had been seriously incensed".[9]

The prince's period of dominance on the council was not concerned only with domestic matters. Relations with France had been reasonably unruffled for some years for the truce established in the reign of Richard II continued in force. However, the domestic situation in France continued to go from bad to worse, as the rivalry between the king's uncles and his younger brother, the Duke of Orléans, grew more acerbic. Each struggled to gain control over Charles VI whose periods of madness struck without warning and incapacitated him from ruling. The rivalry was particularly acute between Louis of Orléans and John of Burgundy and, in 1407, John arranged the murder of his cousin in a Paris street. The Duke of Burgundy consolidated his own power in Paris for the time being, but he made more vicious the internecine warfare which was to plague France for another twenty years, and to give the English an opportunity for intervention and conquest which Prince Henry at least was not slow to exploit. In the summer of 1411 Duke John was challenged by Charles of Orléans, Louis' oldest son and heir, with an army which included forces drawn from those other lords who supported Orléans – Armagnac, Albret, Bourbon, and Berry: John decided that he needed help and turned to ask for aid from England. Henry was delighted to be given this opportunity and dispatched a force which included such important nobles as the Earl of Arundel, Gilbert Umfraville, and Sir John Oldcastle. They went to Paris to meet the Duke of Burgundy and fought with the Burgundians against the Orléanists who had won the bridge of St-Cloud just west of Paris. The English and Burgundian allies recaptured St-Cloud and killed many of their opponents while the rest of the Orléans army broke up. In a prefiguration of Henry's later methods of operating in France the prince not only sent effective troops, he also armed his ambassadors with power to arrange a marriage between him and one of the daughters of the Duke of Burgundy, but nothing came of this.

The tortuosities of the English policy with regard to France between 1411 and 1413 illustrate the struggle for power that was also going on in England, although it was not as deadly, or as bloody, as the struggle in France. At the end of 1411 King Henry temporarily threw off his illness, regained his old decisiveness and once more took control of the council. The prince and his supporters were removed and Arundel returned as chancellor. This brought about quick changes in policy, since the king and the prince favoured opposing factions in France and the Orléans connection now felt it could appeal for help against the Burgundians. It was on Henry IV's initiative that diplomatic negotiations began in the winter of 1412 between the king and the ambassadors of Berry, Bourbon, Orléans, Armagnac and Alençon. A treaty was arrived at by the middle of May, providing for the restoration of Aquitaine to the English, and for English help against the French king, temporarily under the Duke of Burgundy's control. By the beginning of June the Duke of York and the king's second son, Thomas, were arranging indentures for a force to serve in France. At a council at Rotherhithe in July 1412, Thomas was created Duke of Clarence and given command of the expedition. The English force landed in the Cotentin in August and joined the Orléanist forces at Bourges, but before any serious fighting developed the feeling among the Orléanist coalition fluctuated once more, this time against English help. Clarence and his forces were bought off and rode south to Bordeaux in the classic pattern of the *chevauchée*, or armed raid, "capturing castles and towns and taking prisoners", and burning and destroying as they went.[10] Clarence spent the winter in Bordeaux and returned to England in the spring on hearing of the death of his father.

Meanwhile Prince Henry, who had withdrawn from the court after his loss of dominance in the council, was the centre of rumours that he was trying to overthrow his father. He wrote from Coventry on 17 June to protest his total fidelity, and his intent to seek further troops only to assist in the expedition to Aquitaine. He also protested against those who slandered him with accusations of misusing the funds committed to him for the payment of the garrison in Calais. His proof against these allegations was brought forward in the council and he was acquitted of this charge.[11] It is difficult to discover exactly what lay behind this breach between the king and the Prince of Wales. The *English Life** suggests that the king suspected his son of wanting to usurp the crown while he was still alive – whether or not this was true, it was widely believed. It was also obvious that the prince was more popular than his tired and ill father, and that his court was thronged, not only by his genuine followers, but also by those opportunist hangers-on who are always to be found where they feel power and patronage will soon be. This must have galled the king and those most loyal to him, and further embittered relations. The biographer draws the curious picture of the prince arriving at the court at Westminster dressed in a blue satin gown, worked in eyelets, with the needles hanging from them,† and wearing the ss collar of gold. Prince Henry sought a private

* The *English Life* was an early-sixteenth-century translation of the official Latin Life by Titus Livius. It includes several stories not mentioned elsewhere which the translator acquired from the Ormonde family.

† It is a possible conjecture that the prince's extraordinary costume was inspired by Bishop Beaufort's connection with Queen's College, Oxford, for on New Year's Day members of that college were presented with threaded needles (an elaborate pun on the name of Eglefield, the founder), and adjured to take them and be thrifty.[12]

interview with his father and knelt before him, saying that he understood that the king was suspicious of him but that if his father felt he had reason for doubt, the prince offered his own dagger with which the king could slay him, for "my life is not so desirous to me that I woulde live one daye that I shoulde be to your displeasure". At this the king's heart was softened and he embraced the prince and restored him to grace and favour.[13] The story seems over-blown and unlikely to our ears, but we must remember that this facile emotionalism was a normal part of the pattern of the time, and such sweeping gestures were both common and unremarkable.

Henry, like many a Prince of Wales since, was a natural target for moral advice and hortatory treatises on the way he should behave. Mention has already been made of the tract sent him by Ullerston, the Oxford scholar, which took a religious view of Christian knighthood and exhorted him to spiritual study. During the last two years of his father's life one of the best-known poets of the day, Thomas Hoccleve, also penned his thoughts for the illumination of the prince. Since Hoccleve was a clerk in the Privy Council office, none too well-paid and the recipient of a pension from King Henry IV, which was frequently in arrears, it is a fair question whether Hoccleve's treatise was meant more for the edification of Henry or the enrichment of Hoccleve. It is primarily a popular compilation in English verse of three very well-known works of instruction: the *Secret of Secrets*, supposedly by Aristotle; the *Concerning the Rule of Princes*, by Giles of Rome; and the *Game of Chess Moralized* by James de Cessolis. Hoccleve's verse has none of the classic qualities of Chaucer, whom he revered as his master, but the work is interesting in its allusions to current events and the feelings of the time. Fortunately, Hoccleve does not stick too closely to his originals. He is most interesting to us when he declaims on the wild extravagances of fashion and draws a vivid, if perhaps exaggerated, picture of the men who walked the streets of London in scarlet gowns twelve yards wide with sleeves hanging to the ground. Hoccleve's casual comment that such men are not of much use in their lord's retinue since they cannot be effective in a street-fight encumbered with such sleeves provides a quick glimpse of the noisy disorder of city streets. He draws also a vivid picture of the labours of the clerks in the Privy Seal office working at the ever growing mass of documents:

> But we labouren in travaillous stilnesse
> We stoupe and stare upon the shepes skyn,
> And kepe most our songe and wordes in[14]

complaining that they were forced to work silently with no help from conversation or song as they bent over their parchments. But most interesting of all is Hoccleve's outspoken complaint against the continuing war with France which he would like to see settled. Unlike the lords, who might see the possibilities of wealth through service and profits, Hoccleve

looks at the results for the poor caught up in the middle of a fight they
do not understand:

> Allas! what peple hath your werre slayne!
> What cornes wastede, and downe trode and shent!
> How many a wyfe and mayde hathe be forlayne,
> Castels doune bete, and tymbred houses brent
> And drawen doune, and alle totore and rent!
> The harme ne may nat rekened be ne tolde;
> This werre wexeth alle to hore and olde.[15]

Henry was given a lot of advice – he does not seem to have paid much
attention to Hoccleve's and it is hard to tell whether all the poet's work
helped very much to make his annuity less tardy.

In the face of all this advice what are we to think of the stories of Henry's
riotous youth? We know that Henry was much in London during these
years and that he had been given a lifetime grant of Coldharbour, the great
house in London beside All Hallows the Less. Conveniently located near
Hay Wharf and London Bridge it had previously belonged to the Black
Prince, and was used for at least one council meeting. We know that his
younger brothers were involved in a brawl in a tavern in Eastcheap, when a
fight developed between two factions from court which had to be broken
up by the responsible officials of the city. This tale may have been stretched
to include Henry himself. The wildest stories, which Shakespeare used,
are of much later provenance, and are distinctly dubious. Henry's contemporaries describe him as "wild and reckless in his youth" or, in a literary
vein, speak of his devotion to both Mars and Venus, but these are not
really very specific or very extreme accusations.[16] It must be remembered
that the current standard of behaviour allowed for a wide latitude in what
we would certainly call breaches of the peace, if not assault. Such happen-
ings did not necessarily suggest that those involved were not regarded as
respectable citizens who could subsequently rise to positions of importance
in the realm. Take, for example, the case of Sir John Pelham who, in 1387,
led a gang in storming a manor house near Cambridge, and forcibly
removed the owner's widowed sister-in-law and a quantity of valuables.
The lady in question was a landed heiress in her own right, and after this
summary abduction Pelham married her. He escaped any punishment,
although some of the smaller fry involved were arrested and one was
hanged.[17] Yet this same Pelham was at the time in the retinue of John of
Gaunt and became a member of parliament, the treasurer of England, and
constable of Pevensey Castle, in charge of some of the most distinguished
of state prisoners including even Queen Joan. It is against the light of
incidents such as these, therefore, that one must look at the accusations of
Henry's "riotous" youth. His conduct was particularly remarked because
he was the king's son, and all agree that his behaviour as king was immedi-

ately and continuously irreproachable. It must be added that the chroniclers' emphasis on his sudden and dramatic conversion at the moment of his accession to the throne owes something to their almost irrepressible instinct to make their histories as dramatic as possible. In medieval terms, the process of creating a legend of heroism or sanctity almost required a striking conversion to high seriousness from previous wildness.

By November of 1412 the king was already very ill. His skin disease had affected his face so that he was repulsive to look at. Although writs were issued for another parliament it never officially met because of the king's health. Henry spent Christmas at Eltham and then returned to London. In February the business of the great council was assented to by the Prince of Wales – he was not a member of the council, but it was obvious that the king was dying and that authority would soon be in the prince's hands.

It is about this period of Henry IV's prolonged final illness that some of the chronicle stories cluster. Henry is supposed to have swooned while making an offering at the shrine of Edward the Confessor at Westminster and he was then carried to the abbot's lodging, the Jerusalem Chamber. The crown had been placed on a cushion by the dying monarch and, according to Monstrelet, the informed Burgundian chronicler, the king was so close to death that his attendants had covered his face with a cloth, thinking him dead. The prince therefore took the crown. But King Henry roused himself once more and, troubled over the absence of the crown, called for the prince. Prince Henry avowed that he had acted in good faith, having been told that his father was dead and that therefore the kingdom and the crown belonged to him as eldest son. But the king sighed and declared that his eldest son had no right, as he himself had had none. The prince's reply is characteristic of his uncompromising belief in himself, untroubled by second thoughts or suspicions: "As you have held it by right of your sword, it is my intent to hold and defend it during my life."[18] Capgrave, an English chronicler, is not quite as dramatic as Monstrelet but he has the king's confessor urging him to repent his usurpation and his execution of Archbishop Scrope. Henry replied with some energy that he had received absolution from the pope for the matter of the archbishop, and, as for the crown, his sons would never suffer him to give it up.[19] However, both these authors, although happily pillaged by the Tudor historians and therefore by Shakespeare, were not contemporary to the matters they describe. The more contemporary chroniclers speak only of the king's deathbed counsels to his son, and these were of the platitudinous variety which every medieval king felt it was necessary to press upon his heir – the importance of justice, the avoidance of all oppression and extortion. The prince was not to be vain of his kingly position but rather to bear it as a burden, defend it well, and give the glory to God. The king was particularly worried that discord might arise between Henry and his brother Clarence since he knew "bothe to be of so grete stomake and courage", but Henry reassured his father about this, promising him that he would love his brothers above all men so long as they were faithful and obedient and, if not, would do them evenhanded justice.[20]

On 20 March Henry IV died and the Prince of Wales became Henry V. All the chroniclers emphasise that there was an immediate change when the impulsive prince became king. One mentions that Henry had a holy hermit brought secretly to him at Westminster where he spent the night after his father's death in penance and prayer with the holy man. Perhaps the final acquisition of the longed-for reality of power had a sobering effect. Certainly from this time on, Henry was, and remained, a monarch concerned always with the business of the kingdom and the extension of his power and rule.

The relationship between Henry of Monmouth and his father is hard to fathom. From all the evidence it certainly seems to have been one of remarkably little emotional involvement. In reality, Henry had seen little of his father during his young years, and his expedition with Richard to Ireland may have left him with warmer feelings for Richard, whom he knew, than for his father, whom he did not. Besides the effect on Henry of Monmouth of the imprisonment and death of King Richard by his own father, there was also the relationship between Henry and Hotspur, who for three years served as his governor in Wales and led him on the first expeditions against the Welsh. Hotspur's death, also in rebellion against Henry's father, must have left the young prince with some difficult emotional conflicts. Nevertheless, it would appear that there was respect and loyalty between the prince and his father, at least during the earlier years of the reign. By 1408, however, Henry of Monmouth's ambition, fuelled by his father's serious illness, had won out over his filial feelings. He avoided open revolt but he obviously chafed at the restraints on his power and ability to manoeuvre which Henry IV continued to impose tenaciously until two months before his death. To use the modern term, the prince was frustrated by his father's policies, by the restriction on his initiative, and there seems to have been no real sorrow at his father's death, only the visible desire to get on with his work as undisputed monarch. Henry IV had been an active and popular young man – wealthy noble, an able combatant, and convinced crusader. He gained the throne and he held it – this latter was really his accomplishment in the light of revolts, financial embarrassments, and general lack of enthusiasm – but he seems to have roused remarkably little affection, either among his subjects or his children.

CHAPTER IV

Crowned King: Rebellion and Heresy

The young man who was crowned King of England in a solemn ceremony at Westminster Abbey on 2 April 1413 in the midst of an untimely spring snowstorm, was a notable contrast to his sickly father. Some of his contemporary biographers provide a sharp portrait of his appearance, although the emotional deductions which they draw from physical characteristics do not necessarily appeal to later generations. They say that he was of more than medium height and handsome. His head was round, with a smooth forehead and a suitably proportioned face. His hair was smooth, brown and thick. His eyes were bright and an enthusiastic clerk insists that they were "dovelike in peace, but leonine in anger". He had a cleft chin and small ears, as well as white, even teeth. His neck was long, his body slender and lean, and he was noted as a remarkably swift runner – he could even run down a wild deer.[1] The picture these contemporaries draw resembles very closely the familiar portrait of Henry V.* The wiry, athletic young king became a changed character with his coronation – and all his contemporaries agree on that too, although they are more or less specific about his actual youthful misdeeds. Their stories range from the late, rather scurrilous gossip picked up by the author of the *English Life*, to the more sober judgment of Walsingham and his followers, who merely stated that Henry on his accession to the throne was immediately changed into another man, remarkable for honesty, modesty, and gravity. The serious-minded monk of St Albans revelled in the symbolism which that spring snowstorm allowed him to add to his rotund phrases.[3]

We know that the coronation was presided over by Thomas Arundel as Archbishop of Canterbury and the rite appears to have been carried out as it had been for Richard II and Henry IV. Henry V followed the usual pattern of gathering a number of noble young squires around him at the

* The portrait dates only from the late fifteenth or early sixteenth century, although it may well have been derived from an earlier, now vanished, votive painting, which would account for the profile view and the position.[2]

Tower of London on the night before the coronation. They were duly
knighted there and accompanied their king to Westminster. Titus Livius
reported with astonishment that the great men of the realm had made an
unprecedented offer to swear the oath of fealty before Henry was even
crowned or had taken the oath to rule well[4] – valuable reinforcement for a
king whose strength and proven ability had to buttress a shaky legal claim.
At this time Henry also installed his own officials, naming the Earl of
Arundel (nephew of the archbishop but with a history of membership in
Henry's party) as treasurer of England. The new king handed the most
important office of chancellor to his uncle, Henry Beaufort, the Bishop of
Winchester – a position which the rich and shrewd bishop seems to have
exploited to ensure the payment of over £800 which the king had borrowed
from him while Prince of Wales.[5] With the appointment of Beaufort and
the Earl of Arundel the king knew that his own unquestioned supporters
were in the positions of power and he turned almost at once with his
characteristic energy to the problems of government which awaited his
decision.

Within a month after his coronation Henry had convened his first
parliament at Westminster. It met in the Painted Chamber for its formal
opening and the expected oration by the Bishop of Winchester. After the
formalities had been observed the king moved briskly to get business under
way. The Commons were adjured to meet in their usual spot, the Chapter
House of Westminster Abbey, at seven o'clock of the morning on Wednesday to choose their Speaker and to present him to the king by eight. From
the beginning of the session the nature of the petitions presented to the
king by the Commons illustrated the temper of the realm. The king asked
for, and received, the customary grants on wool, wool-fells, and skins to
be used for the defence of the realm for four years and customs duties on
wines for a year from Michaelmas. A petition put forward by Rhys ap
Thomas sought the removal of the disabilities imposed on Welshmen in
England by the statute of 1401. Rhys reminded the king that Henry himself was a Welshman, born of a father and mother born in Wales. It seems
unlikely that Henry was touched by this naïve appeal to his birth in Monmouth, but his cooler judgment could recognise that the Welsh were no
longer a danger to the peace of the realm and the petition was allowed.
A series of petitions also underlined the basic xenophobia characteristic of
England at this time. The Commons wanted the aliens thrown out of the
realm. They were anxious that no Frenchman should have or enjoy any
benefice in the realm, and those already in possession must buy letters
patent to make them denizens. The Statute of Provisors was to be strictly
enforced – this, of course, was a useful weapon in the king's hands against
papal filling of benefices which he himself wanted to exploit.[6]

While parliament was continuing its sessions through the end of May
and into the beginning of June, Henry was also taking the first steps in his

council to refashion his administration. On 22 May, for example, John Catterick, soon to start his upward spiral through ever more desirable bishoprics, was constituted king's proctor at the Roman curia, and the lieutenant of Calais and another royal protonotary were given power to deal with the Aragonese ambassadors. But the council was not only interested in such administrative minutiae. In the course of several meetings in June and July they wanted to discuss the major questions which faced the new king, the state of affairs with Scotland and the marches, the problems of Aquitaine, the relationships with France and Ireland, and the desire to keep the sea safe for merchants. There also seems to have been some discussion as to where the king should spend the summer. His council's advice was that he should stay near London in the place that suited him best, so that he could more easily receive the news from each county. In this way he could make the best provision for the defence of each part of the realm.[7]

Henry had other more personal concerns as well. Before the end of May he had ordered, and paid a coppersmith of London the sum of £43 to design and make an image in copper of his mother, ornamented with various arms of the kings of England. This was to be placed over Mary de Bohun's tomb in the king's college at Leicester.[8] One is inclined to feel that Henry was not so much moved by spontaneous affection for the young mother whom he could hardly remember, but rather by the desire to make sure that she was honoured as was suitable for the mother of a king. He also presided at the solemn burial of his father in Canterbury Cathedral, since Henry IV had expressed the desire to be buried near the Becket shrine, and made provision for the reburial of Richard II. After his unexplained death Richard had been hurriedly buried at King's Langley, some twenty miles northwest of London, in the Dominican church which adjoined the royal manor there. On 8 December Henry had Richard's body brought back to Westminster for ceremonial reburial in the tomb next to his beloved Anne of Bohemia, where he had wished to lie. It is impossible to know whether this move was prompted, as the *Brut* suggests, by the desire to be cleansed of his father's sin, or, as seems more likely, by the real affection he felt for Richard. Walsingham suggests – and the St Albans monk was both informed and near at hand – that Henry felt he owed as much veneration to Richard as to his father in the flesh. The procession was carried out with all the expected solemnity for such an important occasion. It is amusing to note, however, that Henry showed no wild extravagance. The banners to be placed on the hearse carrying Richard were hurriedly borrowed from Henry IV's tomb at Canterbury, and the wax which remained from the partly burned candles was melted down and delivered to the clerk of the king's spicery for the use of the royal household.[9]

One issue which had been simmering steadily below the surface during the reign of Henry IV was fated to burst into full-scale eruption at the very beginning of Henry V's reign. All during his father's time there had been a deep current of anti-clericalism, and signs of an attachment to Lollardy among many of the country knights who agreed with its arguments against the church's possessions. Their feelings had surfaced several times in the suggestion in various parliaments of Henry IV that the king's expenses in the rebellion in Wales and the north could best be covered by the expedient of confiscating all the goods of the church. The suggestion had been rejected but it represented a widespread feeling in the country. The trial and burning of John Badby in 1410 illustrated the continued existence of Lollard opinions and the insistence of Archbishop Arundel, with the support of the king, on stamping out this heresy. In August of his first year as king, Henry issued a strong proclamation against "the pestilent seed of Lollardy and evil doctrine", and emphasised his desire to defend the Catholic faith and to maintain the laws and ordinances of the church and the realm.[10] Lollard preaching was encouraging sedition and discontent throughout the realm, and Henry had to take a firm stand. The matter came to a head when the suspicion of heresy touched one of the king's own friends and loyal captains, John Oldcastle.[11]

Sir John Oldcastle, Lord Cobham, was about ten years older than his king. He had been born in Herefordshire of a family that was rising in the world, and he continued the upward climb. He had served Henry IV in his expedition to Scotland in 1400 and had fought against Owen Glendower and the Welsh. During this period he became attached to the household of the Prince of Wales and began accumulating further marks of esteem – an annuity of 100 marks and an appointment as sheriff of Herefordshire in 1406–7. Then, as a sign of his growing importance, he married the heiress, Joan de la Pole. He was his wife's fourth husband, and she brought Oldcastle both wealth and position, for she had inherited not only from her father but also from her maternal grandfather, Lord Cobham, one of the most important landowners of Kent. In 1409 Oldcastle was summoned to parliament as a baron, and he continued to follow the natural pattern of his class, taking part in an Anglo-French tournament at Lille in 1409 and, in 1411, being one of the captains sent by the Prince of Wales to help the Duke of Burgundy recover Paris.

However, his involvement in these normal activities did not keep Oldcastle from a growing absorption in Lollardy. By the spring of 1410 one of his chaplains was preaching heresy in several parishes in Kent, right under the watchful and suspicious eye of Archbishop Arundel. The churches were interdicted, but the sentence was quickly raised out of respect for Lady Joan, Oldcastle's wife. By this time Oldcastle himself seemed intent on proving his adherence to the movement. In September he wrote a congratulatory letter to a Bohemian noble who was a prominent supporter of Hus, and a year later he wrote to King Wencelas of Bohemia in the same terms, even mentioning that he had been carrying on a correspondence with Hus. It is not surprising that at the convocation which began on 6 March 1413 the clergy encouraged further exploration into the people around Oldcastle. John Lay, suspect as a heretic, was interrogated and said he had celebrated mass that morning in Oldcastle's presence. A later search of an illuminator's shop in Paternoster Row turned up some hard evidence – a number of heretical tracts belonging to Oldcastle – for which the archbishop had obviously been looking.

Arundel's problem was how to deal with a matter so potentially explosive, since Oldcastle was known as a friend and intimate of the king. Henry was informed of the archbishop's suspicions and the stage was set for a confrontation which took place at the royal manor of Kennington, with both the king and Oldcastle present. The orthodox king was shocked by the heretical passages in the tracts which had been confiscated, but Sir John was unruffled and proceeded to excuse himself to the satisfaction of the king, but not to that of the clergy present. During the subsequent discussions among the clergy, the lower clergy pushed for immediate trial and condemnation, but the more worldlywise prelates were circumspect, and paid another visit to the king at Kennington. Henry then took the matter into his own hands and asked the clergy to await the result of his personal appeal to Oldcastle. But whatever his arguments they were not sufficient to prevail with his captain and by August Henry wrote to Archbishop Arundel that he could cite Oldcastle for trial. By this time, all appearances of civility and co-operation had vanished. Oldcastle refused to accept any citation or to appear before the court which sat on 11 September at the archbishop's castle at Leeds, Kent. He was, therefore, excommunicated in his absence and once again cited to appear on 23 September to show why further proceedings should not be taken against him.

Some time during these first weeks of September, Oldcastle was arrested and imprisoned in the Tower, for it was the Keeper of the Tower who brought him to the Chapter House at St Paul's for the second hearing where the archbishop, aided by the bishops of Winchester and London, was waiting to hear the case. When asked to seek absolution, he paid no attention but produced his own profession of faith which he proceeded to read to the court. The document was a clever one, and specifically designed to give the impression of agreeing with Catholic doctrine, while not in reality doing so. The archbishop was not at all convinced, and Sir John refused to alter his statement in any way. The court then decided to frame and put their own questions to Oldcastle and to require a full and complete answer the following Monday (25 September). At the hearing on Monday Oldcastle seems to have decided that he must at length declare himself without circumlocutions. He threw off any ambiguous appearance of adherence to official doctrine, roundly denounced the pope as antichrist, and declared that no prelate should be obeyed unless he was proved to be an imitator of Christ. Despite all Arundel's attempts – and they seem to have been sincere and strenuous – Oldcastle insisted on remaining obdurate in his beliefs. The church court condemned him and he was to be handed over to the secular arm as an incorrigible heretic. However, before secular justice could take its course, the king made one last effort for his friend. He urged that sentence should be delayed for forty days, during which time Oldcastle was to be imprisoned in the Tower in hopes of changing his mind. Oldcastle used the time in a way the king had not anticipated. Instead of being brought to see the error of his ways he gained the assistance of Lollard sympathisers in the city, and on 19 October escaped from the Tower and hid with one William Parcheminer, a Lollard bookseller who lived near St Sepulchre's, Smithfield.

By this time Oldcastle's insistence on his Wycliffite beliefs had led him beyond the original Lollard attack on clerical possessions and riches, beyond the original concept of preaching and a campaign of peaceful persuasion, to direct attack, not only on the church but also on the king and the lay lords who did not share the Lollards' point of view. To put it bluntly Oldcastle was now contemplating active treason. His conspiracy was a cunning one and called for a fair measure of knowledge of the king's movements and also for the ability to call in Lollard sympathisers from various parts of the country. Henry and his brothers went to Eltham to spend Christmas and Epiphany. Perhaps consciously harking back to the attempt on Henry IV in the first Christmas of his reign, Oldcastle plotted to have certain conspirators, disguised as mummers, appear before the court at Eltham and capture the whole royal family. But the king was on guard for such a contingency. He had notified his spies to be on the lookout for any conspiracies, and his prescience was rewarded. After the rebellion had been put down Thomas Burton, "king's spy", was paid 100s as a special reward for his great pains and diligence and for his attentive watchfulness to the operations of the rebellious Lollards, and because he let the king know fully what their intentions were.[12] The mayor of London was also warned, whether by the king or by another informer, so that at ten o'clock of Epiphany night he, with a strong force chosen from the aldermen and the men of the watch, went to the sign of the Axe, outside Bishopsgate, which was owned by a Lollard carpenter. There they captured the carpenter himself and some seven other would-be mummers, including one of Oldcastle's own squires. They were taken to Eltham and appeared before the king, but in a very different fashion from what they had proposed. They were induced to confess and were apparently put immediately into chains, for the exchequer reports payment for four pairs of fetters, two pairs of manacles, and six other varieties of irons, all with locks, which had been sent to Sir Thomas Erpingham as steward of the king's household "for the traitors lately taken at Eltham".[13]

Despite the capture of these conspirators and the failure of the first half of Oldcastle's plan, he appears to have made no effort to call off the rallying of the Lollards' outside London in the early morning of Wednesday 10 January. It may be that it was already too late to put off those supporters coming up from the country. The king himself seems to have returned to Westminster on 8 January, passing through London on his way from Eltham. From the security of his palace at Westminster Henry planned the further movements in the dismantling of the potentially dangerous conspiracy. The London Lollards were already discouraged by the sight of the king and the knowledge that he had escaped from the ambush arranged for him so, on the crucial night when they should have appeared at St Giles' Fields in strength, they did not leave the safety of the city. The king himself had arranged for the guard of the city gates and had set his troops to cover the principal approaches to the Fields, the arranged point of meeting for all the conspirators. Henry reserved for his own personal command the army covering the road to Westminster. The result was a triumph for the king's organisation and attention to detail. Many of the Lollard supporters coming up from the country walked all unknowingly into the trap laid by the king and were easily caught. There seems to have been relatively little real fighting although there was a great deal of confusion. It would appear that many of the Lollards escaped in the darkness, but the king's troops captured some eighty individuals, although the richest prize, Oldcastle himself, escaped. The major threat to Henry V's possession of the crown ended in a confused midnight skirmish.

Religious dissent and sedition had joined hands and it is difficult to try and disentangle the fair share of each in the uprising. However, from the records of the trials and executions which took place with great rapidity, it would appear that political conspiracy was a greater motive force than religious heresy, for of the some forty conspirators that were executed within the next weeks only seven were burnt, the accepted penalty for heresy. The remainder were merely hanged as traitors. The king made determined efforts to have Oldcastle surrendered, but the loyalty that surrounded him kept the Lollard knight free for another few years. Archbishop Arundel died in February before he could be sure that the Lollard threat to orthodoxy, which he had countered with great vigour, was really on the wane, but he could at least be comforted by the knowledge that the immediate danger to King Henry was over.

By the end of March the commissions of enquiry around the country had done their task, the main conspirators, apart from Oldcastle, had been captured and executed, and the king had decided on general clemency for those remaining. Very wisely too, the king had issued general orders that no one was to be arrested or to have his goods and chattels seized on mere suspicion of Lollardy without the authority of the king or his ministers. He reminded the sheriffs that many men strove to accuse persons of misdeeds so that they could themselves enjoy their goods. The passion for justice, the characteristic which was so marked in Henry, appears in the tone of this proclamation for it declared that "the king wishes that no man have cause for undue fear and that men accused be punished by the laws of the realm and not otherwise".[14] The terms of the pardons which were finally distributed to many of the remaining prisoners in November 1414 suggest at least the propaganda estimate of the wide-ranging purposes of the conspiracy: the conspirators had intended to kill the king and his brothers; to occupy, spoil, and knock down all churches and religious houses and their goods; and to make John Oldcastle regent.[15] The king's offer of pardon to rebels who had been sentenced to death marks the depth of his conviction that the worst of the danger was over, and that clemency would sooner heal and unite the country. In fact, clemency was even offered to Oldcastle himself. Although he had been formally outlawed in June 1414, Henry decided by the end of the year, as he planned his invasion of France and sought the tranquillity of his realm, to offer pardon to his old friend. In December 1414, and again two months later, the king offered to pardon Oldcastle if he came out of hiding and surrendered. Henry's offer went unheeded and Oldcastle remained at large after the king had left for France.

Looking back on the reign of Henry V, illumined as it is for us by the brilliance of his later military victories, we tend to forget that in 1413–14 the reality was a great deal less glorious. Henry IV had usurped the throne. He had maintained himself on it despite some serious efforts to dislodge him, but Henry V's title was none too secure. There seems little doubt that there were several important pockets of antagonism to him. The Lollards who now made a holy cause of their opposition to the king, the convinced supporters of Richard II, and those embroiled in various dynastic hatreds – all accounted for a general current of unease and for the fact that Oldcastle was able to remain at liberty until 1417, despite a price on his head of 1,000 marks. The reports of various incidents give body to this sense of unease.

The most important of all these was the Southampton Plot which was disclosed to the king just before he left for France in the summer of 1415. Richard, Earl of Cambridge and younger brother of the Duke of York, was the instigator of this plan to kill the king and his brothers and put the Earl of March, Richard II's legitimate heir, on the throne. Cambridge was part of the Percy connection and the plans for the uprising were reminiscent of earlier years: the young Percy would raise the north, the Scots would assist, and Glendower and Oldcastle would unite the west. The ringleaders in the plot – Cambridge himself, Thomas Gray, and Henry Lord Scrope – were all from the north with its tradition of unrest under Lancastrian rule. Scrope was the most surprising person to find in such a plot. Treasurer of England, Knight of the Garter, close personal friend of King Henry – even to sharing his chamber – he was an unlikely conspirator.

But he was also the nephew of Archbishop Scrope of York, executed after the failure of the 1405 conspiracy, and this and other family ties seem to have, in the end, outweighed his loyalty to the king. Some of the chroniclers suggest that French gold was behind the plot, hoping to achieve the abandonment of the expedition, but the banked fires of northern hostility and opportunism are a sufficient explanation in themselves. Besides, the French do not seem to have been sufficiently co-ordinated to act so effectively. The original conspirators were at first unsuspected. The Earl of Cambridge had even indented with the king to take a sizeable force of some 220 men to France and had come to Southampton, ostensibly to take ship. There is some question as to when the Earl of March actually joined the conspiracy, but, in any case, he disclosed it to the king at Porchester the night before the assassinations were meant to occur. In giving away his confederates he saved his own skin. Henry reacted quickly, coolly and with immediate severity. Cambridge, Scrope, and Gray were seized, tried, condemned and executed for treason – Gray immediately and Scrope and Cambridge, having requested trial by their peers, within five days. The sentences were softened from the full harshness of the penalties for treason. All three were only beheaded, not hanged, and only Scrope, whose treachery Henry must have felt most keenly, was drawn in ignomiry through the streets of Southampton to the place of execution.[16]

The king did not allow the necessary hard decisions or any feeling of personal loss to interfere with the planned departure of his expedition. Although the plot came to nothing it appears to have encouraged the Lollards who hoped to rouse more general enthusiasm when the king was safely out of the realm on his way to France. There was still much loose and dangerous talk, according to the St Albans' chronicler, who recorded how the malcontents continued "to raise their tails, vomit blasphemies about the king, to speak out bombastically, and to post on the doors of churches and elsewhere scattered threats in written documents".[17] Oldcastle himself hoped to seize the opportunity to incite rebellion again, and was known to have been entertained in August at Chesterton (War.) by the former vicar. But, though individual cases of rebellion and heresy* were discovered, the Lollards were unable to co-ordinate their efforts or launch another uprising.

Nevertheless, they continued to look for any possible means of publicity and support. There was the case of Thomas Lucas, for example, once a Fellow of Merton, who was brought to trial in the Easter term of 1417 for "conspiring the king's deposition or death". He had sent a letter to the Emperor Sigismund during the imperial visit to England which put

---

* There was the unusual case of the extraordinarily modern Lollard who had constituted his daughter a priest and had her celebrate mass in his own house. He was seized, examined, and having been convicted of "running into such madness" and heresy was burnt at London in 1415.[18]

forward the Lollard arguments against possessioners and, in addition, claimed that Richard II was alive in Edinburgh. Lucas then broadcast his accusations by scattering bills with these accusations in the streets of London and Canterbury. The indictment also suggests that Lucas had acted with, counselled and abetted all the works of Oldcastle, "both in opinions of Lollardy and in all his other evil deeds, treacherously purposed and imagined . . . towards the king".[19]

The inevitable end to the Lollard upheaval came with the capture of John Oldcastle in the autumn of 1417. During that summer the wanted man had fled to western Herefordshire and the Welsh border where he still had old retainers and a nest of loyal supporters. At the end of August he stayed for a time at Almeley, his original land-holding. As he had travelled with servants and horses his presence must have been obvious to the villagers who, however, did not give away their long-time lord. The village cobbler was later arraigned on the charge of having provided the fugitive with meat and drink, although the jury claimed not to know whether he had also provided him with boots. It appears that one of the government supporters, who was connected with Oldcastle by marriage, put the government forces on Oldcastle's trail, but he may simultaneously have warned the fugitive and encouraged him to leave. Oldcastle fled again, this time to North Wales, where he had been in contact with one of Glendower's sons who was still out of the king's allegiance and might be plotting for Welsh independence. In the end it was the Welsh supporters of the Lord of Powys who captured him at Welshpool. The struggle seems to have involved several of the onlookers as well, as during the fight to subdue him one of the women hit him on the shin with a stool and injured, perhaps broke, his leg, so that he had to be carried in a cart from Welshpool to London. Most of the chroniclers report Oldcastle's arrest with self-righteous glee, calling him "infernal satellite and cursed heretic", "prynce of Erytykes and cheff leder and mayntenere of all the lollardys in the reme".[20]

The Duke of Bedford, then regent of the kingdom for Henry who was busily occupied in his campaign in Normandy, was responsible for having Oldcastle brought immediately before parliament. There the original indictment was read to him, and he was asked if he wished to excuse himself and show any reason why he did not merit death. In the usual Lollard manner, Oldcastle instead began to preach to his accusers. Bedford and the justiciar insisted that he answer the question and Oldcastle, according to the St Albans' chronicler, proudly repudiated their right to judge him since, he said, his liege lord, King Richard, was living in Scotland.[21] No further leniency could be shown after such a blatant denial of the king's rights: Oldcastle was ordered to be dragged without delay to St Giles' Fields, hung on the gallows there and burnt while hanging. His death took place on 14 December 1417.

With the execution of Oldcastle the Lollard movement passed into obscurity. The doctrines of Wycliffe and his immediate followers had originally enjoyed considerable intellectual acceptance among important scholars at Oxford and had gained a fair body of adherents among the landowners, those men who have been called "Lollard knights". In fact, the story of the abortive rebellion of 1414 and of the stamping out of the embers of dissent in the following years illustrates the fact that the sect was becoming politically unimportant, and that it was also easily seduced to treason. The king's rapid dismantling of the conspiracy and revolt removed the few leaders of some education and social importance whom the movement had managed to attract. There continued to be Lollards, but no further Oldcastles or Oxford masters. Lollardy had been discredited and eked out an underground existence which had little effect on the intellectual or social life of the country. In disarming Oldcastle and his followers and putting down the Southampton Plot Henry had met the major challenges to his rule, and, by speed and careful organisation, had proved them hollow threats. The rebellions put down, he could turn to the subject that had already begun to dominate his interests – France.

CHAPTER V

Preparations for War: Diplomatic Manoeuvres

Although the Lollard rebellion called for immediate action by the king, the internal problems of conspiracy and treason do not seem to have been the major objects of his concern. Henry was an ambitious and legalistic prince, and he saw in the troubled situation in France the ideal conditions for a return to Edward III's policy of war and conquest there. The possibilities of intervention in French affairs had been sharply delineated for him during his years on the council, while he was still Prince of Wales, when he and his father had successively lent aid to the opposing factions. It must certainly have been obvious to the watchful Henry that the moment for English intervention, and for a careful policy of forcing concessions by pitting one faction against the other, had undoubtedly arrived. Henry might be determined on war – and this was certainly true by 1414 – but it was the ultimate weapon, only to be used when he had exhausted all other forms of persuasion and threats.

The period between Henry's accession and the departure of the first expedition to France in the summer of 1415 was marked by a tremendous flurry of diplomatic activity. The king's gifts for organisation and the planning of detail are particularly obvious in the complex series of diplomatic manoeuvres which he orchestrated in those two years and which produced an extraordinary list of English demands on France.

Soon after his accession he moved to safeguard the current situation. In July he named an embassy to treat with the Duke of Burgundy as Count of Flanders concerning a truce in Flanders. This move was inspired by the commercial needs of both the English burgesses and the Flemish weavers, whose economic interests were important to both the king and the duke. At the same time the same ambassadors were empowered to deal with France, but only concerning Picardy – a logical extension of a truce with Flanders. This was achieved by the end of the summer, and in October a safe-conduct was issued for the French ambassadors to come to England to discuss extending the truce of Leulinghen. In January a one-year truce was arranged. Meanwhile Henry had been clearing the ground by negotiating a truce with Brittany, which he hoped would lessen the attacks on English shipping in the Channel, and one with Castile.

It was only in the winter of 1414 that the king seems to have felt prepared to reopen with the French the whole vexed question of English claims in France. From this time on French and English ambassadors travelled frequently between the two courts, armed with proper letters of credence, bearing detailed instructions, and protesting their vehement desire to arrive at a peaceful solution for all the problems at issue between England and France.* Both parties in France were looking for English assistance against each other and the Orléanist party especially offered concessions and inducements, but Henry's demands were impossibly high, and must certainly have raised questions about his good faith. The French concern about the English intentions is easily understood. A memorandum drawn up in January 1415 summarised the terms of the claims which had been put forward by English embassies in France during the previous year. The English had first demanded the lordship of Normandy, Anjou, Touraine and Maine, and the homage of Brittany and Flanders, in addition to everything included in the Treaty of Bretigny and further lands to the north between the river Somme and Gravelines. After a period of negotiation, they added to the lands included in the Treaty of Bretigny half of the county of Provence with the castles and lordships of Beaufort and Nogent, and the staggering sum of eight million crowns† – six million for the unpaid ransom owed for King John who had been captured by the English at Poitiers in 1356, and two million as a dower with Catherine, youngest daughter of the French king, who would marry Henry. The French negotiators had countered these extravagant demands with an offer of a considerable increase of lands in the south, bordering the English

* It is an interesting sidelight on the growing nationalism in language that the English ambassadors had begun to insist that any accord must be written in Latin, rather than merely in French. As a result of this insistence, the truce which was made in January 1414 was drawn up in both Latin and French. The reasoning behind the English demand is illuminated by Froissart's comment, made twenty years before, on the difficulties the English experienced at conferences where only French was used for "they were not so well used to the finesse and double meanings of that language, as the natives who turned and twisted it to their own advantage at pleasure."[1]

† An estimation of the varying values of separate kinds of coins, some of which were only units of accounting, makes the financial statistics of the Middle Ages particularly confusing. It is, however, possible to have a rough idea of corresponding values. The crown, or *écu*, was worth approximately 3s 4d in London, or half the value of an English noble. In 1414 it was worth about 22 *sous* (s.), 6 *deniers* (d.) *tournois*. The French moneys most commonly found in accounts are the *livre tournois* (the pound of Tours), and the *livre parisis* (the pound of Paris). These are usually abbreviated l.t., and l.p. The *livre parisis* was 25 per cent higher than the *livre tournois*, and, at the end of Henry's reign, 1 pound sterling was worth roughly 9 l.t.[2]

holdings in Aquitaine, and the sum of 800,000 crowns, plus dresses, jewels, and household furniture for Catherine.[3]

What were the legal grounds for these extensive English claims? For the last fifty years any English demands had been based primarily on the terms of the Treaty of Bretigny. Signed in 1360 when the French had barely begun to recover from the capture of King John the Good and the disastrous defeats of Crécy and Poitiers, the treaty was generous but not abject. It gave the English king full sovereignty over the duchy of Aquitaine, which was further increased by the addition of Poitou, Quercy, the Limousin and the Agenais. In the north the English territories included Calais and its march (captured by Edward III in 1347), and the counties of Ponthieu, Guines and Montreuil. In return for these concessions, plus the large ransom for the captured king, Edward III promised to give up his claim to the French throne. This claim was founded on the English argument that the right to the French throne passed to Edward's mother, Isabella, daughter of King Philip the Fair, when the male line of Capetians became extinct in 1328, and that her son had rightfully inherited it. The French, faced with the possibility of a foreign monarch in 1328, had agreed to accept a Valois, the nearest direct male heir through the male line, and bolstered their tactical decision with the legal reinforcement of the supposed Salic law, i.e., that succession to the throne through the female line was forbidden.

Unfortunately the two essential points of the treaty – Edward's sovereignty over the enlarged duchy of Aquitaine, and his consequent renunciation of his claim to the throne of France – were put to one side, and never formally ratified or put into effect. During the following years the French continued their aggressive practices in regard to the English possessions in Aquitaine, and the cautious policy of Charles V and the good generalship of Du Guesclin gradually made good most of the major French losses. By 1376 the English had only managed to retain a foothold in a relatively narrow coastal strip of Gascony, centring around Bordeaux, and the French had again declared their confiscation of Aquitaine and had even given the title of Duke of Aquitaine to one of the French princes. Under such circumstances, it is not surprising that Edward III and his successors did not formally abandon their claim to the French throne, though the whole matter stood in abeyance during the reigns of Richard II and Henry IV. The more extensive English claims of 1414 not only revived the demand for the crown by Edward III, but also stated a legal right to the original lands of William the Conqueror and his English successors in Normandy, as well as the Plantagenet inheritance of Henry II. To accede to them, even in part, would have totally dismembered France.

The *Liber Metricus*, the laudatory verse life of Henry by the monk Thomas of Elmham, provides a contemporary propaganda version of the English case.[4] Elmham countered the French reliance on the Salic law which he called that "fictitious decree" by bringing forward various Biblical precedents for maternal inheritance. He concluded with the triumphant statement that Jesus Christ was king of the Jews through inheritance from his mother, so that the king of England, by a like inheritance, could properly join to his own title the lilies of France. The claim to Normandy – strategically most valuable because it controlled the Seine valley, and thus the access to Paris – was passed over rather rapidly as belonging to the English king by the right of his ancestors. It was certainly the part of France about which Henry V seems to have felt most strongly and which was most useful to him tactically. The English propagandist refused to recognise the legality of the confiscation of Normandy, and of all the other Plantagenet lands outside Aquitaine, by Philip Augustus two centuries before, although it had been formally accepted by Henry III in the Treaty of Paris in 1259. The rationale was distinctly dubious so it is not surprising that all this English emphasis on the essential legitimacy of their claims and the English king's rights in France ultimately provoked the Archbishop of Bourges, exasperated after a long and fruitless period of negotiations, to sharp retort. He pointed out to King Henry, most undiplomatically, that not only was Charles VI the true king of France and that Henry had no right to anything in France, but that he even had no right to the kingdom of England and that the king of France should rather treat with the true heirs of the late King Richard. Henry's anger at the ambassador's presumption was unbridled, but he refused to abate in any way his "legitimate" claims.[5]

Much of this emphasis on proving the rights and legitimacy of the English claims strikes us as hypocritical and irrelevant, especially when it is obvious to us – and must also have become obvious to the king's contemporaries – that he was primarily planning for war. However, for the men of the fifteenth century it was necessary to prove that one's cause was a righteous one. In an age which was steeped in religious sentiments and practices, it was essential to be able to believe that God was on one's side. Although the unworthy and the unrighteous might gain the victory for a time, general opinion in the fifteenth century believed the final victory would surely rest with the righteous. This attitude saturated much of the literature of the time, for even the strictly practical military treatises laid considerable emphasis on the importance of waging a just war. As a contemporary poetic propagandist of Henry's time put it:

> God doth batayle, and not ye;
> Though ye fought, God doth the dede.[6]

King Henry himself was only voicing one of the more extreme examples of this attitude when he preached at his prisoners after Agincourt, and attempted to "console" them with the self-righteous statement that God had given him the victory because of the sins of the French nation.[7]

It was obvious to the king's close advisers in the winter of 1414 that Henry was seriously planning to reopen the negotiations with the French king. Six clerks in the office of the Privy Seal were duly ordered to make copies of all the truces concluded in the times of the king's ancestors, so that the ambassadors dispatched to Paris should have a more complete knowledge of all the relevant background.[8] Nevertheless the spring parliament gave no real hint of his plans. Henry had moved to Kenilworth from Westminster soon after the Oldcastle rebellion had been put down. Henry had always had a special fondness for the great red sandstone fortress where his grandfather, John of Gaunt, had made so many improvements and where Henry himself had spent some of his childhood. It was perhaps during these weeks of February and March that he thought of adding his own improvement to the castle grounds. The king ordered the creation of a "pleasance", at the edge of the lake which could be reached by boat from the castle, and had built what the sixteenth-century writers called a "praty banketynge house of timbre", probably on the model of Richard II's island summer-house at Sheen. Elmham describes Henry as having decided on a garden for his solace, placed where the foxes had been used to hide in the marsh between the brambles and the thorns. The initiative to create "Pleasant Mareys", as it was called, was inflated by his eulogists to be a symbol of his success in putting down the crafty deceits of the French king, so like the foxes of Kenilworth.[9]

Henry had summoned his spring parliament to meet at Leicester, an unusual spot. The king may have felt that London was rather unquiet in the aftermath of the Lollard conspiracy and that trouble might erupt between the citizens and the great throng of lords and commons and their retinues gathered for the meeting of parliament. He may also have felt that it was more likely that parliament would do its business quickly if it had to meet in the confining conditions of a small and crowded town. Leicester had no suitable building for such a large gathering, so the king ordered one constructed. Although it was a large structure, some one hundred and twenty feet long and eighty feet wide, the royal mandate must have stirred the workmen to speed, for the building was roofed and finished in only twenty-four days.[10] The rather makeshift arrangements for the parliament did not deter it from transacting considerable business. The Commons had several issues very much in mind and they hoped that the choice as Speaker of Sir Walter Hungerford, well known as a trusted and faithful servant of Henry V and a former steward of the duchy of Lancaster, would help to ensure the success of their petitions. They urged that statutes should be expressed in terms of the petitions on which they were based, and the king agreed not to change the meaning of successful petitions, an important advance in parliamentary power. The acute problems of public disorder and lawlessness which were plaguing the country required, parliament felt, further measures to strengthen the existing laws. Amongst their efforts were new enactments against the widespread piracy. As well, bearing in mind the dangers of the Oldcastle rebellion, they passed a further, still more stringent, statute against the heretics.[11]

In another move which testified to the ever-growing nationalism of the English, and their perpetual suspicion of all foreigners, the Commons petitioned the king for the total suppression of the alien priories, i.e., those convents or cells of widely varying size and closeness of connection which answered ultimately to a mother-house outside of England. The process of confiscating the lands and profits of these priories had been begun by Edward I in 1295, during a war with France, although they had been returned when hostilities stopped. Edward's example had been followed by his successors during the active periods of war all during the fourteenth century. Many of the larger houses had evaded these confiscations by paying large sums for expensive charters which recognised them as denizens of England. The smaller cells, or monastic granges which had only a few monks serving primarily as estate agents, could not afford this expensive process and often remained in the hands of the king's officials or were sold. The act of 1414 for the total suppression of the priories was not, therefore, something altogether new. It was merely a further episode in a long-drawn-out legal process which was primarily inspired by an anti-foreign rather than an anti-clerical bias, and, in fact, most of the revenues so acquired went to various religious foundations in England.[12]

Nothing overt was said in this parliament about a resumption of war with France, but the thought seems to have been much at the back of men's minds. The king took advantage of the solemn occasion to name his two youngest brothers dukes – John was made Duke of Bedford and Humphrey, Duke of Gloucester. The brothers were now seasoned adults of twenty-five and twenty-four, and both were to serve their brother faithfully in his military plans. Bedford especially was Henry's trusted lieutenant and main support during the king's life, and he tried desperately to carry out Henry's vision of conquest after the king's early death. The certainty of negotiations and the possibility of war must have been fostered during the meeting of parliament by the appearance of messengers from both the Armagnac and Burgundian factions in France. The French do not seem to have done much serious business but the Burgundians dealt with a lengthy draft of a proposal for a military alliance between their duke and King Henry. The draft survives, along with the questions asked by the English officials and the Burgundian replies, but no formal agreement was arrived at.[13] King Henry had also sent solemn messengers to both sides but it became more and more apparent that this was a matter of calculated manoeuvre rather than a genuine attempt at serious negotiation. The deviousness of the king's plans seem to have been hidden from even his ambassadors for the St Albans' chronicler says pithily: "Frequently both these messengers in France and the messengers sent into England were utterly lulled into the hope of peace."[14]

The famous story of the condescending French gift of tennis balls to King Henry, suggesting that he was more apt for sport than war, seems to belong to the spring of 1414. It appears first in the chronicle of John Strecche, a canon of Kenilworth who was especially well placed to pick up the colourful and exaggerated pieces of gossip which naturally flowed from the royal household when it was in residence at the castle, as it was at this time. His version of the tale had the French, overcome with pride, *predicting* that they would send Henry "little balls to play with, and soft cushions to rest on, until what time he should grow to man's strength".[15] The story bears the marks of hearsay gossip, and it is not to be found in any of the serious chroniclers, either French or English, although it is included in Elmham's poetic life. Naturally, such a colourful story was picked up by later writers, including the early-sixteenth-century author of the *English Life*, and thus was passed on to Shakespeare. There are several reasons which militate against its acceptance. The king of France, and his ambassadors, were attempting to pacify Henry and, in fact, went a long way to try and meet his claims. If the story referred to an actual happening, it would inevitably have been regarded as such an insult to the king's honour that negotiations would have been broken off. They were not, and no reference was ever made to it in the royal correspondence or by the responsible persons of any embassy. It would appear that John Strecche had picked up the account of some casual boasting among the retinue of the French ambassadors who came to Leicester. They hoped to prick the arrogance of the English and the story seems to have circulated in the spate of gossip which inevitably followed the royal retinue. Although it was the inspiration for a magnificent Shakespearean speech its authenticity is most dubious.

By the autumn of 1414 it was obvious that Henry was planning to reopen the war, no matter how much diplomatic manoeuvring he attempted. In the October convocation of the clergy in London the king was granted two-tenths on clerical incomes – one to be paid on the Feast of the Purification (2 February) 1415, and the second on the same feast in 1416. Parliament met again in Westminster on 19 November, and Bishop Beaufort as chancellor immediately set the tone of the meeting. The bishop's opening sermon was devoted to support of the king's desire to recover the inheritance and the rights of his crown, and emphasised that this was the suitable time, with the aid of God, to achieve his purpose. The bishop was sufficiently worldlywise to insist that beyond the aid of God, the king also needed "sage and loyal counsel of his lieges, strong and true assistance of his men, and copious subsidies of money from his subjects".[16] The Commons were enough in agreement to be willing to vote two-fifteenths on the same terms as the tenths of the clergy, but there is an interesting warning to the king in the records of the Privy Council. According to this, a plea was made to King Henry by all the estates that before he made any voyage he should send ambassadors to seek right and justice for so Christian a prince should eschew the shedding of Christian blood. The king seems to have pointed to the efforts already made by his ambassadors, and his own willingness to accept less than all his rights, and argued that it was only because of a failure of justice that he was proposing the expedition. It is obvious from the tone of the council's memo that many of its members were not truly enthusiastic, although they agreed to "be redy with oure bodyes to do you the service that we may as fer as we oughte".[17]

It is interesting to note the suggestion of hesitation in renewing the war with France, since so much emphasis has been put on the general English enthusiasm for the war. In this case, the king was certainly determined on war, believing that the fatal divisions in France favoured his success. Some lords and knights also regarded the waging of war as their normal pattern of existence, for successful campaigns brought them not only honour and prestige, but also very tangible economic advantages. This was a general attitude in western Europe at this time and it is exemplified in a treatise of advice for his son written by Ghillebert de Lannoy.* Ghillebert's practical advice emphasised that the use of war was one of the best ways by which a brave and virtuous man of good reputation could arrive at great and honourable riches. The Burgundian knight laid particular emphasis on the profit which accrued from taking noble and wealthy prisoners. Even one such captive, he asserted, could enrich his captor so greatly that he would become, and remain, rich all his life, and even pass on great wealth to his heirs. The knight added cannily that if your reputation is high, it is also much easier to make a rich and profitable marriage.[18] The common soldiers too were encouraged by the tales of booty and the possibility of captives so that they were willing to accept, at least for a time, the harsh conditions of medieval warfare. Yet the enthusiasm of the professionals was not the only sentiment. The council's desire "to eschew the shedding of Christian blood" was perhaps the commonplace of the churchmen but Hoccleve, the Privy Council clerk and poet, put into more emotional terms the achievements so dearly bought:

> Whan ye have stryven and foughten alle your fille,
> Pees folwe mote; but goode were it or than
> That pees were hade; what lust have ye, to spille,
> The bloode that Crist withe his blood bought . . .[19]

* Ghillebert de Lannoy was a year older than King Henry and a member of a well-known family which provided several high officials for the Duke of Burgundy. He was typical of the knight errant, who sought campaigns and opportunities for glory in all corners of Europe and the Middle East. He fought at Agincourt, and in 1420 was standard-bearer for the Duke of Burgundy. An indefatigable traveller, he visited shrines and made pilgrimages when neither war nor diplomacy afforded opportunities for his voyages.

Sceptism was fairly general too among the merchants and the common people, at least until their emotions had been fired by victories. For them royal wars meant increased taxation and forced loans which bore heavily on their resources. The indiscreet speech of a drunken French doublet-maker in Orleans could find its echo on the other side of the Channel, especially among Lollard sympathisers:

> *Estront, estront de roy et de roy*! We have no king but God! Do you think they've got rightfully what they've got? They tax me and tax me and it hurts them because they can't have everything that belongs to us. What's the king got to do, taking what I earn with my needle away from me? I'd rather the king was dead, I'd rather all kings were dead than have my son have a pain in his little finger.[20]

But the grumblings of the common people had little influence on the ambitions of kings.

However, even after the public statement in parliament that the king proposed to gain his rights in France by force if necessary, the movements backwards and forwards of the French and English ambassadors continued in a pattern as stylised, and as inconclusive, as the figures of a formal dance.* The French court was not really paying serious attention to events in England. Much time and energy had been spent, especially by the dauphin, in trying to work out a suitable peace with the Burgundians, who at the moment were out of royal favour and removed from control of Paris. A formal peace between the dauphin and Duke John was solemnised on 22 February 1415, and the rejoicings over the possibilities of internal peace probably accounted for the particularly elegant and expensive spectacles which greeted the English ambassadors when they arrived at the beginning of February. King Charles had arranged for several days of jousting and, since he was in one of his lucid periods, took part himself. The combats were actually held in one of the main streets of Paris, the Grande Rue St-Antoine, which bordered the king's favourite palace, the Hôtel St-Pol. It was a most elegant occasion, for the participants' garments and horse trappings were trimmed with sable, and the dancers at the feasts which ended each day's festivities were clothed in cloaks of gold embroidery. Le Fèvre de St-Rémy, the French chronicler who gives the most detailed account of the festivities, had particular reason to remember the richness and elegance with satisfaction as, at the end of the three day celebration,

---

* The king's old friend, Richard Courtenay, by now Bishop of Norwich, served on several of these embassies, and seems to have had enough leisure to pursue several other interests. In 1414 he and Bishop Langley interviewed the Celestines in Paris, a religious order which King Henry was thinking of establishing in England. As well, Courtenay was in touch with Master John Fusoris, a doctor and astrologer of Paris, from whom he tried to acquire some astronomical instruments, including astrolabes for himself and the king. The bishop became sufficiently friendly with Fusoris that he tried to persuade him to come to England.[21]

the cloaks and other trappings were given to the attendant minstrels, trumpeters, and officers-at-arms, of which he was one.[22] The feasts were more seriously attended to than the English ambassadors who returned home, not having mitigated their demands. The French had found the English claims so excessive that they refused to believe they were put forward seriously.

Immediately upon the return of his ambassadors from France, Henry continued his policy of alternate negotiation and threat. On 7 April he wrote once more to Charles reiterating his desire for peace and for the marriage with Catherine, adding that in order to achieve these ends he has been willing to abate his just claims. He complained that the French ambassadors insisted that they did not have full powers and urged Charles to be sure and send quickly ambassadors who did. Before King Henry could have received an answer from Charles, he wrote again, on 15 April, mentioning the safe-conducts which he was dispatching for the named French ambassadors and urging their speedy action. The tone of this letter is more menacing than that of 7 April, and emphasises the dangers to the peace of Europe in a division between England and France at a time of schism in the church.[23] These letters with their high-minded insistence on the legality of the English claims and the king's great desire for peace must be glossed by the king's decisions in the council in the week of April 12–18, which placed the country on a war footing and set the rates of pay for the members of the expedition. Meanwhile Charles' ambassadors were preparing for the trip to the English court. The embassy included the Archbishop of Bourges, the Bishop of Lisieux, the Count of Vendôme, the Baron of Ivry and the Lord of Braquemont, as well as Master Jean André and Gontier Col, the king's secretary.* Col obviously served as secretary for the embassy, and we are fortunate to have his detailed account of the negotiations, written immediately on his return to France.[24] Col apologised to the archbishop, to whom he had sent the letter, that his horses had all been seasick from the Channel crossing, and so he was delayed in his return to Paris. He wanted the archbishop to have at once a full account of all that went on – obviously so that he would be fully informed when he met the king and council to report. Col's memorandum is at once a fascinating description of the exceedingly formal pattern demanded of embassies in those days and a vivid reminder of the importance of the personal influence and intervention of the king himself in the deliberations.

The ambassadors had left Paris on 4 June. It may have taken them the whole month of May to organise their departure, as the final safe-conduct

---

* Gontier Col was a mature man of over sixty, who had been a favoured protégé of the Duke of Berry. He served as secretary to the French king while the Orléanists were in power and was killed in the massacres which followed the Burgundian entry into Paris in 1418.

allowed for a retinue of some 360 persons.[25] They had gone first to London but the king had already left, so they were brought to Winchester where Henry was staying in the palace of Bishop Beaufort before departing for Southampton. It must have been obvious to the French as they rode through London and the summer richness of the English fields that England was preparing for war not peace, since the arrangements for the embarkation of an expedition were easy to see. Nevertheless, both sides continued to play out their required parts. The Archbishop of Bourges preached the opening sermon on the eminently suitable text, "Peace to you and your house", and the formalities were carried out with practised politeness, although Bishop Beaufort, the chancellor, warned the French that the king wanted all negotiations concluded within a week of their arrival.

The ambassadors were taken into the presence of the king on Thursday, and Col draws a vivid picture of the encounter. Henry was leaning on a dresser in his chamber with a silk pillow under his arm, surrounded by his closest advisers and supporters. Both sides seem to have made set speeches, to have advanced and retreated to previously prepared positions, but whether negotiations meant a real exchange of views, much less any genuine attempt to arrive at a working compromise, is more than doubtful. One inevitably arrives at the impression that this was one more meeting which Henry wished to put on the record for propaganda purposes, to prove how hard he had tried to obtain his claims by "the way of justice" before he took to the sword. But this secret aim was not disclosed, for the French ambassadors during the week of meetings were frequently encouraged by the Duke of York and Richard Courtenay, the Bishop of Norwich, that all went well and agreement was near. The final English demand was that Catherine, with all her jewels and a dowry of 600,000 francs should be delivered to Calais by Michaelmas, and that the lands agreed upon should be turned over at the same time. Such a date, less than three months away, seemed to the French ambassadors quite impossible. They said plaintively that it would not be possible to find so great a sum of gold in so short a time in order to make the jewels and coin the currency. By Saturday 6 July it was obvious that the charade would be played no further. At six in the evening the French ambassadors were called to the king's presence and found him seated in his hall, surrounded by prelates and men of war, foreign ambassadors from Aragon and Burgundy and a great press of people. The Archbishop of Canterbury, Henry Chichele, then read a carefully prepared memorandum in Latin which rehearsed King Henry's many efforts and embassies, and insisted that he had been kept from his hereditary rights unjustly and for too long a time. It accused the French king of being unwilling to search for a firm and fair peace, and called on all the inhabitants of heaven and earth to witness the failure of the French king to render him justice, and therefore his obligation to search for his rights in another way.[26]

Henry made every effort to exploit these diplomatic efforts to the utmost. After he left Winchester, on his way to Southampton, he drew aside to the abbey of Tichfield and there had all the treaties transcribed that Henry IV had made with the princes of France in 1412, which had recognised many of the English claims, and from which the French princes had unceremoniously withdrawn when they felt able to deal with Burgundy by themselves. As his chaplain describes it, he had these transcripts sent to the Council at Constance, to Sigismund and the other Catholic princes "so that all Christianity might know how French duplicity had injured him, and how he was almost unwillingly forced to raise his standard against the rebels".[27] This was a calculated and shrewd effort to influence public opinion in the councils of princes, and used a highly selective gleaning of past events to give a further veil of legality to the invasion which was now so imminent.

The French ambassadors were under no delusions of peace. They arrived back in Paris at the end of July to report on their abortive mission and they warned the king and council that Henry's conciliatory letters screened his aggressive intentions, "while he amused our king with his honeyed words, he raised troops from all sides to destroy his kingdom".[28] They added that they had learned during their stay in England from officers in charge of the troops, that Henry had already raised 6,000 men-at-arms and 50,000 archers, as well as a considerable number of foot-soldiers and craftsmen. These men had all been embarked at Southampton, but no one knew their destination although they had heard that Henry had resolved to attack Harfleur because of his passion to conquer Normandy.

Their warning against the "honeyed words" of the king was borne out by the tenor of Henry's final letter to Charles, written from Southampton on 28 July, just before he embarked. The tone of the letter is one of aggrieved innocence and emphasises how much Henry was willing to give up in the cause of peace – "the possession of a state which belongs to us by hereditary right" and the willingness to remit 50,000 crowns of the sum offered with Catherine in marriage "to shew that we are more inclined to peace than avarice". Charles' answer was written from Paris at the end of August when Henry was already besieging Harfleur, and, in its turn, lays emphasis on his constant desire for peace and his efforts to achieve it. Only in his reply to Henry's demand for justice and Catherine's hand does a tart note emerge: "it does not appear that the means which you have adopted . . . are proper, honorable, or usual in such a case".[29]

The French ambassadors had had more success in their survey of military preparations in England than they had had in their peace-making mission. It was imperative for the welfare of France that the opposing factions should work together to counter the danger of the English invasion.

However, Henry's careful diplomatic manoeuvres and his shrewd use of propaganda stood him in good stead. He was met not by a united France but by a sorely divided nation in which the necessary decisions were constantly delayed. Henry had great gifts as a careful and precise organiser, and his plans for his military organisation were as firmly laid and as meticulously pursued as his tortuous pattern of fruitless embassies.

CHAPTER VI

Preparations for War:
Military Organisation

Modern generals are presumed to have acquired a knowledge of military theory, garnered from earlier experts, and most successful military leaders have been fascinated by the exploits of historic conquerors. Medieval commanders had fewer formal methods of acquiring knowledge than their present-day counterparts, but they too had a number of informative treatises to which they could turn for both theoretical and practical advice about warfare. Certainly the most widely known was Vegetius' *De Re Militari*, written in the fourth century but recognised as an authority all through the Middle Ages. It suffered the usual fate of most medieval standard works for it was frequently pillaged by other authors. Giles of Rome, for example, used large chunks of it in his popular and highly respected treatise on the education of princes, and from there it resurfaced, third-hand, in many other instructional works. However, it was of such immediate practical use to the large upper class, who had a vested interest in the skills of warfare, that the whole work was translated into French as early as the thirteenth century, at a time when French was truly a lingua franca for most of the nobility of Europe. In 1408 Lord Thomas Berkeley ordered an English translation which formed part of a manuscript that included several other technical discussions of military subjects, such as how to array a knight in his armour, the rules of jousts and tournaments, and the oath taken by a herald on appointment; as well as more domestic material on how to calculate expenses by the day and the year, a calendar with astrological tables, and how to foretell the weather.[1]

Christine de Pisan, that prolific author and first professional woman of letters in France, made a new translation of Vegetius into French at about the same time as the English one ordered by Lord Berkeley. In her version she also included material from other more up-to-date treatises on siege-craft, and a collection of cases culled from a popular fourteenth-century textbook of military law. Her work was brightened by examples which she drew from the military history of her own time, and by the addition of contemporary technical information on such new developments as cannons. Although she claimed to put forward her treatise with some diffidence, fearing she might be considered presumptuous for delving into men's matters, she invoked the example and assistance of Minerva, the goddess of war, and proudly reminded her readers that she, like Minerva, was an Italian woman. Whether it was due to Minerva's auspices or more prosaically to Christine's favoured position at the French court, her book retained its influence and popularity in both England and France all during the fifteenth century and was translated and printed by Caxton as one of his first works. Christine's connections were certainly influential on both sides of the Channel. Henry IV had tried to entice her to England, sending two of his heralds to her with a warm invitation to his court and the promise to treat her generously. She preferred to remain in France where she felt more at home and where the princes of the royal blood were most generous to her. It has been suggested that her eulogistic life of Charles V was encouraged by the Duke of Burgundy as a manual of suitable royal behaviour for the guidance of the dilettante and pleasure-loving dauphin Louis, who had real need of treatises in both statecraft and military matters.[2]

Besides these theoretical works, the occasional military engineer might collect and record his knowledge of the contemporary technology in his speciality. Conrad Kyeser of Eichstatt, for example, wrote in 1405 the delightful manuscript known as *Bellifortis* which is a compendium of the most ingenious military technology of his time. Conrad described, and illustrated, such things as folding bridges to be carried with the army, collapsible scaling ladders more easily transported to sieges, armoured carts – oddly reminiscent of a crude tank – early cannons, and engines with cunningly anchored hooks to pull down the most stoutly anchored city gates. He included several recipes for Greek fire, that inflammatory substance so much used in medieval sieges, and in less prosaic vein pictured a flying dragon which might be used to overawe the enemy and suggested equipment to get soldiers across rivers under water – rather complicated arrangements of air bottles and sponges.[3]

King Henry, even before his campaigns in France, was a successful field commander with a store of practical knowledge acquired during his long and arduous campaigns in Wales. From all his actions, however, it is equally obvious that he had a considerable grasp of the theoretical framework which supported medieval ideas of warfare. His diplomatic documents show how carefully he insisted on justifying his campaigns in France as part of a "just war", and thus one in which he could claim that God was on his side. Despite its appeal to the final sanction of God's judgment, the medieval concept of the just war was essentially a legal, rather than a moral, one. Such a war had to meet certain definite requirements: it must be fought by laymen, its aim must be to try and redress some injury, there must be no alternative way to settle the dispute, and its protagonist must be moved by a genuine desire for justice. Above all, there was the insistence that it be waged by one with sufficient authority. By the beginning of the fifteenth century the lawyers had already restricted the possibility of just war to one waged by a sovereign prince, which also made it what was described as "public war". Public, as opposed to feudal, war permitted burning and ravaging, and the taking of spoils and captives, who were then allowed to ransom themselves. These rather arid legal technicalities had very real and practical bearing on both the commencement and the waging of war.[4]

The need to prepare a case within the lawyers' categories can be observed in the nature and style of the diplomatic documents leading up to Henry's invasion of France. It was also imperative for a conscientious commander to try and keep the actions of his soldiers within the accepted bounds. Since the seizure of goods and the taking of captives made war one of the best ways in which a soldier or a noble could achieve sudden prosperity, efforts at controlling pillage and unreasonable seizures were often disregarded. Nevertheless, Henry reiterated military ordinances for his army which not only laid down strict regulations to try and protect genuine non-combatants such as the clergy and women, but also attempted to regulate the problem of looting. Kinds of booty were differentiated and the pillaging of church goods – inevitably of particular appeal since church plate was normally of gold or silver – was made punishable by death. Henry not only proclaimed such laws: he acted on them. On the march to Calais when one soldier was caught in possession of a stolen sacred vessel he was immediately strung up and the army marched past the gallows where he hung as a salutary public warning.[5] The taking of captives was also strictly regulated. By Henry's time the king was entitled to take a third of the ransoms and spoils from all indentured soldiers. The individual soldier paid a third of his captures to his own captain, and the captain was then responsible for paying over a third of this as well as a third of his own spoils to the king. As well, most especially important prisoners – those of royal blood or of the higher nobility – were awarded to the king. Since the pattern was set and well known there was little conflict over this division, although there were often great struggles on the field of battle as to who had claimed a potentially valuable prisoner first.

Another more sophisticated method of distributing the dangers and rewards of war were the contracts between soldiers which made them "brothers-at-arms". Such agreements were genuine legal bonds, sometimes for life, sometimes for a specific period, which were usually arrived at by a solemn oath or by sealed letters. Their terms normally provided that the brothers-at-arms should share equally in all gains of war, and should also contribute equally to ransoms if one of them became a captive. If both were taken prisoner, one served as hostage and the other went to raise the ransom for both. All classes of soldiers might become brothers-at-arms –

the Duke of Clarence made such a contract with the Duke of Orléans,
though he specifically reserved his allegiance to the English king. Occasionally the contracts were more obviously business relationships. For example,
in a specific agreement made between two of Henry's captains, Nicholas
Molyneux and John Winter, the two agreed that all their gains of war
should be pooled and sent home to await their return in the coffer of the
church of St Thomas Acon in London. Whoever returned to England first
was to be responsible for the investment of their winnings to their joint
advantage, and when they returned to England they would then divide
equally whatever they had purchased or put by. The survivor was to take
all, although a dower of one-sixth was reserved for the widow.[6] Such
professedly business partnerships seem to have been relatively unusual
and attracted the most opportunist adventurers, but they could, and did,
provide considerable profits for certain individuals in England, even during
the last unsuccessful phase of the Hundred Years War.

Ransoms were potentially the most valuable of all profits from war.
Although there was a theoretical requirement to set a reasonable price for a
ransom – among knights it was considered traditional that the ransom
should be a full year's revenues of the captive's estates – in practice there
was no way of establishing a fixed rule. Even if they were kept at reasonable amounts, ransoms were especially valuable because the right and the
obligation did not disappear with the death of the principals. In many
cases, such inherited rights or liabilities dragged on through a procession
of heirs. Nor were prisoners automatically freed when a war was ended,
since they were regarded as the private property of a specific person, and
not a public group belonging to the enemy as a whole, whose status would
change when a peace was signed. Although the average knight or noble
could arrange his ransom by striking a satisfactory financial bargain, such
important prisoners as the Duke of Orléans, who was captured at Agincourt, could be held in England for twenty-five years primarily for political
reasons. Even when Charles of Orléans was finally freed in 1440 his ransom
was the enormous sum of 260,000 crowns, and required the assistance of
the French royal treasury for its payment.

This complex of accepted private rights within a public context is
puzzling to the present-day mind, accustomed to the over-riding power of
the state. We find it even more difficult to understand the problem which
even the men of the Middle Ages often found awkward, that is, the right
of certain individuals to refuse to engage in certain wars or in specific
battles because of conflicting personal relationships. Allegiances to a feudal
or sovereign lord were usually the most important limiting factors, but
there were also the personal bonds created by the acceptance of pensions
or honours, or even by an accidental hand-to-hand fight in a mine which
made enemies into brothers-at-arms. These personal ties often made
it awkward, and on occasion made it impossible for a knight to fight

when his benefactor or connection was present in person on the opposite side.

Fortunately there was a "law of arms" which was a genuine if rudimentary international law, and which applied equally to all men-at-arms. In fact, the constable of any sovereign prince, who was the normal judge of military offences, was not necessarily restricted to the soldiers of his own prince but could do justice to all those subject to military law wherever the code was accepted. This code, with its developments and accretions, was most intelligibly put by such men as Honoré de Bonet, the fourteenth-century French prior whose casebook of military law, *The Tree of Battles*, was an excellent popularisation of the accepted principles of his day and was immediately and continuously consulted by kings and great lords.[7] Also, the long period of warfare between England and France, and the inevitable need for trained men to deal with many of the problems of military etiquette and law helped to encourage the development in both numbers and functions of those men often referred to as the officers-at-arms – the heralds and pursuivants.

By the middle of the Hundred Years War the heralds had become important officials. Their office arose originally out of tournaments where they had served as marshals and organisers. During the early days they had been linked with minstrels but gradually they took on a more exalted function which they guarded jealously. They were supposed to know the combatants and their background and gradually, under the conditions of sporadic war, extended both their functions and their status, for they fulfilled both diplomatic and military missions. Any noble could name his own herald and invest him with his coat of arms. Chaucer suggests that the principal purpose of such heralds was to sing the praises of their noble employer,[8] but only heralds in the employ of sovereign princes could serve as kings-at-arms and wear the distinctive crown with lozenges which was a badge of their position. Although heralds were created by specific princes or magnates, they had a special non-combatant and privileged status. A herald's coat of arms was sufficient protection for him anywhere, although he might also carry a white wand as a sign of his personal immunity. Heralds of opposing princes often worked co-operatively as when the French and English surveyed together the field of Agincourt. A feeling of professional detachment was natural to heralds, for they tended to look on battles as primarily a legitimate pastime by which the nobility was able to prove its valour. For heralds, too many victories might be self-defeating, as one of the speakers remarks in a mid-fifteenth-century debate between the heralds of France and England. He claimed that if one side always gained the victories the war would be too soon won and ended wistfully," which would not be to the advantage of the office of the afore-mentioned herald".[9] It is perhaps this professional interest in war and the opportunity to have immediate information about battles which accounts for the appearance of so many heralds among the contemporary chroniclers.

Obviously heralds were particularly useful in times of war. They were skilled in identifying knights by their arms, and were often responsible for identifying the dead. As messengers, they were given the task of summoning a town to surrender – a formal prerequisite before a captain could begin the siege. They carried the challenge for a pitched battle from a prince to his enemy and formally certified the victor. On a less exalted plane, they obtained safe-conducts for ambassadors or for soldiers who wanted to joust or parley with the enemy. They might help to negotiate ransoms for prisoners by arranging terms with their relatives at home. In some cases, they even served on embassies themselves. For example, when Ghillebert de Lannoy made his two-year trip to the east for the Duke of Burgundy and the English king, he took Artois King-of-Arms with him as his trusted second. In more peaceful times, they were often commissioned to carry a king's formal communications to other reigning princes. As, for example, Aquitaine King-of-Arms was ordered by King Henry to carry a letter to the emperor at Constance and Gloucester Herald sent off to the Spanish peninsula with letters for the kings of Castile, Portugal, Aragon, and Navarre. The heralds served as distinguished messengers rather than negotiators on matters of substance.[10]

The herald's code of conduct was a demanding one. He was bound by his oath of office to be true to his prince and to keep all secrets that he learned, except treason – this he was bound to disclose. He should aid gentlemen-at-arms in other lands who had lost their goods and help all gentlewomen who were in need. In order to maintain his proper dignity and seriousness, the herald was bound to forsake all places of dishonesty and chance, common taverns and places of debate.[11] Pursuivants were really apprentice heralds. They had to be able to read and write, and they served for several years without taking an oath. If they failed to give satisfaction they could lose office without being dishonoured, but normally after a period of apprenticeship they would take the herald's oath and be invested with the coat of arms. From a letter written by the Anjou King-of-Arms around the beginning of the fifteenth century it is apparent that some pursuivants had been abusing their immunities by spying out military plans for their masters when they went on embassies. The herald reported with indignation that such a practice was contrary to honour, faith, reason and the law of the office of arms.[12]

The career of William Bruges, chief in the office of arms during Henry V's reign, provides a living example of the way theory was carried out in practice. William Bruges was the son of Richard Bruges, who had served John of Gaunt and accompanied Bolingbroke on his voyage to Prussia. When Bolingbroke seized the throne Richard Bruges became Lancaster King-of-Arms, but he died soon after Henry V's accession. Meanwhile his son had served the Prince of Wales as Chester Herald, had been named Aquitaine King-of-Arms after the coronation, and in July 1415, when Henry was reviving the Order of the Garter, was named Garter King-of-Arms. His position was a prestigious one. He was able to feast the Emperor Sigismund at his own house in Kentishtown during the emperor's visit to England, and, as well, had his own lodgings in Windsor Castle. Before 1420 he submitted a petition to the king which pointed out those things the heralds themselves felt were important. Only men of honour and good character who were the king's lieges should be appointed, and once they had renounced the calling, they should not be allowed to return to it. Control was to be exercised over access to the office of herald. No one was to be received without the king's licence and present members should be asked their view of the candidate. No king-of-arms or herald, or even pursuivant, was to be created without taking the solemn oath. On the important matter of largess, Bruges petitioned the king to allow only the heralds to cry the praises of knights and receive largess for so doing. Referring to an obvious bone of contention between the two he urged that minstrels were to be restrained from usurping the herald's function. The king himself was to distribute largess to his heralds on the four great feasts of the year, and perhaps on the feast of St George as well.[13] We have no record of any royal answer to this petition but it is obvious from its terms that the heralds were becoming a professional body, and regarded themselves and their functions seriously.

However, although the trappings and formalities of fifteenth-century warfare may look unfamiliar to modern eyes, the basic requirement for a major military adventure then as now was money. The king had two main sources of supply open to him. He could call on the people of England for grants beyond the normal revenues of the realm – and these he had already received in the autumn of 1414 when both the parliament and the convocation agreed to the imposition of two-fifteenths and two-tenths on moveables. Only the financial specialist can make the difficult effort to understand the financial systems of medieval English kings, and even they find the task overwhelming. One of the most respected has written ruefully: "He who essays to reduce to intelligibility the credit instruments of the Middle Ages condemns himself to much drudgery without necessarily emerging from his labours with a clearer mind."[14] He could fairly add that it is almost equally difficult for his readers to gain the necessary illumination. Apart from normal revenues, and such extra grants as could be forced or cajoled from parliament or the clergy, the king was forced to rely on loans. The process by which all possible avenues were explored to demand loans, even from those who were unwilling, is vividly illustrated in the minutes of the Council for 25 May 1415. That afternoon at the house of the Dominicans of London the chancellor, the treasurer, the Earl of Dorset, and the guardian of the Privy Seal interviewed representatives from the Florentine, Venetian and Luccan companies of merchants living in London. The chancellor's speech minced no words. He reminded them, as alien merchants, that they had an obligation to assist the sovereign of the country in which they gained wealth and advantage by making loans to him when he needed the money, and, to reinforce the vigour of his message he warned them that if they did not, they would be put in jail to await the king's will. On this threatening note Bishop Beaufort then announced that the Florentines were expected to loan £1,200, the Venetians, £1,000, and the Luccans, £200. The merchants at first refused and seem to have later negotiated a diminution in the royal demands from pounds to marks, that is, a lessening of the sum required by a third.[15] The City of London too aided the king's cause, whether willingly or under menaces such as those which threatened the Italian merchants. For the 10,000 marks the mayor and commonalty of the City of London loaned to the king they received one of Henry's jewelled collars, made of interlinked crowns and antelopes and garnished with pearls and diamonds, which they were to hold until the king had repaid his loan. In actual fact, the king got it back before the promised repayment. Later they provided another 10,000 marks on the surety of the wool customs. The king's jewel house must have been sadly depleted by his series of loans because he consistently used his jewels and plate as surety. The Patent Rolls are full of the details of the objects surrendered, such as the gold tabernacle which had belonged to John of Gaunt and which was handed to Thomas Langley, Bishop of Durham, as security for the loan which he and the priory of Durham and the Archbishop of York had made to the king.[16] Many of these loans were not finally cleared away till the reign of Henry's son, and in many cases payment was not made in full.

While the king, and the members of his council, were exploring and exploiting all the possible avenues for the provision of funds for the king's expedition, Henry had already set the rates of payment for those retained for his voyage. By the fifteenth century the old concept of a feudal levy which was bound to serve its lord for forty days had been replaced by a paid force based on a complicated series of indentures. Captains indented to serve the king with a certain number of accompanying men-at-arms and archers, at specific rates of pay and for a definite period. The king's forces had become a contract army. The rates of pay took social standing into consideration. Henry V's rates were proclaimed as 13s 4d per day for a duke, 6s 8d for an earl, 4s for a baron, and 2s for a knight. The king further provided that if his voyage was made to France, each esquire man-at-arms would have 12d a day, and each archer 6d, but if the voyage was made to Aquitaine the nobles would receive the same wages as for France but the man-at-arms would receive forty marks a year, and the archers twenty marks.[17] At this time indentures were normally made for a year, and the usual ratio was three archers to every man-at-arms. Wages were to be paid quarterly, and half the amount due for the first quarter was paid as an advance when the indenture was signed. The indenture also specified the date on which the captain making the contract, and the men he had agreed to recruit, had to be present at a named port, equipped, ready to sail and prepared to muster before the king's officers who would be appointed to review the contingents and prove that the terms of the indenture had been met.

The series of indentures continued to be drawn up all through the spring and early summer of 1415, as Henry gradually built up the nucleus of his army. But there were also indentures for certain special services which the king realised he needed as well as his usual fighting men. Sir John Greyndon, for example, led a group of 120 miners, an essential constituent of any siege army. Other auxiliary workmen, such as masons, carpenters, smiths and carters also swelled the numbers. Henry was anxious to make use of that relatively new military weapon, the cannon, and was accompanied by four master gunners with their assistants and servants, some seventy-five men in all. The king's physician, Master Nicholas Colnet, accompanied by three archers, indented for a year's service, and Thomas Merstede and William Bradwardyn led a contingent of some twenty surgeons. Apart from all these related trades which provided support of one kind or another to the fighting men, there were representatives of the lighter side of life. Even on such a campaign Henry's own retinue included a group of eighteen minstrels, who were paid at the same rate as the men-at-arms, i.e., 12*d* a day; his chief heralds – Leicester, Guyenne, and Ireland kings-of-arms; four painters who were to decorate the king's banners; some thirty members of the king's chapel; as well as a small number of clerks who undoubtedly served as the king's secretaries.[18]

Once the active forces for the army had begun to be recruited, the king then turned to the problem of providing for such a large force. It is always difficult, if not impossible, to make accurate estimates of the number of men in medieval armies. Even for such a campaign as that of Harfleur and Agincourt, which has an extraordinary amount of available documentation, there are still major gaps. Medieval chroniclers loved round numbers and had little idea of accurate statistics. However, there seems to be a general acceptance of the estimate that Henry's army on this first expedition to France was between eight and ten thousand men. So much had to be provided for this number of men that the problem of supply and transport was naturally acute. Froissart, with his inimitable ability to draw a lively picture, described what the scene was like when the French had been planning an invasion of England some thirty years before, and the scene must have been much the same in the summer of 1415 though the English may not have been so enthusiastic about the garlic:

Whoever had been at Damme, Bruges, or Sluys at this time, and had seen how busily all were engaged in loading the vessels with hay in trusses, garlic, onions, biscuits in sacks, pease, beans, cheese-bowls, barley, oats, rye, wheat, wax candles, housings, shoes, boots, helmets, spurs, knives, hatchets, wedges, packages, hooks, wooden pegs, boxes filled with ointments, tow, bandages, coverlids for sleeping on, horse-shoe nails, bottles of verjuice and vinegar, iron stone ware, pewter and wooden pots and dishes, candlesticks, basins, vases, fat pigs, hasters, kitchen furniture, utensils for the buttery, and for the other offices and every article for man and beast, would have been struck with astonishment.[19]

Although in a brief expedition the army would expect to live off the land once it had landed and could sack the countryside, such preparations were necessary for food had to be provided for the men during the voyage, as well as during those days when they were waiting for the signal to depart. By the end of May the king had already ordered the sheriff of Southampton to have the brewers and bakers of Winchester and Southampton and the other surrounding towns brew and bake for the coming of the king and his retinue. At the same time he also sent out orders for the delivery of 800 oxen to the main departure points to serve for victualling. Despite such measures, there was inevitably conflict between the local population and the gathering soldiers. A royal order to the sheriff of Wiltshire at the end of July speaks of the English and Welsh soldiers who have taken food and will not pay for it. The sheriff is to try and make them pay, and if they refuse his request, he is to compel them "as best and most peaceably he may . . . so that no second loud complaint shall reach the king".[20]

Probably the greatest problem for any English king planning a full-scale invasion of the Continent was the provision of ships. Henry himself was very interested in having a good fleet and, as his reign progressed, devoted considerable funds to setting up a navy whose ship-masters received an annuity from the king. For his first expedition, however, he had only two great ships, the *Holigost* and the *Trinity Royal*, of about 750 and 540 tons respectively. The *Holigost* had just been built at Southampton and the king was merely providing for its finishing touches when he ordered a carver to make a swan and an antelope in timber for the ship and a painter to decorate it with "swans and antelopes and divers arms, also with the royal motto".[21] Although we do not know the exact nature of the *Holigost* or the *Trinity Royal* we are fortunate enough to have a detailed description of the much larger *Grace Dieu* which the king ordered built at Southampton in 1416–18. In 1430 it was inspected by a Florentine galley captain whose guide was William Soper, the man who had been in charge of Henry's ships. The Florentine was much impressed by the *Grace Dieu* and reported that he had never seen so large and splendid a construction. Having taken careful measurements, he described the ship as about $176\frac{1}{2}$ feet long and about 96 feet in the beam, with a mast that was 21 feet in circumference and 196½ feet high. From the galley of the prow to the water was about 50 feet, and he added that he had been told that when she was at sea still another corridor was raised above this. The *Grace Dieu* must have been close to completion by July 1418 when the king's council ordered the Bishop of Bangor to Southampton to consecrate the newly built ship, but the final touches were much delayed. It was only in May 1420 that Duke Humphrey wrote enthusiastically to his brother that the *Grace Dieu* was completely ready and was "the fairest that ever man saugh".[22]

Although such great ships could carry the king and his immediate household, a great number of other craft were needed to transport the men-at-arms, the archers, their horses and supplies. This need was filled by requisition. In March of 1415 the king was already ordering the Admiral of England, his step-uncle Thomas Beaufort, Earl of Dorset, and his lieutenants to require all "ships, barges, balingers and other vessels" of twenty tons or more in any ports of the realm to be brought to Southampton by 8 May. At the same time, no ships or vessels of the same size which were then in port, no matter to what country they belonged, were to be allowed to leave port without the king's special leave.[23] Obviously they too were to be pressed into service. The need for such ships was essentially a limited one. Perhaps the closest modern parallel is that of the fleet of small ships at Dunkirk which gathered in the Channel ports and sailed to the French coast to transport the stranded English army after the fall of France in 1940. They brought back the soldiers and then disbanded. In much the same way most of Henry's makeshift navy transported the army and its supplies and then thankfully withdrew to carry on its normal merchant occupations. However, the king not only needed to requisition ships but also sailors, since even his own ships normally carried only a skeleton crew. The sailors were often tempted to avoid the king's commission and, upon occasion, the king or his council issued orders for the arrest and imprisonment of the recalcitrant mariners "els we schall gete no men to do the kyng Cervise when he hath nede".[24] It is not surprising that such orders are so frequently found in the records as the problems of supplying and reinforcing a large army on foreign soil were especially acute during the first years of the French expeditions. Once Henry had made good his bridgehead in Normandy and had more and more Norman territory under his control he found it easier to supply and equip his army from the land he had conquered. During the first expedition the army had to live off its own supplies or off the land – and found both these alternatives difficult.

Once the force had been armed and provisioned, and ships had been assembled, the task of loading the convoy with its supplies and men and equipment began. This process was a lengthy one and many of the soldiers had to spend some time on their ships before the whole flotilla was ready and the signal could be given that the king himself had embarked and

departure was at hand. For most the destination was still a secret. Would
it be France or Aquitaine? The natural choices were Calais or Bordeaux,
the English footholds where they could operate from the security of a
familiar base. Calais had been jealously safeguarded by the English in any
discussions with the French ever since its capture by Edward III. Froissart
put the English point of view succinctly when he said, "The commons of
England loved Calais more than any town in the world; saying that as
long as they are masters of Calais, they carry the keys of France at their
girdle."[25] In the years since its capture Calais had been made one of the
most strongly fortified places in the north of France. The town itself was
surrounded by walls and towers, outside of which lay marshes and water-
courses. Inland there were outlying castles, as well as strong fortifications
at the bridge where the main road crossed the river Hammes, with a
complicated system of sluices which could be used to flood the surrounding
countryside in case of attack. The cost of maintaining this whole complex
was very high – almost a third of the king's ordinary revenue – and was
normally financed by the wool trade which used Calais as its staple.
Henry IV had had difficulty in paying the large garrison – some 800 men
in time of peace, and 1,000 in time of war. Their wages had to be high,
for as a garrison force they did not enjoy the usual soldier's opportunity
for plunder and they occupied an exposed position.[26]

Despite the longstanding truce between the English and French, at the
beginning of the century the French had continued to plan attacks on
the English strongpoint, and the St Albans' chronicler describes one of the
more unusual schemes. Planned to destroy Calais, it called for the building
of some extraordinary "machines" at St Omer, twenty-five miles away.
One held a number of jars, containing poison, serpents, scorpions, and
toads, which were designed to break when thrown. It was hoped that the
resultant smell and venom would break the spirit of the defenders. The
inhabitants of Calais were naturally much disturbed by the rumours they
heard of this plan and promised a reward to a young man of the town who
undertook to destroy the unusual artillery. His raid was so successful, and
his fire so widespread, that he not only burnt the offending apparatus but
destroyed almost the whole city with its monastery.[27] The story sounds
inherently improbable and suggests the flying dragon of Conrad Kyeser,
but it must be remembered that the most effective result of the early
artillery was the terror that the noise and the fire induced in people.
Because of the defects in workmanship of the early cannon it was almost
impossible to be quite sure what the trajectory of a projectile might be or
how far it would go.

When King Henry was considering the alternative destinations for his
invading force, Calais had the advantage of proximity to England and the
security of a well-established base on the French side of the Channel, but
it was a considerable distance from the parts of France which most

interested the king. As well, it adjoined the lands of the Duke of Burgundy, who was also Count of Flanders. Henry did not wish to provide the duke with any grounds for joining the French king in opposition to the English. It was imperative for his success that the Burgundians did not attempt to counter his plans directly. As for Aquitaine, it is interesting to see how little it ever figured in Henry's calculations. The pattern of disinterest in Bordeaux, which was so obvious during the reign of Henry IV, was continued by Henry V. Although the king had been careful to draw up the indentures of his first French expedition in such a way as to safeguard his freedom of action – and perhaps to further confuse the French about his actual target – it was unlikely that he would attempt a conquest of France from the southern outpost of Bordeaux. It was even further distant than Calais from the heart of France, and it called for a longer, more costly voyage with the attendant difficulty of finding enough sufficiently large ships to transport all his force across the Bay of Biscay. Nevertheless, Henry's final decision must have surprised many of his captains. The English army would head for neither Calais nor Aquitaine, instead it would attack Normandy directly and besiege Harfleur.

CHAPTER VII

First Expedition to France

When Henry left his lodging at Porchester on 7 August, he went on board his ship, the *Trinity*, which was anchored between Southampton and Portsmouth. As soon as he had embarked, he had the mast erected to display his readiness to sail and as a signal to the other ships that were dispersed in the various harbours along the coast that they should join him at once. By this time Henry had focused all his energies on the task ahead of him. He had dealt summarily and harshly with the Scrope–Cambridge conspiracy which had aimed at his life and the abandonment of the expedition, and which had been discovered to the king by the Earl of March, a last-minute and unwilling member of the plan. Almost without trial, the Earl of Cambridge and Sir Thomas Gray were beheaded at Southampton on 5 August, and Lord Henry Scrope, who had been one of the greatest familiars of the king, was executed with even more ignominy. Despite the worry of many of his lords that the king's absence, as well as any aftermath of the conspiracy, might encourage the Lollards and others who opposed the king to take advantage of his absence, Henry would not be turned from his immediate design. He sent his herald to King Charles of France with a final, essentially formal, demand for his rights. Since contemporary military etiquette required an offer of peace to any country or city you proposed to attack and take by force, Henry was not making a genuine offer but merely pursuing his carefully legalistic way. His letter insisted that he did not want to spill blood but did want everything that his ambassadors had asked for, as they were his by right, though, as a token of his constant desire for peace, he would abate 50,000 crowns from the sum demanded for Catherine's dowry. Obviously such a document was completely self-serving, but it did fulfil the fiction that his proper demands had been unreasonably denied, and that therefore he had the privilege of demanding his rights by the force of arms.[1]

His departure from Southampton was marked by two incidents which the superstitious interpreted in opposite ways. While the fleet was gathering, three of the larger ships caught fire and burned with the loss of almost everyone in them. The fire was so intense that even when the ships had been practically consumed, their timbers still burnt in the water with a clear flame. Some asked if this was a message from heaven to discourage the expedition. Undismayed by the portent, the king's ship led the great flotilla of some 1,500 ships of all sizes out past the Isle of Wight and into the Channel on 11 August, while swans could be seen swimming among the boats. Their presence was regarded as a good omen by all on board.[2]

By this time the ships' captains had been informed of the king's plans and the haphazard navy headed for Harfleur, the great port at the mouth of the Seine on the Norman coast. Late in the afternoon of 13 August the English force entered the mouth of the river and cast anchor at the village of Chef de Caux, about three miles from Harfleur. The king's ship immediately hoisted the banner of council, calling all the captains on board. Henry ordered them that no one, on pain of death, should land before he did, but that preparations should be made for a landing on the following day. In the meantime, the king sent the Earl of Huntingdon at the head of a scouting party to explore the country, so as to discover a suitable site for the army and investigate the possibilities of requisitioning supplies. Early the next morning, "with the sun showing a pretty dawn", Henry disembarked with the major part of his army and pitched camp on the side of a hill near Harfleur in a spot which was flanked by woods and orchards. Rather to the chronicler's surprise, the English disembarkation was not opposed by the French, although the beach was very rocky and offered good possibilities of defence if they had so wished.[3] The road was now clear for Henry to besiege Harfleur and, on the following day, the English forces moved off to invest the city.

Harfleur was a rich prize for any besieging force. Second only to Rouen, it was the great port of Normandy, with a large stock of artillery and other equipment used for the French ships of war. Its natural position was a fine one. About five miles from the present port of Le Havre, Harfleur was protected on the west by a high line of chalk cliffs. The town itself was bisected by the Lezarde, a tributary of the Seine, and was well ditched, with good walls and bulwarks. The tides along the Norman coast are extreme and only at high tide did the Seine fill the harbour which was protected with a chain rather than a mole. The surrounding flat land was marshy, making the city difficult to besiege, and the walls and towers were in good shape. It is tempting to wonder if Henry's decision to direct his expedition to Harfleur was influenced by reports he had received from two of his ambassadors the year before. Both Master Henry Ware and Lord Richard Grey of Codnor returned from their long embassy to the French court in the autumn of 1414 by way of Harfleur, and no doubt reported to the king the observations they had made on the state of the town and its defences as they and their retinues waited for a passage to England.[4]

Northern France, 1415–1422

The Sire de Gaucourt commanded the forces of Harfleur, which had lately been strengthened with 400 picked men-at-arms, in addition to the usual garrison. His men had taken up the pavement to discourage the easy movement of the attackers on the road between Montivilliers (some seven miles north) and Harfleur, which led over marshy ground. The English army was divided into two main camps, one under the captaincy of the king himself, and the other under the Duke of Clarence. Henry commanded the force closer to the sea, his brother that on the Rouen side of the river, with a guarded passage between them. As the *English Life* put it nostalgically, when all the tents and pavilions and halls of the besiegers were set up it seemed "a right greate and mightie Citty".[5] The English gained an early advantage by intercepting and capturing at sea the reinforcements of gunpowder and shot which the French king had sent to the town's defenders, but despite this success the besiegers did not have an easy task. The English miners had great difficulty in getting close enough to the walls over the marshy land to try and weaken the outlying defences, or even to attempt to fill up the ditches with brush and wood so that an assault could be made. The various accounts of the siege all lay heavy stress on the large amount of artillery employed by the attackers and on the devastation it caused, but it was some time before the English could move close enough to permit its effective use, since the early guns were noted both for their short range and their inaccuracy. However, the French chroniclers put particular emphasis on the size of the stones thrown, and the dire effects of the resulting smoke and noise. One describes the bombardment as discharging "enormous stones in the middle of clouds of thick smoke, and with such a terrifying noise, that one would have believed them vomited from hell".[6] The defenders had attempted to armour the barbican with great tree trunks, almost as tall as the city walls, plastered with mud and earth to lessen the effectiveness of the guns; but the cumulative effect of the constant bombardment with its accompanying noise, dirt, and the destruction of walls and buildings within the town seems to have been remarkably effective.

Nevertheless, the city held out for a month and Henry had almost decided on the necessity of a frontal assault. In his newsletter to the City of London, on the day of Harfleur's formal surrender, Henry informed the Londoners that he had proposed to attack the city on Wednesday 18 September, but that the defenders had asked for a truce. He added that he was specially pleased that they had met his demands, since he had not thought "they would so lightly agree to that conclusion".[7] The king gave them only five days to try and gain assistance for the beleaguered town, and they were forced to surrender twenty-four of their most important men as hostages. Although messengers were sent to Vernon to urge the dauphin to assist them, no help could be obtained and the terms of the truce had to be carried out. On 22 September the king, crowned and in state, accepted the formal surrender of the town in a symbolically humiliating ceremony, receiving the keys of the city from the kneeling governor. Henry made his formal entry into Harfleur to give thanks for his victory at the church of St Martin, whose handsome bell-tower must have served as a landmark during the siege. In token of his humble appreciation of God's goodness, the king entered the church barefooted and barelegged.

These formalities properly attended to, the king then turned to making Harfleur into an English base. Henry named his uncle, the Earl of Dorset, captain of the town, with a garrison of some 1,500 to 2,000 men, including both men-at-arms and archers. He took 300 prisoners from the French knights and men-at-arms who had defended the town, though he assured them that he knew that they had been for a long time oppressed and overworked but that he had come into "his own" country and "his own" kingdom to put them in such freedom and liberty as had existed under the rule of St Louis. The French chronicler who reports this adds realistically that nevertheless they were all held for ransom.[8] However, Henry did allow them their freedom for the moment – and gave a clue as to his further plans – once they had sworn on oath to yield themselves at Calais on 11 November. The king's settlement with Harfleur prefigured his later pattern in his successful sieges of other Norman towns. Those who took the oath of allegiance were allowed to remain and retain their goods and possessions, the clergy were allowed to go free. Those of some standing who refused to accept Henry were sent to England for ransom, while the poorer inhabitants and the women and children were forcibly evacuated with only their clothes and the few possessions they could carry. In their place, the king proposed to "stuffe the toun" with English. In pursuit of this policy, he sent orders to England offering any craftsman who would come and live there the right to have a house and household for himself and his heirs. Such advantageous terms were necessary as much vital repair work was essential in the town, both for comfort and for defence against any French attempt to reconquer the place. Many seem to have taken up the offer, and faithful supporters obviously received favoured patronage. Thus, Richard Bokelond of London was granted the inn called the Peacock, because he had brought two vessels to the king's assistance during the siege.[9] Such measures of English reinforcement were particularly necessary since during the siege the army had suffered heavily from dysentery, that perpetual accompaniment to medieval campaigns. Conditions were especially bad at Harfleur, for the marshy land, the poor sanitation, and the army's unbridled indulgence in unripe fruit and sharp new wine all encouraged the disease. Henry's old friend, Richard Courtenay, Bishop of Norwich and keeper of the king's jewels, died; so too did Michael de la Pole, the Earl of Suffolk. Prostrated by illness, the Duke of Clarence, the Earl of Arundel, and the Earl Marshal, as well as some 2,000 less distinguished soldiers, returned immediately to England.

The problem which now faced Henry was to decide on his next move. Even before the final surrender of Harfleur, the king had made the proper overture, in the terms of the chivalry of the time, by sending his personal challenge to the dauphin to submit all his claims on the kingdom of France to decision by single combat between himself and the dauphin. Whoever won would have the crown of France after the death of Charles VI.[10] Henry announced that he would wait in Harfleur for eight days for a response to this message, but no response came from either the king or the dauphin. Indeed, it seems unlikely that any was really expected. Henry's formally expressed desire to avoid the shedding of Christian blood was perhaps sincere, but it was not ever allowed to stand in the way of his peremptory acquisition of everything that he felt was his right.

Meanwhile he and his council discussed what he should do. The siege had been unexpectedly time-consuming, as well as costly in men and material. Most of the council, made pessimistic by the loss of so many men to dysentery, and the number required as garrison in Harfleur, as well as by the lateness of the season, felt that the king should return to England at once by sea. The king was opposed to this faction. He certainly did not feel that the mere capture of Harfleur, valuable port and base though it was, was an adequate return for nearly two years of planning and organisation and the expenditure of large sums of money. The chronicler's comment that "he greatly desired to see those lands, whereof he sought to be lord"[11] represents his cool acceptance of a daring gamble and his belief that it was unwise to give the French the idea that the English had fled home to avoid combat. Against the weight of advice he ordered the departure from Harfleur of his much reduced and weakened army, now probably about 5,000 men, planning to march overland to Calais.[12] It seems obvious that the king had already taken this decision when he set the rendezvous at Calais for his Harfleur prisoners, and that the council was unable to shake him in his brave but not prudent intention. The distance itself was not great – some 160 miles – and could normally be marched by an army in about eight days, if all went well. However, such a timetable presumed that Henry would be able to use the Blanche-Taque ford over the Somme, the river which was the major natural obstacle between him and Calais, and that he would be able to avoid a direct confrontation with a fresher French army far superior in size.

In fact, the French council was discussing this very point when they gathered in Rouen at the beginning of October. Their scouts had informed them of the illness in the English force and of its small size. The more seasoned commanders, Boucicaut, d'Albret and others, advised against seeking a pitched battle with its inevitable hazards. They recommended that Henry should be allowed to gain Calais and return to England, while the French threw all their forces against Harfleur to recapture it. Such cautious suggestions, reminiscent of the successful tactics of Du Guesclin against Edward III's high tide of conquest, did not appeal to the rasher, more warlike spirits, such as the Duke of Bourbon. They insisted that the French army, probably three to four times the size of the English force, should search out and destroy its bedraggled opponents. Arrogant in their pride of birth, the French nobles even disdained the armed contingents offered by the towns, dismissing them as "unnecessary little merchants". Once this decision had been made, d'Albret led the vanguard to Abbeville, where his men could check any English crossing of the Somme. Meanwhile the main body of the French army left Rouen about the middle of October to arrive at Amiens by the 17th.

Henry's army had left Harfleur on 8 October, marching to Arques and Eu near the coast, and covering about twenty miles a day. The French along the route withdrew within their fortified castles, or sent out small skirmishing parties to harass them. The general pattern of both armies was tartly described in the journal of a Paris bourgeois: "They devastated and robbed all the countryside. So did the French troops; they did as much harm to the poor people as the English did and that was all they did do."[13] From Eu Henry had planned to cross Blanche-Taque ford, which had been Edward III's escape route before Crécy. This would put him on the direct road to Calais, and he had sent orders forward to this stronghold that a force from there should sally forth to protect the ford. D'Albret's men had been able to repel and scatter the small English party and the French troops had been busy rendering all the local bridges and fords impassable. The straight road to Calais was barred and the king had no choice but to march up the valley of the Somme, searching for a crossing place. The army passed near Amiens and lodged at Boves, a village with many vines and a quantity of wine in its cellars. The hard-pressed English soldiers fell upon this booty, until the angry king forbade it, claiming that they were not merely filling their bottles, but making bottles of their stomachs. Henry was able to obtain from the captain of the castle there a considerable quantity of bread, of which the army was in short supply and which was more essential for the army's wellbeing. Still there seemed no way to cross the Somme and the king decided on a bold move. Instead of following the river valley where the Somme looped to the north, he cut directly across the neck of the loop to Nesle, hoping that this far up the river the French forces might not have been so thorough in their destruction. His gamble was justified. French prisoners told him of a little-known passage over the river at Bethencourt and Voyenne, which had been ordered to be guarded by the men of St Quentin. They had left the ford in such shape that with the use of boards from knocked down houses, ladders and hurdles, the causeway could be built up to make a rude but passable bridge. On 19 October the king himself supervised the passing over of the army – first the vanguard with the archers and a standard, then their horses, and after that the other two battles. It took them till nightfall, but the crossing was achieved with only a minor skirmish, and the road was again open to Calais.

Meanwhile the vanguard of the French army, under d'Albret, had moved east from Abbeville to parallel the English march on the other side of the Somme. They had gone to Corbie and then on to Péronne, where they were joined by the main force which had marched there from Rouen and Amiens. From now on the French and English armies were to march almost parallel, with the French to the north and slightly to the west. The English realised the inevitability of battle when they crossed the traces of the great French force at Péronne. The conviction deepened with the appearance of the French heralds giving notice of battle. The king heard them out impassively and sent them back with presents, but without an answer. He then sent two of his own heralds with the reply that he was heading for his kingdom of England from Harfleur, and if the French princes wanted to fight there was no need to name a day or a place, as he could be found in the open field at any time.

The encounter was to come soon. On 24 October Henry and his tired men marched to Blangy on the Ternoise river – still another of the small streams which criss-cross the flat plains of northern France. There was a brief skirmish at the bridge where a party of French tried to prevent their crossing, but failed. As the English forces began to straggle across the bridge, the Duke of York's spies, who were riding ahead of the main army, saw from the height of land the "multitudes" of Frenchmen who had crossed the Ternoise at Anvin, a few miles northwest. They filled the valley between Agincourt and Ruisseauville and lay directly across the English road to Calais. It was obvious that battle was inevitable. The king took up his quarters at Maisoncelles, a small village just south of Agincourt. Fearing an immediate French attack, he prepared his army for battle, and kept them in the field until evening came and he could be sure that the contest would not come that day. One French authority states that during this time negotiations went on and that Henry offered to restore Harfleur and to pay reparation for damages if his army was given free passage.[14] The story is not corroborated from the English side, though it seems most plausible in face of the enormous odds which Henry could see only too well faced his exhausted and dispirited men. In any case, nothing came of this and both sides settled for the night in the fields and woods, drenched by a continuous cold rain. The two camps, barely a mile apart, presented contrasting scenes. The French army, with its multitude of men, horses, and supplies, was sure of its victory. Some of the more arrogant soldiers even played at dice to determine who would profit by the English prisoners. The tired, hungry, and rain-sodden English waited with trepidation for the morning. As the chaplains circulated through the host, the soldiers made their peace with God, expecting death, and kept their watches around their meagre fires. St-Rémy, the herald who was present at the battle, commented on one difference between the English and the French. Unlike the music-loving English, the French had no musical instruments to rejoice them and, he added, there was the ominous portent that in the great French host no horse was heard to neigh.[15]

The field of Agincourt is for the English-speaking almost a part of mythology. The remembrance of Shakespeare and, more recently, the visual impact of the impressive film of *Henry V* have coloured historical judgment with emotional memories. The reality is at once more evocative and less glamorous. The site of the battle has changed little over the centuries. For the present-day observer looking at the fields, still planted to wheat and bordered by woods, the pattern of battle described in the chroniclers' accounts almost draws itself on the rough triangle lying between the villages of Maisoncelles, Agincourt and Tramecourt. It is easy to appreciate the inevitable effect of continuous rain and innumerable horses' hooves on the soft, tilled ground, turning it into a muddy quagmire in which the heavily armoured Frenchmen sank above their ankles and their horses had to strain to the uttermost to develop even a slow, lumbering charge. The physical condition of the English was worse than that of the French. They had been marching some fifteen miles a day for the last two and a half weeks, under difficult conditions and with inadequate supplies. Many suffered from dysentery. Food and drink were in very short supply. They were fortunate only in their generalship. Henry may have been unwise in his obstinate insistence on this unproductive *chevauchée* to Calais, but once committed he bent his considerable powers of leadership and organisation to the task of keeping his army safe, in good order and good heart. Shakespeare's night scene, in which the disguised king talks unrecognised with his soldiers, has no source in the chronicles, but it mirrors what is known to have been Henry's common practice. Certainly the king managed to inspire his soldiers with some of his own supreme self-confidence and conviction that God was on their side, since they fought a righteous war.

At daybreak, after he had heard three masses, King Henry, fully armed and with his helmet distinguished by a golden circlet, mounted his grey horse and set his troops up in their battle formation. A small rearguard – all he could afford – was detailed to watch the baggage and the king also ordered the chaplains and some of his sick to this slightly protected position.* It was from this vantage point, on a slight rise at the rear of the army, that the unknown chaplain who wrote one of the best accounts of this expedition sat on his horse and observed the whole passage of the battle. The field had certain advantages for the English, and the French seem to have been injudicious in their choice of site. It was narrow enough so that

* The baggage had already been plundered by unruly French men-at-arms and peasants, and some of the king's jewels and plate, including a valuable sword, had been stolen.

Henry's line could fill the space, albeit thinly, between the woods of Trame-court and Agincourt which defined the field, and provided a backdrop for the wings of archers. These dismounted and unarmoured men were further protected by a frieze of sharpened sticks, thrust into the ground in front of them at such an angle that their points offered some resistance to the charge of the horsemen. The main body of the soldiers were drawn up in the usual three battles, with the king in the centre. The number of fighting men at Agincourt, both English and French, is a matter of considerable debate. It is beyond dispute, however, that there was an enormous im-balance between the English and French forces, probably of the general nature of four to one. Absolute accuracy is impossible: perhaps the most useful attitude to adopt is that of the king's biographer who, when uncertain whose authority he should adopt, suggests "but let everie man give credence to whether part he will, and I will returne to my matter".[16]

Once the troops were drawn up to the king's satisfaction he turned to his companions to ask the time. They answered "Prime", i.e., the first canonical hour around sunrise, and the king was heartened: "Now is it good tyme, for alle England prayeth for us."[17] Henry then rode in front of the lines to address his men. It was usual – in fact, enjoined in the military treatises – for a commander to exhort his soldiers before the battle, and Henry bent every effort to inspire his men. He reminded them that they had come to France to recover a rightful heritage, and that their quarrel was founded on good and just cause. With proud chauvinism he adjured them to remember that they were born in England and should hope to return there with great glory and praise. His own ancestors had won noble battles from the French and, on this day, every man should aid with his body the honour of the crown of England.[18] Thereupon the English readied themselves for the French onslaught.

The French had had far more difficulty in deployment. Their much larger numbers and the nature of the field provided them with inadequate space for manoeuvre and, in fact, denied them proper use of their numerical superiority. As well, since there was no one recognised commander, there was considerable rivalry among the many distinguished noblemen, all of whom insisted on their right to a place in the vanguard, without con-sideration of tactics but only of their individual prestige. The French front line ultimately consisted of the dukes of Bourbon and Orléans, the Count of Eu, and Constable d'Albret and Marshal Boucicaut, with their contingents. Alençon and Bar formed a second line with the French crossbow-men, while mounted men-at-arms flanked the sides and formed a rearguard.

Once the armies were in position, they remained motionless for some time. It appeared that the French were not eager to commence the battle, perhaps believing that the sight of their might would so discourage the English army that they would be happy to yield. The inaction worried

King Henry. He knew that his troops must fight that day, for they had reached the limit of their endurance and were poised for one last great effort. If necessary, he must begin the attack. In the middle of the morning, Sir Thomas Erpingham rearranged the archers' wedge-shaped formations, which protected each battle, and then threw his baton into the air as a signal that all was ready. The king ordered his chaplains to their prayers, the heralds to their observation posts and gave the cry which formally declared the beginning of battle: "In the name of Almighty God and St George, avaunt Banner, and St George this day be thine help."[19] In accordance with accepted practice, the soldiers knelt and kissed the ground on which they had made a cross, as a sign of their willingness to die there rather than flee.

The king and the other mounted men dismounted and marched forward on foot, while the archers, once they arrived within bowshot, prepared to fire on the French horsemen who had been deputed to ride them down. The French were still using the tactics of Crécy and Poitiers, and once again they had seriously under-estimated the value of the longbow and the lethal effect of a continuous rain of arrows. The English bowmen easily found their targets, maddening the horses who fell before they could charge the lines, throwing their riders and adding to the difficulties of the oncoming foot column. Protected by their bristling stakes, the archers fired with a speed and accuracy which the French crossbowmen could not begin to match. The already overcrowded French front line was further compressed by the constant arrow fire, which pushed the men on the wings towards the relative safety of the centre, and destroyed the ability for swift and unfettered action of the French nobles who had fought so tenaciously for the honour of leading the vanguard. Nevertheless, the sheer weight of their first charge forced the English centre to recoil somewhat, but as the hand-to-hand combat began, it became evident that the French were fatally handicapped. Tired from marching on muddy ground in heavy armour, held back by the writhing horses which had been brought down by bow-fire, they had not even sufficient room to raise their weapons against their opponents. As well, once a man burdened with the weight of full armour fell to the ground, he found it almost impossible to rise again, and many men died, not of wounds, but of suffocation, as they were ground into the mud by the eager fighters pushing up behind them. Individual French nobles fought bravely and made many attempts to cut down King Henry – his helmet was dented and he lost one of the ornaments from his crown during the fierce hand-to-hand struggles. But it soon became evident that French bravery was not enough. The piles of French dead rose in front of the English positions and the archers, abandoning their bows, seized axes, hatchets, or any other available weapon, leaped upon the growing mass of bodies, and killed or took prisoner the flower of the French nobility.

A coherent story of such a battle is impossible, since in the confused and struggling mass there are a multitude of individual stories gathered by different observers. One tells of Duke Humphrey, the king's youngest brother, being wounded and brought to the ground by the Duke of Alençon. Immediately the king bestrode his brother's body, fighting off his assailants until Humphrey could be dragged to safety. Alençon recognised himself vanquished, took off his helmet to declare his identity and proclaim himself the king's prisoner. Before Henry could take the outstretched hand, Alençon was cut down by an impetuous English man-at-arms.[20] The Duke of Brabant was so anxious to join the fray that he outdistanced his own supporters and arrived at the field not fully armed. He hastily put on his chamberlain's armour, and made a makeshift surcoat from a banner seized from a trumpet. He too was captured and since his appearance gave no hint of the richness of the prize, he too was immediately slain.[21] There is also the tale of Lord Jacques de Heilly, who had been for some time a prisoner in England but had secretly escaped and returned to France. Just before the battle he accosted King Henry, for he was anxious to engage in single combat with any who claimed that he would fly from the battle. Henry turned him aside – this was no time for single combats – and added that he hoped that the renegade lord would be recaptured or killed that day, as by his escape he had dishonoured the order of knighthood. In fact, the fugitive knight was one of the Frenchmen slain.[22]

Although the first two lines of the French had attacked and been conquered, the mounted rearguard still sat in position, observing the struggle until it seemed that they were finally preparing to attack. The prospect worried the king. So many prisoners had been taken that there was a very real danger that they would turn against their captors under the pressure of another attack. Henry felt that their existence was a liability to his small force and gave the order to kill them all, except for those of the very highest degree. This has always been held against him as inhumanly cruel, but it was in conformity with the realities and conventions of medieval warfare. The soldiers refused the command, coveting the rich ransoms the prisoners could bring, and the king detailed a force of archers to see to it. Most of the unfortunates had their throats cut, but other rough and ready methods were also used. Ghillebert de Lannoy who had been wounded, captured and thrust into a little hut with other wounded captives, tells how in his case the English merely set fire to the hut. Since he had suffered only a minor wound he managed to crawl out safely, but it is obvious that his companions were not so lucky. It is an interesting insight into current attitudes that Lannoy was grateful for his recapture by Sir John Cornwall, a distinguished English noble married to the king's aunt, for his status ennobled Lannoy's capture. What really enraged so many of the French nobles was that they had to recognise "armed varlets as the conquerors and masters of their life and liberty".[23]

When the French rearguard saw the willingness of the English to continue the fight, they broke ranks and refused to continue the attack. The last threat had been overcome and the field belonged to the English. With his usual passion for the accomplishment of the formalities, Henry called over Montjoie, the chief French herald, to certify his victory in the presence of the attendant heralds from both sides, and also inquired the name of the castle that could be seen through the woods to the west. The heralds told him "Agincourt", and Henry immediately declared that since all battles ought to bear the name of the nearest fortress, "this shall now and forever be called the battle of Agincourt". The king, as always, claimed that "it is not we who have made this great slaughter, but the omnipotent God and, as we believe, for the sins of the French."[24] Henry later spoke in the same vein to his noble prisoners, who must have found his self-righteous piety difficult to swallow, despite their careful and respectful treatment. As he said to Charles of Orléans, he knew that God had given him the victory over the French, not because he deserved it but because God wished to punish them for their sins and vices. The king was not alone in his belief in divine help. Some of his soldiers claimed to have seen St George during the battle, hovering over the English army and fighting with them against the French. The chronicler who tells the story says simply: "Thus Almighti God and Seint George brought our enemyes to grounde, and yaf us the victory that day."[25]

Thus ended the battle which had started as a punitive expedition by the French, and ended as the greatest disaster suffered by French arms in their own kingdom during the Middle Ages. The casualties were as unequal as the forces had been. On the English side, only the Duke of York; the young Earl of Suffolk, whose father had died at Harfleur; Davy Gamme, the loyal Welshman who had fought with the king and been knighted by him; and a few other knights were lost, as well as a relatively small number of "other ranks". On the French side, the list of dead and captured read like a roll-call of the nobility of France. Killed were the dukes of Alençon, Brabant, and Bar, the Count of Nevers, the Archbishop of Sens, and d'Albret, the constable of France. Among the captives of first rank were the dukes of Orléans and Bourbon, the Earl of Richmond, the counts of Eu and Vendôme, and Marshal Boucicaut, the famous soldier and knight errant. Certainly the princes of the blood suffered grievously from their undisciplined jostling for the pride of place in the battle, and an already divided and factionalised France was deprived of many of its natural leaders. The growing importance of the Burgundian faction, with its encouragement of a state of civil war in France, was reinforced by the casualties of Agincourt. The Duke of Burgundy had withheld himself from the battle, and had ordered his retainers to keep his son from joining the French forces, to the Count of Charolais' lifelong chagrin, but the duke lost two brothers, the impetuous Duke of Brabant and the Count of Nevers. Charles VI had succeeded in keeping the young and ineffective dauphin from the battle, but his nephew, the Duke of Orléans, was to remain a prisoner in England for twenty-five years.

It is against this backdrop of widespread loss that we can set Christine de Pisan's consoling poem, dedicated to Marie de Berry, one of her special patrons at the court. Christine puts into human terms the suffering that the battle brought to the great families of France in her description of Marie's situation. Her third husband, the Duke of Bourbon, was captured and died a prisoner twenty years later without ever returning to France. Her son by her second marriage, the Count of Eu, was also captured but was finally released after a captivity of twenty years. Her son-in-law, the Count of Nevers, was killed, as were several close cousins. No wonder Christine fell back on the necessity of counselling patience in adversity.[26]

The night after the battle Henry spent at Maisoncelles, and on Saturday morning he and his tired but exhilarated men marched across the battle-field of the previous day as they took the open road to Calais. In the field lay heaps of naked corpses, stripped of their armour and valuables by the English soldiers, and of even their clothes by the peasants. Many of the wounded died where they lay or in the shelter of the woods or hedgerows. The servants of the lords and knights searched for the bodies of their masters and took them away for decent burial, either at Hesdin or Ruisseau-ville or in their own lands. Nevertheless, many corpses still remained and the Count of Charolais arranged for the digging of a pit some twenty-five yards square where nearly 6,000 bodies were placed. The common grave was blessed and surrounded by a thick hedge to prevent its desecration by dogs or wolves.* Meanwhile the English army marched slowly on to Calais, some forty miles away, anticipating riches from their prisoners and booty but still desperately short of food and horses. At the castle of Guines, the first English stronghold of the territory of Calais some six miles away from the town itself, Henry paused with his prisoners while the common soldiers went on to Calais. Despite their exploits they were not very wel-come guests, as food was short. Many of the disillusioned soldiers sold their prisoners cheaply to obtain bread at profiteering prices.

On 29 October Henry made his formal, victorious entry into Calais to be greeted with Te Deums and loud praises. On the same day, early in the morning, the first news of the victory reached London where enthusiasm ran high. Church bells were rung, a ceremonial procession of thanksgiving from St Paul's to Westminster was hastily organised, led by Queen Joan and her lords, and the newly chosen mayor of London and his aldermen with representatives of all the city's crafts. They offered thanks and gifts at the shrine of Edward the Confessor. The king's council took immediate

* The spot is still marked by a memorial cross and inscription erected by the local lords of Tramecourt whose ancestors fought for France at Agincourt. The family maintains the tradition. During World War II, the current count and his oldest son led the resistance there, and died in a German concentration camp.

advantage of the popular enthusiasm. When parliament met the following Monday Bishop Beaufort's opening sermon provided a suitably edited version of the king's exploits. He praised his capture of Harfleur, "the strongest city of this part of the world" and "his glorious and marvellous victory" at Agincourt, against all odds, but emphasised that the king needed more money for the continuance of such victories. The dazzled Commons agreed to advance the payment of the previously voted tenth and fifteenth from February to December. As well, they granted to the king for life the usual subsidy on wool, fells, and hides, and the tax on wines and imports which normally the king had had to ask for each year in parliament. With some remaining caution, they insisted that these life-time grants should not be regarded as a precedent for kings to come. In a continuing generous mood they also agreed to a whole fifteenth and tenth, to be used for the defence of the realm, and to be paid in the following November.[27]

Meanwhile the king remained in Calais. It would appear that Henry himself as well as his exhausted army had been physically affected by the campaign. Even before the battle Master Robert Benham was sent from England to Calais with various medicines ordered "for the health of the king's person" as well as for others in the army.[28] During the interval the king appears to have debated with his nobles whether he should continue the struggle against the French by attacking the nearby fortress of Ardres. On this occasion he allowed himself to be persuaded that further efforts with a worn-out army would be unnecessary and unwise. Having made a list of all the prisoners taken, including those from Harfleur who had appeared on the agreed date to fulfil their oath, the king made ready to sail for England. On 16 November, accompanied by his most distinguished prisoners, he took ship for Dover. An autumn gale in the Channel gave the small ships an extremely rough crossing and the French nobles, unused to sea voyages, suffered so dreadfully from seasickness that they groaningly compared their sufferings to those of the day of battle. Their discomfiture was all the greater because the king was totally unaffected by the ship's motion and remained cheerful and composed. After a day's rest in Dover the royal procession moved on to Canterbury, to give thanks at the shrine of St Thomas, and then on through Rochester to the king's favourite manor of Eltham, just outside London.

His formal welcome to London took place on Saturday 23 November. Early that morning the mayor and citizens of London came out to meet Henry on Blackheath and to accompany him from there to the city. The king's entry into London was the occasion for one of the elaborate pageants which medieval men found so satisfying and which must have added enormously to the colour of life. The tower at the approach to London Bridge was crowned by two huge figures, carrying the keys of the city and a staff. Temporary columns carried a lion, supporting the royal banner, and an antelope (one of Henry's favourite badges) hung with the royal arms and holding a sceptre. Then came a representation of St George, surrounded by boys dressed in white and singing like the angelic host. But all ingenuity was not exhausted by the elaborate structures on London Bridge. As the king passed up Cornhill and along Cheapside he saw that the conduits, running wine in honour of the occasion, were adorned with hangings, pavilions, temporary towers filled with elderly prophets, who let fly little birds as the procession passed by, singing boys and carolling virgins. The king rode soberly through this colourful extravaganza and the pushing, cheering crowds, dressed in a plain gown, with his eyes cast down, giving as his panegyrists admiringly said "thanks to God and not to man". The distinguished French prisoners marching behind under guard added to the suggestion of a Roman triumph. Henry paused at St Paul's to be greeted by the bishops and to make his offering of thanksgiving, and then rode on to his palace at Westminster.[29]

Did the thoughtful king remember his other ride from Eltham to Westminster, less than two years before, when he and his retinue had to move quickly and forcefully through uncertain crowds to suppress dissent in London and isolate the Lollard conspirators and the rebellious John Oldcastle? Good leadership, determination, and an element of luck had given him victory then. The same qualities had achieved the spectacular victory of Agincourt, but the king was enough of a realist to know that despite the panegyrics and noisy popular enthusiasm the spectacular victory had not, in sober fact, improved his military position in France. Even its most decisive result – the death or capture of so many leading French nobles – had not left France unable, or unwilling to fight. If the king was truly serious in his conviction of his rights and his purpose to conquer France then there must be another expedition. The second time he must achieve more than one town captured and one brilliant but inconclusive battle in which victory had resulted more from his enemies' mistakes than his own plans.

CHAPTER VIII

The King, the English Church, and the Council of Constance

Henry V was a Christian king in the model of his age. According to the more sober chroniclers he was generous, pious, assiduous in his religious exercises, aided the clergy, and fought vigorously against all enemies of the faith and the church. These virtues, remarkable though they are, pale in the more florid rhetoric of his panegyrists, one of whom compares the king favourably to a wide gamut of Biblical and literary heroes, ranging from Moses and David to Hector, Cicero, and Gawain.[1] Much of even the sober chronicler's praise can be discounted as the respectful platitudes found in funeral orations for the mighty, but Henry's own deeds reinforce his reputation for orthodoxy, particular care for the clergy, and generous gifts to the church. Nevertheless, this very orthodox and pious king ruled a country which contained many heretics and many clerics who were living most secular lives. A contemporary preacher who delighted in complex allegories and also greatly admired his masterful king drew two disparate views of the spiritual state of the England of his day. In one sermon he had a pessimistic picture of England, reinforced by his hatred and fear of Lollards. He described it as a fortified town typifying the city of sin, where priests in secular clothes stood ready to fire arrows of evil-speaking from the tower of pride, while they were reinforced by laymen and women in the most extravagant of contemporary fashions. The city of sin, he went on to say, was so full of an immense army of Lollards that it was beyond the art of the heralds to count them. Indeed, he added soberly, the "serpentine venom" of Lollardy had so weakened the kingdom that the slightest breeze from Wales was likely to blow it over.[2] His other view of England, "that plenteous realm", as "a great ship which sailed for many a day in the sea of Prosperity" was more hopeful. In working out his allegory he carefully described the various parts of the ship as being made up of the various classes in the realm, all of whom were needed, but he put his trust in the skill of "oure maister mariner, oure worthi prince". Nevertheless, he saw clearly that all was not well:

The love of the people is turned away from God: devotion is withdrawe wellnigh in every rank. Neither Regular nor Secular lives as he ought. Our conversation and mode of living is not as it was. The cloth is of another hue. Our life is not like the life of our fathers of old. Many brekkes are in every part of the ship. Neither clergy, nor barony, nor commons can excuse themselves of sin . . . Therefore the master mariner, oure sovereyn lord . . . desiringe from his heart the wele and honour of us all, besied hem by great means to repair the brekkes of our ship and rere up agen our spirit to God.[3]

What was the reality of the state of the church in England during Henry's reign, and how did the king see his responsibility to it? It is, of course, a platitude that the men of the early fifteenth century lived in a world which was saturated with the externals of religious observance – the multitude of churches and masses, the large number of clergy, both secular and religious, the popularity of religious processions and pilgrimages. But even a casual glance at the attitudes exhibited by Chaucer's pilgrims or the inhabitants of Langland's "fair field of folk" make it obvious that much of the religious superstructure was merely taken for granted as part of the accepted background of life. Conventional religious practice required no individual initiative and did not necessarily imply any personal commitment. A look at the hierarchy of the day provides still another impression of decent formalism. There were no particularly saintly men among Henry's bishops, but no scandalous appointments either. Bishop Beaufort was not in the typical mould – and indeed had been made a bishop before Henry IV came to the throne – but he was the king's uncle, in the very wealthy see of Winchester, and was essentially an ambitious ecclesiastical politician who devoted himself almost equally to his own advancement and enrichment and to upholding the Lancastrian succession. Generally, Henry's bishops were able, well-educated administrators who had worked hard for the king as clerks, negotiators, and ambassadors and were ultimately rewarded for their labours with bishoprics. They were conscientious bishops according to their lights, but they saw their duties in the pattern of their own interests and abilities. They devoted their skills to the administration of the rights and lands of their dioceses, to the proper functioning of their courts rather than to the spiritual inspiration of their people. Much the same criticism could be made of the monks, especially the Benedictines, whose energies were almost completely absorbed in maintaining their estates and privileges against all comers.

Nevertheless, apart from these formalised, perhaps ossified, structures, there was still much genuine individual devotion and religious ferment, not only among the clergy but also among the laity. For example, the number of manuscripts of Richard Rolle's works described in the wills and inventories of the fifteenth century testifies to the widespread popularity in lay society of that mystic and hermit. *The Book of Margery Kempe*, an extra-ordinary autobiography, describes in colloquial and vigorous prose the burning personal devotion of a common-place townswoman from Lynn which impelled her to far-ranging pilgrimages, floods of devotional tears during sermons, and a fearless capacity to treat even archbishops as an equal.[4] Margery Kempe was certainly atypical in her flamboyance and volubility, but she was undoubtedly representative of a large group of truly devout and orthodox individuals whose faith was the important core of their lives. However, as we have already seen, many of the devout were not orthodox. Large numbers of the growing class of small tradesmen and craftsmen had been converted by popular preachers to ideas derived from the teachings of John Wycliffe. His diatribes against the established clergy and their wealth, especially in the cruder forms preached by his followers, struck a sympathetic chord among the skilled artisans of the towns and also among some of the landed knights. Part of the attraction of these Lollard ideas was their burning anti-clericalism and anti-papalism, which appealed strongly to the xenophobic emotions of an England roused by generations of chronic war, and also to the deeply held English conviction that their churches and monasteries were being despoiled for the benefit of rapacious foreigners. The Lollard element in the population, deprived of its natural leaders after the putting down of Oldcastle's rebellion, was never again a serious political danger, but it was a continuing submerged current in the religious life of the time.

King Henry's own religious practices seemed conventional. He showed generosity to the church in ways formalised by long usage, and was par-ticularly lavish in his gifts to Westminster Abbey, which in many ways he seems to have regarded as the religious focus for the rightful celebration of the mystique of the monarchy. By the end of the first year of his reign he had had Richard II reburied there and also returned a valuable ruby ring which Richard had presented to the shrine of Edward the Confessor. He considered it a personal obligation to grant 1,000 marks a year for the construction and repair of the nave, which had not yet been completed. His detailed instructions for his tomb and the chantry chapel to be built above it, contained in the will he made before leaving for France in 1415, and his choice of its prominent position, dwarfing the shrine of Edward the Confessor, suggest a concern for royal glorification, almost for apotheo-sis. In a more usual pattern of royal beneficence, both spiritual and material, he gave handsome gifts to the altar and sent venison from the royal forests to the monks' table.[5]

In one way his good works did not follow the contemporary norm. The powerful and wealthy of the early fifteenth century usually endowed schools or chantries: Henry founded the last monasteries in medieval England. However, the impetus for these foundations was not his own initiative, but his desire to carry out the task enjoined on his father by the

Henry V, by an unknown artist

Hoccleve presenting the *De Regimine Principum* to Prince Henry (*Arundel MS. 38, f. 37*)

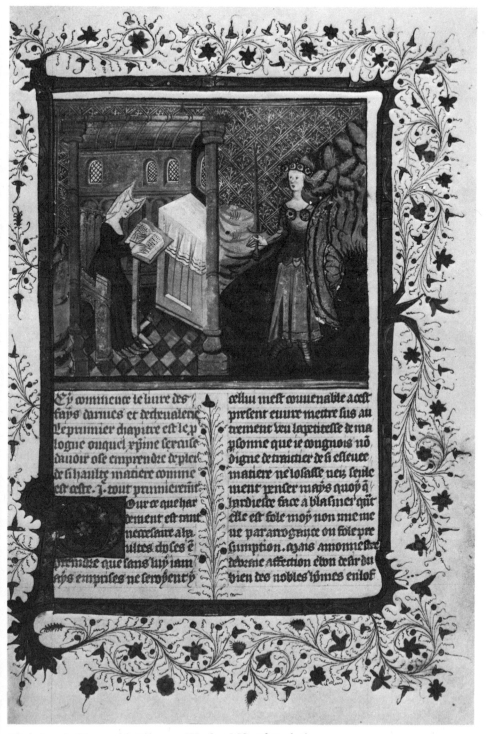

Christine de Pisan with Minerva (*Harley MS. 4605, f. 3*)

St George and the Garter King-of-Arms, William Bruges, from the Bruges Garter Book
(*Stowe MS. 594, f. 5v*)

Charles of Orléans in the Tower after Agincourt (*Royal MS. 16.F.II, f. 73*)

The siege of Rouen, 29 July 1418–19 January 1419 (*Cotton MS. Julius E IV, Art VI, f. 19v*)

An Arbalétrier and an Estradiot – early-fifteenth-century French soldiers

A copy of a contemporary French engraving of a fifteenth-century siege catapult

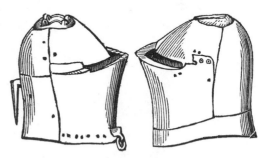

Tournament or tilting helms of the time of Henry V

The effigy of Henry V (completed in 1971) on his tomb in Westminster Abbey. The head was modelled by the sculptor (Louise Bolt) from contemporary chronicle descriptions and the familiar portrait

pope after the settlement of the controversy caused by the execution of Archbishop Scrope. Henry IV, beset by many problems, and always in financial difficulties, did nothing further during his reign, but his son took action to fulfil his father's obligation soon after his own accession to the throne. Henry V had a particular fondness for the royal manor at Sheen and carefully rebuilt it – a necessary task for Richard II had ordered its total destruction after the death there of his beloved queen. When Henry set about its rebuilding he ordered stone from Caen and Yorkshire, as well as nearby Surrey and Oxfordshire, and also re-used the materials from the manor of Byfleet which he himself had occupied as Prince of Wales, but which was now torn down to add to Sheen. It was probably because of his fondness for Sheen that he decided to make these new religious foundations there. The first was a Carthusian Priory which was known as the House of Jesus of Bethlehem by Sheen, and which was richly endowed with revenues taken from the confiscated English lands of some of the alien priories. From the beginning the house was distinguished and devout, with some forty monks, but it disappeared completely at the time of the dissolution. The curious searcher of today must be satisfied with a wall plaque in a lane running from Richmond Green to the river, which marks the western boundary of the priory.

Just across the river from Sheen, at Twickenham, Henry laid the foundation stone of the second house, which was confided to the Brigettines. The choice of this recently founded order from Sweden seems to have been suggested by its links with the king's sister. Philippa had married King Eric of Denmark and the lady in charge of her household was a granddaughter of St Bridget, while Philippa herself had close ties with the mother-house at Vadstena. The house was more difficult than the Charterhouse to establish in running order. The Brigettines were a double order of both men and women, although each house had more women than men, and some changes were required to adapt their constitution to the English scene. As well, the original site proved too small and too wet and, in 1431, the community moved a few miles downstream to Syon.* The third foundation was also projected at Sheen and was to be made up of Celestines, a French order with whom Bishops Courtenay and Langley had been in touch during their embassy in Paris in 1414. This plan floundered on the dual obstacles of financing and general anti-French feeling.[6]

Henry had a genuine concern with the proper regularity of monastic life and the weakening of monastic ideals among the Benedictines, and even his

* Nothing now remains of the old buildings in the secular glories of Syon House which occupies its site, but the religious community has maintained a continuous existence. It fled to the Continent after the dissolution of the monasteries but is now re-established at South Brent, Devon. The Syon Cope, probably the greatest of medieval English embroideries, belonged to this house and took its name from it, although it was made before its foundation.

absorption in his wars in France was not allowed to shoulder it aside completely. In 1421 the king called a general chapter of the black monks, to meet at Westminster on 5 May, at the same time as parliament and convocation. Henry was already poised to return to France to continue the struggle there and would never return alive to England, but he took the time to address the assembly of monks. In his speech he reminded them that the benefactions which they had received from his royal ancestors and other founders had been prompted by a conviction of the value of the prayers of men of austere and regular life. Although he still valued their prayers, perhaps if they would return to the careful observance of their rule they would once more be as effectual as they once had been. To urge the monks along the path of reform the king put forward certain proposals, drawn up on the advice of the Carthusian prior of Mt Grace, which tried to attack the outstanding recognised abuses, and appointed his own secretary, Edmund Lacy, the Bishop of Exeter, and the prior of Mt Grace, to confer with six delegates of the monks on the suggested articles of reform. Despite the fact that the articles were a moderate and practical attack on well-recognised abuses, the committee of monks was not enthusiastic. When the king's personal pressure was removed, after his return to France, nothing was done. The abbot of St Albans finally issued a report in the finest tradition of all reports designed to shelve further inconvenient action. It acclaimed with resonant periods the high ideals of monastic regularity, but carefully avoided any programme of genuine reform.[7]

However, the king was not only concerned with the public welfare of religion in his realm, he took his own religious duties seriously. The calibre of the men whom he appointed as his confessors indicates that he was not willing to accept the uneducated or the unworthy. Stephen Patrington, his first choice after his accession, was a middle-aged and highly respected Carmelite friar who had been prior of the convent at Oxford and had his doctorate in theology. Patrington had a long history of opposition to Wycliffe's ideas and had even been the spokesman of the dissatisfaction of the Oxford friars with Wycliffe, to John of Gaunt, his original protector. For some years Patrington had served as provincial of the English Carmelites, though he gave up that position when he became the king's confessor. The king maintained him according to his station. Patrington was originally allowed nearly £70 a year for the maintenance of himself, a companion, their servingmen, four horses and a hackney and four grooms. In 1415 the king rewarded him with the bishopric of St David's, a poor Welsh diocese whose bishops rarely resided but which was seen as a traditional stepping-stone to higher places. Before Patrington's death at the end of December 1417 his translation to the see of Chichester had been arranged but was not completed in time.[8]

The importance of a confessor impelled the king, soon after Patrington's death and while he was busily occupied with the siege of Falaise, to write to Archbishop Chichele requesting him to send him "a gode man and a clerk of divinite" to fill that office while he was abroad. Chichele's choice was Thomas Dyss, a Dominican and a master of divinity from Cambridge, who was released by his provincial for this new assignment.[9] Still another Carmelite, Thomas Netter, also seems to have served at some time as Henry's confessor. He was a protégé of Patrington and especially strongly opposed to the Lollards. In fact, he is reputed to have criticised Henry for his inaction in this respect in a sermon against the Lollards preached at St Paul's Cross. For a time he was part of the English delegation at the council of Constance. Netter certainly reinforced, and perhaps strengthened, the king's dislike and distrust of the Lollards but he did not encourage persecution. At the king's request he mobilised his great learning and ability in defence of orthodoxy, trying to convince rather than condemn. It was Netter who preached at Henry's funeral and who served until his death as confessor for young Henry VI.[10]

This royal interest in the outstanding religious men of his day is further illustrated by Henry's acquaintance with the famous Dominican friar, Vincent Ferrer. Brother Vincent had been preaching in Brittany in 1418 and had encouraged a religious revival there. He was obviously a forceful personality: it was said of him that his preaching was so sweet and gentle that he never bored his listeners although he prolonged his sermons for many hours. Hearing of his fame, the king asked him to come to Caen. Vincent accepted the king's invitation to preach before him, but is said to have covered his face with the hood of his habit so as not to be intimidated by any signs of the king's or the court's disapproval. It was a bold sermon for such an audience. The friar praised the king for his condemnation of Oldcastle, but reproached him for his oppression of the people and for his destruction of Christians who had not even offended him. The king, outwardly unperturbed, had the friar brought before him and explained his own conviction, "I am the scourge of God, sent to punish the people of God for their sins." The two then talked secretly together for some hours and appear to have parted with mutual admiration. The king offered Vincent rich gifts which the friar would not accept, so Henry then pressed on him the complete altar furnishings for the chapel where he said mass, and begged him to return. Afterwards the king wrote to a friend of the profound impression that the friar had made on him, and his desire that some English religious, with training in theology, could be found who would follow Vincent and then return to preach in England with some of his spirit and power. The friar had been equally impressed by the king. As Vincent left the king's presence he passed through the hall where the king's household and military leaders were, and he paused to adjure them to serve their king well and truly. He told them that he had previously believed that the king was the greatest tyrant of all Christian princes, but now he was convinced that he was the most perfect and acceptable to God, that his quarrel was so just and true that undoubtedly God would be his aid in all these wars.[11]

Henry's conviction that he was the elect of God, specially chosen to carry out the divine designs, permeated much of his life and may have been responsible for his particular interest in the possibilities of reviving the crusade. The long tale of western crusading efforts against the Muslims was coming to an inglorious end. By the 1390s the revitalised Turks had succeeded in pushing beyond Asia Minor into Europe and had reached the Danube where they threatened the kingdoms of Eastern Europe. The last of the great crusading armies, containing contingents from almost every part of Europe, was mobilised to oppose them but this international force was no more united than the quarrelling armies of the Second Crusade in the twelfth century. The perpetual disputes over precedence and tactics, as well as the ungovernable insistence of all the eminent knights on displaying their own individual bravery at no matter what cost to reasonable strategy, led to the inevitable result. In the battle of Nicopolis (1396) the Turks practically wiped out the crusading army, saving only those of the greatest importance from whom they could expect fat ransoms. King Sigismund of Hungary managed to escape, but John of Nevers, the son and heir of the Duke of Burgundy, was captured, as were such other distinguished Frenchmen as Enguerrand de Coucy and Marshal Boucicaut. The ransoms were ultimately paid, primarily by King Sigismund and the Duke of Burgundy who provided more than a million francs for this purpose, and the last of the disillusioned crusaders trickled back to Europe. Over three centuries of crusading effort had brought no permanent success but only such erosion of Christian power that the ultimate fall of Constantinople had become inevitable. The Turk was established in Europe and had gained control of the eastern Mediterranean.

It was in such an atmosphere of defeatism and of the breakdown of the old ideas of a universal Christendom that Henry seems to have nurtured the hope that, as soon as he had obtained his rights in France, he would lead a new and important crusade to the east. His ideas were shared by Duke Philip the Good of Burgundy, who must have heard tales from his father about the disastrous battle of Nicopolis and may have felt the need to try and redeem that fiasco. During the long siege of Melun in 1420, the king and the duke discussed their dream, and both promised to go to the Holy Land.[12] They were serious enough in their intent to send Ghillebert de Lannoy, a distinguished Burgundian knight who at Melun shared the duke's tent and was his standard-bearer, on a military reconnaissance mission. In May of 1421 Ghillebert set out from Sluys on an overland trip through Prussia, Poland, the Ukraine, and the Crimea. His instructions had been to make a serious study of the main points of defence near the Holy Land, and from the Crimea he went on by ship to Constantinople, Rhodes, and the main harbours of the eastern Mediterranean. He explored widely and conscientiously, and then wrote a careful report on the cities of Egypt and Syria – whether they were walled or not, the conditions of navigation and access, the types of fortification, and even the depths of the Nile.[13]

The English king and the Duke of Burgundy seem to have had more in mind than just the acquisition of strategic information, and the ceremonial presentation of King Henry's gifts to the rulers of the countries through which their envoy passed.* They appear to have genuinely desired to play a part in ending the scandal of the longstanding divisions between east and west in Christendom, for they commissioned their envoy to impress on the Greek emperor their urgent wish to advance the union of the Roman and Greek churches. Lannoy found himself in the company of papal ambassadors who were there on the same mission, and spent many days explaining his master's position. Unfortunately nothing was achieved for, despite the surface politeness, the problems were too deep and too emotionally rooted to be solved by such casual diplomacy. Nevertheless, we must give Henry due credit for a serious and genuine desire to do something about the state of Christendom and an effort to make his dreams a reality. Looking back, influenced by our knowledge of his premature death and what actually took place, we may dismiss his dreams as insubstantial fantasies. But from his viewpoint, trusting his own youth and undoubted military and organisational abilities, Henry could reasonably and genuinely hope to improve the state of Christendom and perhaps even have legitimate confidence in the possibility of altering the military pattern in the Near East.

The king was not only interested in the great design. His attention, even in religious matters, extended also to specific matters of detail. Henry had a particular devotion to St George, and it was at his request that at a church council held soon after his accession the feast of St George was made a double, requiring special observance. It was in the name of St George too that he fought at Agincourt and when the Emperor Sigismund came to England in 1416 he endeared himself to Henry by bringing a finely worked image and the heart of St George to be offered at Windsor, at St George's chapel.[14] As well, the king paid special attention throughout his reign to the proper conduct of services by his household chapel. In 1413 he had twenty-seven chaplains and clerks (including choristers), of whom four were composers. Even during the hard-fought campaigns in France Henry was anxious to have with him his accustomed household chapel, with its ability to sing the services properly, and orders came back to England to send

---

* The most interesting of these was a gold clock which Lannoy could not deliver to the Emperor of Turkey to whom it was addressed, since he had died before his arrival. All during the rest of his extensive voyage he carried the valuable gift with him and, in 1423 when he returned to Europe and went to London to report to the council on the charge which Henry V had given him, he brought along the undeliverable gold clock and solemnly returned it to the infant king's council.

over organists and impress boy choristers for the king's chapel in Normandy. Undoubtedly, much of the king's personal interest in his chapel
was due to his own serious and quasi-professional involvement in church
music – the present weight of evidence suggests that he actually composed
some himself – but it also bespeaks a continuing concern for the proper
performance of the king's private devotions and religious observances.[15]

It is obviously impossible in the fifteenth-century frame of reference to
discuss Henry's relations with the English church, or even his own religious
life, without sketching the wider ecclesiastical background of the contemporary state of Christendom. Unfortunately the situation was shocking.
The papacy, the institutional expression of the organic unity of western
Christendom, was in scandalous disarray. The long residence of a series of
French-sponsored and French-supported popes in Avignon, rather than
Rome, had led by easy stages to open schism when, in 1378, opposing
factions of cardinals elected both a Roman pope and an Avignonese pope.
Both claimed the full primacy of Peter and rival obediences immediately
established themselves on political lines. The Avignonese pope, for ex-
ample, was naturally supported and recognised by the French, and those
other countries where French influence was paramount: Scotland, Castile,
Aragon, and the minor German principalities bordering on France.
The Roman popes found their supporters among the states opposing the
French hegemony: the Empire, Hungary, England, and Scandinavia. The
inadequacies of the popes and the inequities of the cumbersome and
expensive system of papal administration and finance were made disas-
trously obvious when two popes claimed the same powers and installed
two equally extortionate bureaucracies. The situation seemed almost
impossible to resolve, since each side marshalled an almost equal economic
and political weight, and no one was able to get both popes to agree on the
calling of a general council of the church which could adjudicate the
opposing claims. Finally, a group of cardinals, independent of both popes
and the emperor, convoked the council of Pisa in 1409. They attempted to
remedy the situation by decreeing the deposition of both the Roman and
the Avignonese popes, and elected their own candidate, Alexander V, who
was vowed to reform. Unfortunately, neither the Avignonese nor the
Roman pope recognised the validity of the council, nor accepted its sentence of deposition. Thus it came about that at the beginning of Henry V's
reign, Europe was distracted and divided by three competing popes – the
Roman Gregory XII, the Avignonese Benedict XIII, and John XXIII,
successor to Alexander V.

General disgust and the disappearance of political support for the various
claimants finally opened the way to ending the impossible situation. Sigismund, King of Hungary, who had been elected Holy Roman Emperor in
1410, was genuinely insistent on the need to end the schism, to put down
the growing heresies, and to reform the church. His earnest political

manoeuvres to get a council convened and active were made more effective by his ability to exert sufficient pressure on John XXIII to force him to issue the necessary papal call for a council at Constance in 1414. The diplomatic exchanges of these years – including the frequent embassies between Sigismund and Henry IV and then Henry V, and Sigismund's alliance with Charles VI of France – were all directed towards rallying support among the reigning princes for the council and paving the way for a return to unity within the church. Henry himself was sufficiently convinced by his ambassadors' reports of Sigismund's high motives that he included in his will of 24 July 1415 (made before he took ship for France) a special legacy for the emperor of the two-edged sword which Henry had received at his coronation for the defence of the faith and the church. He bequeathed it to Sigismund because he was, in the king's opinion, the most faithful defender of the church and of the faith.[16]

The English delegation to Constance was a mixture of distinguished ecclesiastics and prominent laymen whom the king frequently used in his diplomatic service. It thus reflected the dual nature of the council as an ecclesiastical and a political arena. The embassy included Bishop Hallum of Salisbury, Bishop Bubwith of Bath and Wells, Bishop Catterick of St David's (soon to be transferred to Lichfield); the abbots of Westminster and St Mary's of York; and John Honyngham, professor of law and royal prothonotary. The laymen were led by the Earl of Warwick, and included Lord Fitzhugh, the king's chamberlain, and Sir Walter Hungerford, his steward of the household. Hallum, the most influential of the English party, had been one of the English representatives at Pisa, an embassy he had shared with Henry Chichele, then newly consecrated Bishop of St David's but now Archbishop of Canterbury and a close and trusted adviser of the king. Hallum was a Lancashire man, once chancellor of Oxford, whose efforts both as bishop at home and as head of the English delegation at Constance were zealously bent on reform and the good order of the church. His eloquent sermon before the council fathers on 8 December 1415 applied the characteristics of the sun to the papacy and episcopacy, denounced the evils and worldliness which eclipsed the sun of the church, and looked forward to the day when it would again break through in all its glory.[17]

Hallum was not merely a zealous reformer and eloquent preacher. His literary interests led him to persuade one of the Italian bishops to make a Latin translation of Dante for him. True to the tradition of Salisbury, he rejoiced in the careful carrying out of the liturgy in all its musical splendour, singing mass himself in Constance Cathedral on the feast of Thomas Becket and providing beautifully sung vespers on the eve of the feast, accompanied by "sweet English hymns on the organ". His death at Constance in September 1417 deprived the council of a strong reforming leadership. He had made a notable impression on the enormous and distinguished assembly gathered in that lakeside city on the Rhine. A fitting

epitaph is recorded by Richental, the wealthy and enthusiastic citizen of
Constance, in whose delightful chronicle the excitement engendered by
the presence of the emperor and so many eminent churchmen never quite
extinguishes his bourgeois concern for the details of everyday living.
Richental wrote of Hallum that:

> He was the bishop who dared to say openly to Pope John, when the
> Pope was at Constance at mid-Lent, that he was not worthy to be pope,
> because of the wicked crimes he had committed, and then recounted
> them to his face. He stood in fear of no man.[18]

The general atmosphere at Constance was less edifying, as witnessed by
the drastic remedy for international contentiousness suggested by an
anonymous observer:

> Recipe for the stomach of St Peter and total healing of the same, issued
> at the Council of Constance. Take twenty-four cardinals, one hundred
> archbishops and prelates, the same number from each nation, and as
> many curials as you can get. Immerse in Rhine water and keep sub-
> merged there for three days. It will be good for St Peter's stomach and
> for the cure of all his diseases.[19]

The Council of Constance is most frequently remembered for its condemnation of John Hus, the famous Bohemian preacher much influenced
by John Wycliffe. Hus combined unorthodox doctrine with an inflammatory nationalism which made him doubly suspect to the German ruling
class and the conservative members of the church hierarchy. Brought to
the council to defend his teachings, Hus had his safe-conduct revoked and
was summarily convicted and burned. Heresy, particularly combined with
social upheaval, was an easy target for the assembled churchmen. Their
real problem, however, was how to achieve both unity and reform within
the church itself. Unanimity on this matter was far more difficult to achieve
and was further complicated by political alignments and rivalries.

The general method of discussion and voting at the council followed the
pattern established at Pisa, and from the beginning illustrated the pervasive
political influences brought to bear. The division of the council fathers
into four nations – the Germans, French, Italians, and English – was so
arranged that each nation had one vote for the whole delegation, no matter
what the discrepancies in size of the various delegations. The plan was
originally designed to keep the great number of Italians from being able to
control the proceedings by their weight of numbers, but the scheme was
particularly attractive to the small English delegation. During the first
months of the council the English and Germans worked closely together,
partly for religious reasons and a mutual desire for reform, and partly
because the English laymen were reinforcing their king's efforts to negotiate
an alliance with Sigismund against the French. Inevitably the cockpit of

the council reverberated with the political quarrels of the component states. The French nation was split by the controversy between those who represented Charles VI, for the moment under Armagnac influence, and those who gave primary allegiance to the Duke of Burgundy. The appearance of a small but haughty Spanish delegation, which insisted that it must be given at least equal precedence with the English, and the return of Sigismund himself with his obvious preference for the English, precipitated a violent controversy. French and English attacked each other vigorously and stalled any progress for some months. Hallum's death in September 1417 provided a useful opportunity for Henry to change the emphasis of his instructions. It allowed the English king to put aside the cause of reform, which Hallum had championed so energetically, and to encourage his delegation to attempt to mediate between the emperor and the cardinals in order to achieve the election of a new pope as quickly as possible. The way was clear, once the prior demand for reform had been shelved, since Gregory had resigned, John had been deposed, and Benedict, deserted by all his supporters, could be disregarded. Henry's motive was obvious. He was primarily anxious that the council achieve the restoration of unity, which he saw as its main objective, so that Sigismund could then turn his energies to fulfilling the terms of the alliance he had made with Henry in September of 1416 and provide the military assistance which Henry needed in Normandy. Through the good offices of Bishop Beaufort, suspiciously close at hand on the first stages of a pilgrimage to Jerusalem, a compromise was worked out between all the parties.[20] The cardinals proceeded to elect a Roman, Odo Colonna, as Martin V, who was supposed to carry on the work of reform.

The council had passed two important decrees: *Sacrosancta*, asserting the superiority of the general council over the pope, and *Frequens*, calling for the holding of general councils at regular intervals. It had restored unity to the church, but it had made little headway in reform, and it had made more bitter the already inimical relations of England and France. In its condemnation and execution of Hus and Jerome of Prague for heresy it provoked a popular religious and patriotic uprising in Bohemia which was to preoccupy Sigismund for much of the rest of his reign, and to negate Henry's hopes of military aid from his alliance with the emperor.

As Martin V began to rebuild papal influence and force after the conclusion of the council, England's relations with him were continually exacerbated by the conflict between papal privileges, as understood by the pope, and their limitations in England by such statutes as Provisors and Praemunire, invoked by suspicious kings. The Statute of Provisors which nullified any appointment made by the pope, at the expense of the regular patron, to a benefice not yet vacant, and Praemunire, which forbade appeals to courts outside the kingdom, cut sharply into papal revenues, accustomed to being generously augmented by the profits of provisions. The kings were enthusiastic supporters of the statute, particularly in regard to the more profitable canonries and prebends. This was not disinterested care for the rights of the ordinary patron but rather a desire to have at their own disposal a reservoir of patronage for royal clerks and administrators whom they could thus reward at no expense to themselves. Even the clerk of the king's kitchen, for example, might be rewarded with the wealthy prebend of Croprede in the diocese of Lincoln for his work in the king's service.[21] Nevertheless, the king would cheerfully accept papal provisions when they were in his favour – his choice for bishoprics, for example, or a special benefice for one of his clerks – but proclaimed his devotion to the statute when this was better adapted to his purpose. Such opportunism is particularly obvious in the answer which was given to the pope's messenger at Mantes in October 1419 when he delivered the papal request that Henry abandon "those statutes of England, prejudicial to the Roman church and pope". Master Philip Morgan, the king's mouthpiece, remarked tartly that the king was very busy recovering his hereditary rights and did not have time for this. As well, the king had taken an oath at his coronation to uphold the statutes of the realm made in parliament, as these had been, and he could make no changes without the assent of the three estates in parliament.[22]

Henry was equally swift in invoking the statutes when Bishop Beaufort was named a cardinal and legate for life by a grateful Martin V soon after his election. Beaufort had not asked the necessary permission from the king to accept the cardinal's hat, and his holding the office of legate would inevitably involve conflict with the rights of Archbishop Chichele, a most loyal servant of the king. Henry reacted vigorously and threatened to invoke the full rigours of the Statute of Praemunire against his uncle, to strip him of all his possessions in England, including his bishopric. There was an uneasy pause for a time, while the king remained unyielding and Beaufort, in an effort to avoid public humiliation, offered to go on pilgrimage and then resign. The quarrel was finally settled in May 1421 by Beaufort's surrender; the bishop not only agreed to abandon the cardinal's hat (which he later accepted after Henry's death) but to provide the financially hard-pressed king with an enormous loan of over £17,000.[23] The king, though orthodox, would brook no papal meddling in the English church.

Dealings with the pope and the curia were inevitably slow and difficult. Letters to and from Rome normally took six to eight weeks, and individual messengers might take longer, or even never arrive. Master John Forster, for example, sent with a special oral message to the pope about the choice of a bishop for the see of Lisieux (for Henry refused to allow a Frenchman to be appointed in the conquered territories), never got to the curia at all. He was captured and detained in France, although he was supposedly protected by safe-conducts from both the king of France and the Duke of Burgundy. William Swan, who served as the proctor of the Archbishop of

Canterbury at the curia for some ten years, spoke feelingly of "the dangerous obstacles and fearful perils of so long and precarious a way".[24]

But the constant volume of business required resident functionaries and occasionally we can glimpse the personality of such a man behind his official papers. Master Thomas Polton, for example, had been named king's proctor at the curia in 1414. At the Council of Constance he delivered the vigorous justification by the English of their right to be considered a nation. He was apparently a difficult and pugnacious man. Swan, who frequently dealt with him in Rome, found him devious, and complained to Archbishop Chichele, "Nobody can ever understand him." There is no doubt he had a strongly developed sense of self-importance, having caused considerable scandal by a brawl at the altar with the Castilian ambassador, the Archbishop of Compostela, over precedence. The unseemly quarrel had offended the pope so much that he undertook proceedings against Polton for disorderly conduct. Nevertheless, Polton, despite his prickly behaviour, made good use of his opportunities for advancement and worked his way upward through three bishoprics – Hereford, Chichester, and Worcester – before his death in 1433.[25]

Of course, not all Henry's relations with the pope were as frosty as those occasioned by Polton's behaviour and the king's suspicion of papal disregard for his proper honour. In February 1419 John Catterick, Bishop of Lichfield and ambassador from Henry to the pope, wrote the king a glowing report of the pope's enthusiasm for Henry's letters and quoted Martin as saying that "not all the theologians in the world had moved him as much as the most sacred eloquence of this our son". In a less flowing vein, the bishop gives a list of the papal bulls which he transmitted, including that for the foundation of Syon, and for such privileges as the right to a portative altar and other equally desirable exemptions. The costs came to over 1,500 florins, but there was some money left from the king's letters of exchange so Catterick, in businesslike fashion, had deposited the residue.[26]

The pattern of England's relations with the papacy during the reign of Henry V was drawn by a dedicated and orthodox, but independent monarch. He strongly opposed heresy and tried to encourage a fitting standard of religious practice within his kingdom. It is obvious that he felt an immediate personal responsibility for the English church which, under the pressure of schism, war and growing national feeling, was becoming less a European and international entity than the ecclesiastical arm of a secular government. The old ideals of a supra-national Christendom still claimed lip-service, and Henry could even be moved by the vision of leading a successful crusade against the infidel; but national antipathies and national interests, both financial and political, more and more determined church policy within the realm.

CHAPTER IX

Once More to France

Although Agincourt had inflicted dreadful casualties on the French, it had by no means deprived them of the ability, or the will, to continue the struggle against the English. Their first efforts would naturally be concentrated against Harfleur as an important, strongly fortified port which the French needed to regain to protect the Norman coast. The English were equally aware of its importance, for a council meeting of 25 November 1415 was mainly devoted to its affairs. The councillors discussed the choice of a "sufficient and discreet person" who would not only pay the captain of the soldiers the quarter's wages of his men but would also be competent to make a quick estimate of the state of the town, especially of the artillery. There were at the time 300 men-at-arms and 900 archers in the garrison and their wages, including the necessary oats for the horses, called for a payment of £3,640. The king's treasury was empty and, as so often with royal financing, the only way to meet such pressing obligations was to borrow against the sum expected from the fifteenth which fell due on 13 December.[1]

The English concern for their defences was more than justified. At the beginning of 1416 Bernard, Count of Armagnac, was named constable of France to replace d'Albret, killed at Agincourt. Armagnac was aggressive and eager to drive the English from France and soon began to gather forces for an attack. In early March the Earl of Dorset, English commander of Harfleur, took most of his fighting force out on an expedition for supplies. They raided the chalk country – the *Pays de Caux* – to the northeast as far as Cany, some twenty-five miles away, which they burned. Their depredations alerted French patrols and at Valmont, on their way back to Harfleur, their route was barred by a much larger French force, led by Armagnac himself. Although Dorset deployed his archers and their pointed stakes in the fashion which had proved so successful at Agincourt, his line of men-at-arms was too thin to withstand the charge of the French horsemen. The success of the French breakthrough was thrown away by their undisciplined rush to loot the baggage which had been put to the rear. Dorset gained sufficient time to rally his men and regroup around a garden where a ditch and a thorn hedge protected him from being run down. English casualties were heavy, but they held their ground till nightfall, when Armagnac withdrew with his troops to Valmont. Recognising the precariousness of their situation, the English force marched under the cover of darkness towards the sea and gained the coast, temporarily throwing off their pursuers. By the time the French troops had again come up with them the English survivors were marching along the seashore towards Harfleur and had turned the Cap de la Hève, some five miles from the town. The French advance guard, spying them from the precipitous chalk cliffs which lined the shore, plunged down the cliffs to do battle and to annihilate the enemy whom they felt was now at their mercy. They had overestimated their strength and the difficulties of their headlong rush to the beach and they were in turn routed by the English. When Armagnac caught up with his advance guard to carry on the battle the English had gained sufficient confidence to charge up the cliffs and to put this force to flight. Armagnac and his remaining men fled towards Rouen – a road that led them past Harfleur – and some of the garrison sallied out to attack the retreating French. Dorset returned in triumph, having transformed a major defeat into a minor victory by good strategic judgment and the endurance of his men. He had succeeded in gaining a breathing space for Harfleur, but his situation there was still critical, as he had lost many men and horses and had not acquired the supplies he needed. Within a month he was writing to the council in vigorous terms, and demanding their help. He emphasised the need for foodstuffs, especially meat, or all the faithful inhabitants would have to return to "a new Lent", and he reminded council of their heavy loss of horses.[2] Orders were issued almost at once and the commanders of the fleet were urged to go to Harfleur with the necessary supplies as quickly as possible.

The spring parliament at Westminster made it obvious that the king's mind was much exercised by the renewal of French attacks, and the defence measures they necessitated. The Bishop of Winchester, who as chancellor preached the opening sermon, emphasised the English triumphs and the incredible obstinacy of the French after such defeats: "Why do not these miserable and hardheaded men see by these terrible divine sentences that they are bound to obey?"[3] However, until the French came to their senses and recognised English rule as God's will, the bishop urged parliament to give the king counsel and help, especially financial help.

It would be interesting to know Henry's inmost thinking at this time. Certainly he regarded Harfleur as an essential base, which must be maintained, along with Calais, as the forward barbicans of the English position. With the support of these two strongholds, if they could also achieve maritime superiority, the English could use the Channel as a moat, a second

line of defence protecting their shores, and cut down if not completely
suppress the frequent French raids on English ports and coastal towns.
Although the security of England was important, it was not in the forefront
of Henry's strategic designs. Agincourt had been an incredible victory for
the English, but it was in no way decisive. No one pitched battle could be
decisive in a land as large and as strongly fortified as France. The un-
resolved question in the spring of 1416 was how far was the king totally
committed to military conquest as the means to achieve the territory he
sought? It would appear that the council continued to press upon the king
at this time their desire to see what could be achieved by negotiation, and
by some slight abatement of Henry's more extravagant claims to the crown
and territories beyond those mentioned in the Treaty of Bretigny.[4] For the
moment, Henry was willing to use diplomatic pressure to exploit the
evident weaknesses of his "adversary of France" and to build his own
political and military strength by judicious alliances.

The situation in France was certainly most favourable to English ambitions. The death of the dauphin Louis at the age of nineteen just two
months after Agincourt had been a further blow to the unstable balance
between the various factions. Although he was self-indulgent and rather
lazy, Louis had maintained a fairly equitable division between the Burgundian and Orléanist parties. His marriage to the daughter of the Duke
of Burgundy had been balanced by his choice as heir of the Duke of Berry,
who had no son. Louis, struggling under the burdens of the mental instability of his father, the fearful Cabochien massacre of 1413 in Paris, and the
hammer-blows of the English, had at least ensured a certain continuity in
royal policy. He was succeeded by his brother, John of Touraine, much
more closely linked to the Burgundian party and less able than his brother
to pursue an independent line. In any case, John too died before any real
policy to unite France could be elaborated. The loose alliance of the princes
of the blood which had served as a counterpoise to the growing weight of
Burgundy had been seriously undermined by the capture of Bourbon and
Orléans at Agincourt, and the death of Alençon. It was further weakened
by the death of the aged, but respected, Duke of Berry in the summer of
1416, and the ensuing deaths of the dauphin John and the Duke of Anjou
in the following spring. Bernard of Armagnac was the only strong figure
left in the Orléanist party to prop up the confused king, the extravagant
queen, and the timid, fourteen-year-old dauphin Charles in constructive
opposition to the ambitions of Burgundy. The situation in France was
such as to encourage Henry in his designs of conquest: the fatal strains of
disunity and lack of leadership made it appear that he could tear the fabric
of France into a pattern which suited his own ambitions.

Since the internecine factions in France were achieving Henry's ends
almost without his aid, the king turned to ensure the reinforcement of his
political and military strength by the gaining of new friends. His first aim

was to arrange an alliance with the Emperor Sigismund, with whom he was already on cordial terms. Henry knew that the success of the Council of Constance was the matter closest to Sigismund's heart, and he had encouraged his English delegation there to co-operate with the Germans. Sigismund, on his side, was anxious to consolidate his position and encourage progress at the council. He hoped to speed conciliar decisions by acting as peacemaker between England and France and thus lessening friction between the "nations" at the council. In pursuit of this plan he arrived in Paris on 1 March 1416 and stayed for some five weeks at the Louvre. The town was fascinated as his large retinue rode through the Porte St-Jacques, headed by the emperor himself in full armour except for his helmet, and with the robe over his armour bearing a cross both front and back with the motto "Oh how merciful is God!"[5] While in Paris Sigismund was ceremoniously feasted by the dauphin, Berry, and Armagnac, and in return he entertained some of the citizens of Paris, but his discussions with the French council were not conclusive. Armagnac led the war party in the council – in these days, he would be described as a hawk rather than a dove – and he was not anxious to come to any terms with England until the capture of Harfleur and the disaster of Agincourt could be avenged. However, the English bargaining strength lay in their possession of so many important French prisoners. In the end this was sufficient to force the council to agree to Sigismund's suggestion that he should be accompanied by French ambassadors on his visit to England. The French had still not taken the measure of King Henry: their feeling seems to have been that Sigismund's primary aim in going to England was to achieve the release of the French prisoners, not necessarily to engage in any other negotiations.

After the emperor left Paris he celebrated Easter (19 April) at Beauvais, and then rode on to Calais where he was welcomed with all reverence by the Earl of Warwick, the captain of the town, and by other English lords. Henry had sent them over to do Sigismund honour and also sent some thirty ships in which to transport the emperor and his retinue. The protocol requirements of such a visit, even in the fifteenth century, were obviously rigid. It is interesting to read the note in the English council memoranda which prescribed exactly which lords were required to go to Dover, and which to Rochester, to greet the emperor. The mayor and aldermen were to welcome him at Blackheath, and the king himself on the south shore at St Thomas Watering, so that the two monarchs could ride together across London Bridge and through the city. The only scene in this elaborate web of courtesy which seems to have been spontaneous was the impulsive action of Gloucester at Dover, when he and some other lords were reported to have ridden into the water with swords drawn before the emperor could disembark. If he came in peace, as a mediator, they said, he was most welcome, but if he claimed any rights as emperor over the realm of England then they would immediately resist him. Naturally, Sigismund disclaimed any such intentions.[6] The warning, though melodramatic, may have been justified as the emperor had aroused ill-will in Paris by attempting to interfere in judgment in a case before *Parlement*.

The king had done all he could to make the visit a notable one. He turned over to Sigismund his own palace of Westminster, where the great hall had been made festive for the emperor. It was hung with cloth of gold and tapestry and glowed with the light of the torches which each of the angels in the great hammerbeam roof held in its hand. Parliament had been adjourned before Easter so that it could return after the distinguished visitor's arrival and greet him for all the people of England. Also, the king had postponed the celebration of the feast of St George and marked the occasion on 24 May by investing the emperor with the Order of the Garter. The ensuing feast was characteristic of medieval celebrations. The king and the emperor were served three "subtleties" which displayed St George being armed by the Virgin and an angel doing up his spurs, his famous fight with the dragon, and finally his entering a castle accompanied by a king's daughter leading a lamb. The need for such unusual delicacies must have added to the difficulties of Henry's purveyors who had already been ordered to take "little pigs and freshwater fish" for so long as the emperor remained in the realm.[7]

But far more important matters were at issue than merely the ceremonial pageantry which masked the serious intent. The emperor had long and detailed discussions with the king's council and with the king in person about his two fundamental interests: the state of the church and the possibility of peace with France. The French embassy, which the emperor had brought with him, was reinforced at the end of May by the arrival of the Count of Holland, an acceptable negotiator for all parties since his daughter was married to dauphin John and he himself was the brother-in-law of the Duke of Burgundy and owed allegiance to the emperor for some of his lands. During June some progress was made in the discussions on peace with France. The English terms were somewhat more conciliatory. On the advice of his council, Henry declared his willingness to waive his claim to the French crown, but insisted on retaining Harfleur and its neighbourhood, as well as the full implementation of the terms of the Treaty of Bretigny. There was for a time some suggestion that Harfleur should be put into the neutral hands of Sigismund and the Count of Holland, but the English Commons were no more willing to give up Harfleur than Calais. On their side, the French were not willing to fulfil the sweeping terms of the Treaty of Bretigny, for they argued that though fortune favoured Henry now, it would not always. Despite all his labours Sigismund could not fulfil his hope of achieving the prelude to a final peace between England and France, but he did succeed in getting both sides to agree to a personal meeting of the principals near Calais to work out terms for a long truce.

The Agincourt prisoners, who had been present at some of the festivities for the emperor, saw a glimmer of hope for their own freedom in such an arrangement and the French ambassadors returned to Paris to discuss the matter with the council. They were accompanied by Sir Thomas Erpingham and John Wakeryng, the Bishop of Norwich, who had been commissioned as the English ambassadors to continue the negotiations.

It was at this critical juncture that further negotiations were undermined by the intransigence of the Count of Armagnac, who strongly opposed any consideration of the English terms or any arrangements for an immediate meeting. Armagnac's primary concern was with the recapture of Harfleur, which he had already begun to besiege, and against which he was also attempting a naval blockade. He considered its eventual fall inevitable and felt that such a success would immeasurably strengthen the French hand. He argued that negotiations should be dragged on as long as possible, in the hope that Harfleur would fall during the talks, and although he encouraged temporising messages from the council talking of peace he pressed on vigorously with his investment of Harfleur. The result was not what he had hoped. King Henry was coldly furious at the attacks on Harfleur during a period of negotiations for peace, and he lost no time in making clear to Sigismund, who had remained in England as his guest, this further evidence of French duplicity. The king was also angered by the insulting French treatment of his ambassadors, who had let him know that they were locked in their lodgings and, indeed, not even provided with sufficient food. During this time Henry had been balancing his negotiations with France by also treating with the Duke of Burgundy. The Earl of Warwick had been sent to the duke at Lille in June and they concluded a fifteen-month truce, though only for the important commercial districts of Flanders and Artois – always of prime concern to the English. More importantly they had also agreed to a personal meeting of the king and the duke in Calais in the autumn.

The French struggle to recapture Harfleur during the summer of 1416 involved a two-pronged effort. Armagnac's forces laid siege from the land side while a French navy, reinforced by several large carracks hired from the Genoese, blockaded the mouth of the Seine to prevent the city being revictualled from England. Since the blockade did not require all their ships, the French also attacked the south coast of England. Henry was enraged by these French manoeuvres, and quickly organised a relieving force which he put under the command of the Duke of Bedford. The fleet was delayed in sailing by fierce contrary winds, and it was not till the middle of August that Bedford at last got a favouring breeze and could sail for Harfleur. The news of the ships' departure was brought to the king at Westminster and he immediately requested prayers for their success from the Charterhouses of London and Sheen, as well as the recluse of Westminster. Henry was acutely conscious of the urgency of the expedition and the need to bend every effort, spiritual as well as material, to ensure the fleet's success.

The battle was crucial to the fate of Harfleur. Some 500 within the town had already died of hunger, and without provisions Dorset could not hold out much longer. Early on the morning of 15 August the two navies grappled and fierce fighting flared for some five hours. The difference in size between the great Genoese carracks and the much smaller English ships is vividly illustrated by the comment in the *English Life* that, when they grappled, those on the carracks' decks could hardly reach down to the English with their longest spears.[8] Ultimately, the English succeeded in boarding the great hulks, and heavy hand-to-hand fighting ensued, with many casualties. The English captured four of the carracks, and another, the largest, was so damaged in the fighting that it soon foundered. After this success, Bedford easily dispersed a few Italian galleys which lay before Harfleur harbour and sailed triumphantly into port with his stock of provisions for the beleaguered town. The English ships were greeted with enthusiasm by Dorset and his weakened men. After a day's rest they turned to attack the troops besieging Harfleur by land, only to find that the besiegers had lost heart at the defeat of their blockading ships and had abandoned their positions. Harfleur was once more safe for the English. The grim results of the battle were to be seen for many days at the mouth of the Seine, where the bodies of the dead floated restlessly in and out on the tide, "as if they sought another burial than that of fishes".[9]

When Bedford returned to England in triumph with his prisoners and the captured ships, he was greeted by his jubilant brother. Harfleur had been rescued and – equally important in Henry's future plans – Sigismund had signed a treaty of mutual help and alliance with him at Canterbury on the very day of the battle. The terms of this treaty were indicative of Sigismund's disappointment at his inability to reconcile France and England, and his recognition of the impossibility of such a reconciliation. The emperor rehearsed his failures to achieve the peace he had come to seek, and laid particular emphasis on the French deceit in opposing his proposals. He blamed them too for a desire to destroy the unity of the church. Because of all these disillusionments he had decided to make a treaty of perpetual friendship with Henry and his heirs to resist attack from any quarter, except that of the pope and the church. Each side was to be free to move against the French king in pursuit of their rights, and each would aid the other in such recovery.[10] No specific mention was made of the provision of military assistance, but certainly Henry was expecting this treaty to bring him this kind of aid from Sigismund. When the first news of Bedford's naval victory came to the king on 21 August he was at Smallhithe, where he was having some ships built, and he immediately took horse and rode to the emperor at Canterbury – some fifteen miles away – to bring him that "most desired and happy news".[11] The outside observer is likely to attribute the king's impatience to share the good news to a desire to reassure Sigismund that he had chosen the winning side.

With the relief of anxiety for Harfleur, there was no reason for delaying any longer the proposed journey to Calais, where Henry and Sigismund had agreed to meet the French ambassadors, and where they were also expecting the Duke of Burgundy. Before Sigismund left England, and perhaps in gratitude for his generous entertainment at the cost of the king, his knights scattered proclamations in the highways and streets praising England. It would appear that the king maintained the same high, and expensive, standard of care for the emperor's comfort and entertainment while at Calais. Royal commands stipulated that tents ornamented with gold and cloths of arras suitable for the monarchs' use be sent over to Calais and the treasurer ordered a large pair of coffers bound with iron to carry the enormous sum of £4,000 from London to meet the necessary expenses there.[12]

On 4 September Henry crossed from Sandwich to Calais, to be met by the emperor who had preceded him across the Channel. The French ambassadors came as arranged to Calais for further negotiations, but the French defeat off Harfleur and the resultant hardening of Henry's attitude, further stiffened by his new treaty with Sigismund, almost precluded any possibility of successful negotiations. The king treated the ambasssadors with frigid politeness but, in return for the French behaviour towards the English ambassadors at Beauvais, confined them to their lodgings, only allowing one of their servants to go out and buy the necessary provisions. A short-term truce for the sea and a small section of northern France was arranged, to last until 2 February 1417, and with this minor accomplishment the French ambassadors were sent on their way.

The turbulent weather in the Channel at the end of September was responsible for another minor naval skirmish, as several enemy carracks appeared before Calais harbour, possibly blown off course by the storm. English ships, under the command of the Earl of Warwick, issued forth to fight them, but the high winds made it almost impossible for the opponents to meet and grapple. One of the storm-tossed carracks was captured at Dartmouth, where it had been driven ashore, and the others went on their way without any serious consequences to either side. Even the town of Calais was oppressed by the storm. The winds were so high that the tent holding the king's chapel, which had been pitched before the camp, broke in half, and only the determined action of the royal servants in manning the guy-ropes prevented the same disaster to the tent which was the temporary royal hall.

The real importance of the meeting at Calais was the opportunity it provided for a three-way conference between the emperor, King Henry and the Duke of Burgundy, John the Fearless. Henry, by now obviously planning a new descent on France, was particularly anxious to secure, if not an alliance, at least an agreement of benevolent neutrality from the duke. John's arrival at Calais was marked by careful protocol. It had been arranged that the Duke of Gloucester was to serve as a hostage while the Duke of Burgundy was in the English city, and this exchange was carried out with the minute ceremonial detailing in which the Middle Ages revelled. The two parties set out simultaneously and met at the borders of the stream which flowed between Calais and St Omer, some twenty-five miles away. They then left the river-banks simultaneously so that the two dukes met and greeted in mid-stream before passing on: Duke John continued to Calais in the company of the Earl of Salisbury, and Duke Humphrey to St Omer with the Count of Foix. The temperamental Duke Humphrey was apparently none too pleased at his role as one of the Burgundian chroniclers reported that when the Count of Charolais, Duke John's son and heir, came to see him the following day, Humphrey annoyed and displeased his host by omitting the usual greetings.[13]

At Calais Duke John paid his respects to the emperor and then had a series of most secret meetings with Henry where, according to the chaplain, "he and the king sat alone in mysterious council". There exists the draft of a treaty which, according to the most recent biographer of Duke John, was prepared for this occasion by the English chancery in hopes that the king might be able to win its acceptance by the duke. It is an astonishing docu-ment, since it recognised the rights the English king claimed in France. According to its terms, Burgundy promised to acknowledge Henry as rightful king of France and promised to support him in his efforts to make good his claims by agreeing to wage war with all his power on their mutual enemies in the kingdom of France. The treaty, which is written as if by John himself, is not in fact sealed, dated, nor written in John's hand-writing.[14] Many earlier historians, especially French ones, have been convinced that this was a genuine treaty and actually put into effect, and they blame this alliance for the invasion of 1417 that overwhelmed France. The best-informed chroniclers were nowhere near so positive in their judgments. The chaplain, who had written from first-hand knowledge of the 1415 campaign in France and who seems to have also accompanied the king to Calais, was much more noncommital:

> What conclusion was reached by these mysterious discussions and
> negotiations did not emerge beyond the royal mind or the reticence of
> the council. I who write know that the feeling of the people was that
> the duke had detained our king all this time with evasions and ambigui-
> ties and had so left him, and that finally, like all Frenchmen, he would
> prove to be a double-dealer, one person in public, and another in
> private.[15]

Waurin, who wrote as an avowed Burgundian supporter, suggested that the real reason the Duke of Burgundy came to Calais was that it provided useful camouflage for his desire to see and speak with the emperor, as well as do homage for his imperial counties of Alost and Burgundy. He added that the French king and council believed that the duke had allied himself with the English, but he had not. All they had agreed on was a prolongation of the commercial truce between their two countries till Michaelmas 1419.[16] The meeting broke up on 13 October, after the usual polite festivities, and Burgundy returned to St Omer, Gloucester to Calais. The emperor realised that he had spent as much time as he could afford in his futile effort to make peace between England and France and that it was urgent for him to return to Constance where any decisions of substance were postponed until his arrival. The seeds of discord which the Treaty of Canterbury sowed between the emperor and the French king were reflected and heightened at the council by the obvious favour with which Sigismund treated the English delegation and the German and English practice of voting together.

Since the autumn weather was still very boisterous the departures from Calais were somewhat delayed. The emperor was afraid to trust to the sea, and equally afraid to trust to the good faith of some of his vassals of Flanders. King Henry took ship from Calais on 16 October, anxious to return to England for the parliament which he had summoned for 19 October, but his passage was even more turbulent than that of the year before when his French prisoners had become so seasick they thought crossing the Channel worse than Agincourt. The winds were so high that many of the ships had to ride at anchor for most of the night until the weather turned and it became cold and calm. The chaplain has a very vivid description indeed of the horrors of such a crossing.[17] Sigismund, who had parted from Henry with great protestations of affection, finally made his way to Dordrecht, accompanied by Sir John Tiptoft, and rewarded liberally the English officers assigned to him during his stay. As a final present he seems to have sent Henry not only some gold cloth, but also a unicorn's horn more than six feet long. As well, when he returned to Constance he bought a magnificent seven-foot candlestick, with a base "as broad as a table for six" and had it taken apart, packed in a hogshead and sent down the Rhine as a further gift for Henry.[18] These presents were perhaps only a reasonable return for the very stiff expense to which Henry had been put for his extravagant guest. The costs were high, but it would seem that the king felt the price was worth paying for the alliance which freed his hands to turn again to the attack on France.

When parliament opened on 19 October in the Painted Chamber at Westminster, it was obvious from the tone of the chancellor's speech that the king was once more gathering his resources for another expedition to France. The chancellor reminded them that it had been impossible to make a just peace and so there must be war, and that required supplies. In response to this pressure, parliament voted a grant of two-tenths and two-fifteenths, of which one and one-half was to be paid on 2 February

1417, and the remaining half on the subsequent 11 November. However, parliament insisted that these grants were made on condition that no other imposition or charges be placed, nor raised from the community of England, at the same time, nor were the days of payment to be abridged or changed in any way. At the same time parliament confirmed the alliance made with Sigismund at Canterbury.[19] The session ended on 20 November with the king's naming of the Earl of Dorset as Duke of Exeter, in recognition of his achievements at Harfleur. The chaplain, who reported this, also affirmed the king's unbreakable intention to cross to France the following summer to break down the obstinacy and "adamantine hardness" of the French.[20]

Further evidence of Henry's warlike intentions is manifested by a long letter from the king to Sir John Tiptoft, who had been appointed in the autumn to accompany the emperor. On 25 January 1417 Henry wrote secretly to Tiptoft in his own hand, giving him information he wished to reach Sigismund's ears only, and swore Tiptoft to secrecy under pain of forfeiture of his lands and goods. The king wanted the emperor to know of the progress of negotiations with the French prisoners and was particularly anxious to pass on, in the most confidential manner, the result of secret talks he had had with the Duke of Bourbon. This was a matter in which Sigismund was intimately concerned. Although the emperor had agreed in France, before crossing to England, to do all he could to obtain the release of the French prisoners, very little had been achieved during the summer months Sigismund had spent in England. Further discussions in January between the king and the prisoners centred around the sending of Ralph de Gaucourt to France under surety, to attempt to arrange peace and their liberation. Bourbon, an excitable and pleasure-loving man in his mid-thirties, had been more affected by his imprisonment in England, and more willing to make extraordinary concessions to achieve his freedom than any of the others. While the Duke of Orléans, as spokesman for the group, had always steadfastly refused to answer Henry's question concerning their acceptance of his rights in France, Bourbon now promised the king in secret, not only to make enormous territorial and financial grants, but to recognise Henry as rightful king of France.

It is obvious that Henry put little stock in all these negotiations, or in the prisoners' real desire for peace, for he informed Tiptoft that they might speak of peace treaties, but they were really only interested in their own deliverance or in the delay of his forthcoming expedition. Henry's own intransigent attitude, which he wishes Tiptoft to make clear to Sigismund, is vividly conveyed by his own words:

Also, ye shal pray my Brother that he suppose not that for any Tretee that they wol make, that I wol leve my Voyage, with Godds Grace; for sekirly, with his Mercy, I shal not faile, but fully holde such Purpose.[21]

Nevertheless, the charade of negotiation, offer and counter-offer continued, and Gaucourt, though not Bourbon, was allowed to go to France to pursue the matter.

The preparations for the expedition were pressed with vigour throughout the winter of 1416–17. The pattern was much the same as before though on this occasion it is obvious that the king was trying to gather an even larger army and a greater quantity of supplies and siege equipment. The variety of the necessary supplies is illustrated by the royal order for six wing-feathers from every goose in the realm (for the archers' arrows) as well as the expected quarters of grain and gammons of bacon.[22] It seems clear that the king had realised that another purely expeditionary force would not achieve what he desired. In 1417 he was embarking on a serious war of conquest with the intention of permanently conquering territory, not merely acquiring a single base and making showy, but inconclusive, forays through French lands. It is, as always, difficult to arrive at any exact figures for his force, but it would appear that the king had mobilised some 10,000 fighting men, as well as the carpenters, miners, gunners, and masons who were the military technicians of the day. To transport this motley assemblage took some 1,500 ships.

The problem of gathering such a fleet was acute. The king, soon after his return from Agincourt, had begun to consider creating his own navy, and he had certainly been encouraging shipbuilding during the last two years, as well as putting to his own use the carracks which Bedford had captured off Harfleur. The king's concern was purely practical and based on military necessity. Unlike his Portuguese cousin, Prince Henry the Navigator, he was not interested in widening or transforming the scope of maritime endeavour. He merely wished to exploit in the most efficient way possible the current maritime technology. The normal practice at this time was to requisition ships as needed. Obviously the huge flotilla needed to transport a large invasion force, with its supplies and horses, was far beyond any normal needs and had to be obtained by extraordinary methods. The rolls for this period are full of wholesale and specific requisitions of ships. These orders applied not only to English ships, but also to foreign merchant ships temporarily in English ports. For example, in June 1417 the mayor and sheriff of Bristol were ordered to requisition two ships from Denmark, one from Deventer, one from Oporto, Portugal, and one from Ireland, as well as one from Chepstow and one from Bristol itself.[23] Since the same practice was carried out in all the ports of England it is easy to see that the transport the king arranged was of a most polyglot nature and presented many problems, including reluctant masters, and rebellious sailors, as well as the long period of time required to mobilise such a force.

Although Henry had to call once more on this kind of fleet for the major effort of getting his army across the Channel, he had already made great strides in building up a force of his own ships of varying sizes, and of providing their masters with annuities for their labours in the king's service. In August 1417 Henry sent an order back to Bishop Langley, then the chancellor, to pay these annuities and detailed the names and types of the ships. His navy then included three great ships: the *Jesus*, the *Trinity Royal*, and the *Holigost*; eight carracks; six smaller ships; nine balingers and a barge. The terms are unfamiliar. The carracks and the great "nefs" were primarily transport ships, large and rather clumsy, but suitable for ocean travel and capable of carrying very large loads. The *Jesus*, which Henry had had built at Smallhithe in Kent, was rated at 1,000 tons: the *Trinity Royal* and the *Holigost* were considerably smaller. The carracks averaged about 500 tons. The balingers were the most generally useful of the ships of the time. Shallow-draught vessels, with oars as well as sails, they were small and easily handled, and proved most useful for the continuous duties of patrolling the seas and maintaining communications and supplies. Henry's balingers ranged in size from 120 tons to about forty. The annuities for their masters were not very large: ten marks for the masters of the great ships and the carracks; 100 shillings for the smaller ships; and five marks for the balingers and the barge.[24] Before the end of his reign Henry's fleet had risen to some thirty ships, all his personal property, but even before his death the navy was being abandoned as no longer essential. As English forces entrenched themselves ever more firmly on French soil they were more able to maintain and equip themselves without requiring a constant flow of supplies from England. The king's will even specified that his ships should be sold to help pay the royal debts.

While the many preparations were still under way, the king rode from Westminster to St Paul's on 25 April to make his offerings and take formal leave of the city. After his prayers at St Paul's he rode slowly through the London streets, greeting both rich and poor, and begging them all to pray for him. After he had prayed at St George's, Southwark, he took formal leave of the mayor. From there he rode by stages to Southampton to await his retinue and the muster of men who had been ordered to be ready at that port by the end of June. While the king was awaiting the final gathering of his troops he heard of still another French attempt on Harfleur. The French had again hired carracks and armed crews from the Genoese and were harassing the English port. The Earl of Huntingdon was given command of an English force to counter-attack. On 29 June, just off the tip of the Cherbourg peninsula, he fought with nine great carracks, defeated them, and captured four. Huntington was particularly fortunate in this engagement as the French admiral, who was captured with all the treasure for paying the quarter's wages, was the Bastard of Bourbon, the natural brother of the Duke of Bourbon, already a prisoner in English hands. This success literally swept the sea for the English invasion forces.

The chronicle descriptions of these naval battles give very little information about their nature, the strategy or tactics used. A decalogue for naval strategy which was contained in Vegetius' treatise on military affairs, which appears to have been the bible of western sailors during the Middle Ages, suggests the methods and practices of the admirals of the day. Vegetius recommended judicious use of naval intelligence, so that one could know when the enemy might be caught napping, and could then take the advantage of pushing him to the coast, where he would have less room to manoeuvre – a matter of considerable concern for sailing ships. Many of Vegetius' other commandments take for granted the ancient method of fighting at sea, which prevailed for so many centuries – to force ships together so that the soldiers on board could then fight hand to hand. The Roman suggests all kinds of ways to make such fighting more difficult. He recommends hurling missiles of pitch, resin, sulphur, and oil, mixed together and wrapped in flaming tow, to set an enemy ship on fire; or blinding an adversary by breaking pots of lime and dust in front of him; or making him lose his footing by throwing pots of soft soap on the decks. All this time the archers were to be encouraged to shoot holes in the sails; the divers to make holes in the side of the boat with augers; while the attacking ship used a metalled beam suspended from the mast as a battering ram, and cut the sail ropes with a sickle.[25] By Henry's time, the archers on ships were occasionally reinforced by small cannon, which helped to destroy masts and sails. In many cases, of course, such tactics were not necessary. Frequently, the mere sight of a sufficient force of opposing vessels was enough to warn away intruders, and many of the earlier engagements during the reign of Henry IV and the first years of Henry V were piratical raids rather than pitched naval battles such as those commanded by Bedford and Huntington. After 1418 Henry's control of the Channel was almost absolute, and the English ships patrolled rather than fought.

By the end of July the army and all its supplies was prepared and ready to sail. The London chronicle suggests the mixed cargoes of the many little ships:

> Ther was alle his Naveye of schippes, with his ordynaunce, gadred and welle stuffyd as longyd to such a ryalle Kinge, with alle maner of vitayles for his pepille, as well for hors as for man, as longyd for such a warriour, that is to say, armure Gonnes, tripgettis, Engynes, sowis, Bastilles, brygges of lethir, scaling laddres, mallis, spades, schouylles, Pykys, bowes and arrowes, bowstrynges, scheftis and pipis fulle of arowes . . . and whanne tyme come, thedir come to hym scheppes lade with gunepowder.[26]

The proud fleet sailed on 24 July, led by the king's great ship with its sail of purple silk, embroidered with the arms of England and France.

Once again Henry had kept his own counsel about the final destination, merely ordering the fleet to follow the royal ships wherever they sailed. Normandy was again his goal, but not the expected and safe port of Harfleur. Henry's strategic sense was more acute, and he proposed to confound his opponents by an unexpected landfall.

CHAPTER X

The Conquest of Lower Normandy

On 1 August 1417 Henry's flotilla followed the king's lead to the estuary of the river Touques, and there, a little distance from the castle of Touques, the force disembarked. The French had not been expecting Henry in this part of Normandy – south of the Seine, more than forty miles and the width of the Seine estuary from the English base of Harfleur. The disarray at Touques, which agreed to surrender almost before a siege could be laid, illustrated their misjudgment. Henry's strategy on this occasion was far more coherent than that displayed in his earlier expedition. It was based both on considerations of terrain and also on his careful exploitation of the advantages accruing to him from the civil strife in France.

His aim was clear and singleminded – to conquer the duchy of Normandy, "his own" duchy about which he felt so strongly, and to occupy it. The strategic value of using Lower Normandy as a springboard of invasion from England and then as a base for further conquest in France was as evident to the intelligent general of the fifteenth century as it was to those of the 1940s. Caen, the second largest town in Normandy, was, even at the beginning of the fifteenth century, an important agricultural market for the produce of the surrounding rich countryside and had a flourishing religious and commercial life. If Caen was captured, many of the surrounding towns such as Bayeux and Lisieux, which were less well fortified, would almost automatically surrender, although other important fortresses such as Falaise and Honfleur would have to be besieged. From Caen as a centre, one force could cut off and subdue the various strongpoints of the Cotentin peninsula, thus aiding the naval as well as the military situation. Another force could sweep towards the south endeavouring to set up a line along the edges of Maine and Anjou, based on Mont-St-Michel (at the western boundary of Normandy and Brittany), Domfront, Alençon, Bellême and Verneuil as anchor points. Once these positions were safely in English hands, the king could then turn northwards to the Seine, knowing that his rear was protected, and aim at the isolation and capture of Rouen, the second largest city of France. Such a plan not only called for a series of sieges to reduce the great castles and fortified towns which dotted the Norman hills and river crossings, but also for an army which did not fatally infuriate the population and reduce its own ability to survive by the pillage and destruction of everything in its path. Henry had been far more careful about the provision of supplies for the army on this expedition, and he planned to use Southampton as a base for reinforcement and reprovisioning.

Henry's plan of conquest was made easier by the bitter struggle raging between the Armagnacs and the Burgundians for the possession of Paris, and of the person of the poor mad Charles VI, in whose name both factions hoped to exercise power. After the death of the dauphin John in April, Charles, the eleventh and youngest child of the king and Isabel of Bavaria, had become dauphin. Although invested with the resounding title of lieutenant-general of the realm, he was a feeble youth completely under the control of the Count of Armagnac and Tanneguy du Chastel, Armagnac's appointee as provost of Paris. All during 1417 the struggle between the Duke of Burgundy and the Armagnacs became more and more acute, as the Duke of Burgundy moved to cut off the lines of communication and supply to the city of Paris by the capture of the surrounding towns of Pontoise, Montlhéry and Chartres. Henry recognised the value of exploiting this bitter conflict to the full, but he also realised he must act with sufficient care to prevent the dauphin's party and the duke being so alarmed by his successes that they laid aside their enmity and combined to oppose him. Monstrelet, the Burgundian chronicler, emphasised the effect of these feuds on the English success:

> The other towns in the duchy were astonished at the facility of King Henry's conquests, for scarcely any place made a defence. This was caused by the divisions that existed among the nobles, some taking part with the king, and others with the Duke of Burgundy, and therefore they were fearful of trusting each other. The constable [Armagnac] had besides drawn off the greater part of the forces in this district to Paris, to be prepared to meet the Duke of Burgundy, whom he daily expected in these parts with a large army.[1]

The English king also endeavoured to make his coming more acceptable to the inhabitants of Normandy by proclaiming strict regulations about the treatment of non-combatants such as religious, women, or the common people who had submitted to him. They were not to be personally molested nor were their goods to be seized. Henry's discipline in this matter was not restricted to proclamations. When one of his own household at Touques captured and robbed a wandering monk the king had the monk brought before him, gave him the opportunity to identify his oppressor, and had his goods returned. He reprimanded his servant and warned the army that conviction for such an offence could mean hanging. The St Albans' chronicler who tells the story suggests that Henry's enforcement was so severe that many of the more guileful Norman peasants took the opportunity to put on ecclesiastical garb so that they could continue their trading and travelling through the English army without any hindrance.[2] However, it would appear that Henry's insistence on a reasonable code of behaviour among his soldiers, considerably higher than that generally current, was remarked and that strategic advantages accrued to him from this fact. The bourgeois of Paris, who wrote such a vivid journal of daily life in the distracted city during this period, described approvingly the behaviour of the English, as compared to that of the Burgundians and the French themselves:

> These men, all honest merchants, reputable men, who had been in the hands of all three and had bought their freedom, solemnly affirmed on oath that the English had been kinder to them than the Burgundians and the Burgundians a hundred times kinder than the troops from Paris, as regards food, ransom, physical suffering, and imprisonment, which had astonished them, as it must all good Christians.[3]

Once a safe landing had been effected King Henry proceeded to move rapidly to implement his plans, pausing only to mark the seriousness of the occasion by knighting some of the young men of the expedition. He turned immediately to safeguard his maritime link when he heard of another French fleet in action and commissioned the Earl of March, with a large complement of archers and men-at-arms, to take some of the English ships and sweep the seas. The earl carried out his orders, capturing some of the ships and putting others to flight, but his return to Normandy was impeded by a heavy storm which battered his ships and sunk some of them. One of the great carracks was so overwhelmed by the storm that it was driven with such force on Southampton that its mast was thrown over the town walls. After the storm died down the earl and his men sailed once more for Normandy and landed at St Vaast-La-Hougue, on the Cotentin peninsula. They planned to ride from there to join the king's forces and their expedition was joined by what the chroniclers call an "Antony pigge", i.e., the runt of a litter, who followed the host all the way and proved his worth as a mascot when he helped them to find a path across the great wash of the Baie des Veys for "atte the last, this pygge and Godde brought hem out all sauf".[4] They even succeeded in capturing a number of French prisoners before they joined the king's forces.

Meanwhile, after receiving the surrender of Touques on 9 August without any bloodshed, the king cleared the way for his move towards Caen by sending one contingent to Lisieux, an almost open city, and another part of his force to Bayeux. Deauville Castle had already been captured by Salisbury. By 13 August the king and the major part of the

army were on the march towards Caen. In discussing his plans with his
nobles the general consensus had been to attack Caen, which was a large
town and one which they did not think could withstand a prolonged siege.
Besides, if it was taken other lesser strongholds would fall more easily. In
proper form, Henry sent his heralds to Caen with the ominous messages
that they should deliver to him the castle and the town which were "his
owne propur heritage and right".[5] The town was too proud of its defence
to surrender so supinely and the plans for a full-dress siege were put into
operation by both sides. Henry sent Clarence ahead of the main body of
the army with a force of 1,000 horsemen to prevent the burning or destruction of the suburbs of the town. This was a standard manoeuvre on both
sides. The defenders in any siege attempted to burn and devastate everything outside the city walls so that the attackers would have less protection
and fewer goods to add to their supplies. The attackers, on the other hand,
were anxious when possible to seize the suburbs intact, since they often
provided them with a useful foothold in their assault on the walls. Such
was the case with Caen where the suburbs included the two famous abbeys
founded by William the Conqueror and his wife Matilda. These were in
fact far more than mere abbeys, since both were near the town walls and
had their own high walls and deep ditches. Clarence's quick foray was just
in time to prevent the wholesale burning of the suburbs. His soldiers
extinguished the fires in the roof thatch just started by the inhabitants and
made themselves masters of the open quarters.[6]

The abbeys were a more serious matter and considerable argument had
gone on in Caen as to whether they should be completely destroyed for the
better protection of the town. The garrison was anxious to do so, but the
inhabitants were particularly proud of their great and famous churches and
resisted the idea. At the last the process of undermining the towers of St
Stephen's had been secretly begun, but the total destruction of his beloved
abbey was more than one of the monks could bear. After he had overheard
the plan, Brother Gerard crept through the army on hands and knees in
the middle of the night till he came to where Clarence was resting, fully
armed but lying on the grass with his head propped up on a woollen cloak.
The monk begged him to come to the rescue of the monastery, which
would otherwise be destroyed, and emphasised how suitable it was that it
should be one descended from the line of kings who founded and endowed
the place who should be the instrument of its rescue. The duke immediately took advantage of this offer and went with his men and scaling ladders
to seize the abbey, a feat he accomplished with ease as there was no real
garrison to oppose him. Clarence had the mines refilled with earth and the
pillars repaired. The telltale monk found refuge in England – no doubt he
was none too welcome among his brethren, though he was handsomely
rewarded by the English.[7] St Stephen's was indeed a rich prize. The abbey
served as headquarters for King Henry himself during the siege: its towers

were used for reconnaissance, and its walls for the heavy guns which the English had brought with them and used with such devastating effect against the city.

The town of Caen had already had experience with English soldiers. It had been taken by the army of Edward III in his first expedition to France in 1346 and, according to Froissart, the inhabitants had then done their best to repel the English, and had killed a considerable number by throwing stones and benches on them from their houses as the soldiers struggled through the narrow streets.[8] Now, some seventy years later, Caen's defences were in much better shape. The city had been walled and ditched, as had the two abbeys and the church of St Sepulchre. It benefited also from the natural protection given by the Orne river, for its main stream and two branches lapped at the foot of the walls on three sides. The castle, whose defences were separate from those of the town, was also very strongly fortified. The town, however, had its weaknesses from a defensive point of view. The meanderings of the Orne had made an island which had not been fortified and which divided the city into two halves. Once captured, this island could lead any enemy to the centre of the town. Even more dangerous was the matter of the abbeys. Although they had been fortified with walls and were meant to be defended by adequate garrisons, they were so close to the main walls of the town itself that if they were captured – as had so fortunately been achieved by Clarence – they put the town under the threat of close and continuous bombardment.

Caen lost most of its ancient quarters during the desperate fighting and shelling of June 1944 but in the post-war rebuilding, the castle, which had been almost submerged by the accretions of centuries, has again been detached from its surroundings. Looking from its restored walls across the busy modern industrial city it is still easy enough to make the imaginative leap to the proud "city of churches" attacked by Henry. The castle stands on a slight height of land with the old town at its feet sloping southward to the Orne. From the castle entrance and the church of St-Pierre which faces it, the main street of the old town runs down to the river to the place on the quays where in earlier days a square tower protected the access to the town. To the west the towers of St Stephen's (the *Abbaye aux Hommes*) still dominate the skyline, and to the east, more heavily damaged but surviving even modern war, lies the Trinity, the *Abbaye aux Dames*. The siege of Caen, which Henry began soon after his arrival before the city on 18 August, was a hard-fought encounter. The English guns were an important factor, and at such short range even the rather clumsy early artillery could wreak tremendous damage – pounding breaches in the city walls, and letting their missiles destroy the houses and terrify the inhabitants within the city. They also caused unexpected damage, for the shock wave of their charges shattered all the windows of St Stephen's – damage that Henry later agreed to replace at his own cost.

The English behaviour at Caen has always been one of the reproaches brought against King Henry, even by his most convinced admirers. It is often argued that he should never have allowed his troops to indulge in such widespread massacre and looting, but this is a relatively modern point of view. To understand his actions, it is worth looking at the sequence of events from the fifteenth-century standpoint. The English heralds' first call upon the city to surrender the city and castle as Henry's by right, the early attempts by the attackers to whittle away the city's resistance, the call to surrender before the final assault, the success of the assault and the savagery which followed, the surrender of the town followed by a further siege of the castle and its surrender under treaty; these steps provide almost a textbook example of the requirements and results of the contemporary laws on sieges. These laws, and the rules which followed from them, were singularly precise, and also remarkably savage. There was good reason for this. In the Middle Ages no permanent victory could be won, or territory really taken over, until the fortresses there had been conquered. Naturally, any invader would use every possible means to make his task easier. He often hoped that threats or bribery might speed his path, while the dreadful consequences of an all-out assault lent vigour to his demands. The defender's will to resist was strengthened by the fact that it was generally reckoned as treason to surrender a fortress if it still had sufficient food and men to withstand attack. The penalty for such treason could be exacted, not only by the commander's own prince, but also by any military tribunal which applied the law of arms. Henry himself did, in fact, so rule against a French commander who gave in to the English troops too easily.

Each siege followed much the same three stages of military activity: the reduction of the suburbs outside the walls, of the town itself, and finally, of the central citadel or castle. Before a siege began the heralds of the attacker were bound to summon the town or castle to surrender, since the attacking prince claimed it as his right, being convinced of the justice of his cause. It was upon this summons and its implicit legal claim that the law was based. If a town or castle refused to surrender, it was denying a prince's right and insulting his majesty, and thus was legitimately subject to dreadful punishment if he was successful. As well, the higher the rank of the besieger the greater the damage done to his majesty by such a refusal. Normally, after the preliminary summons, a siege proceeded to breach or undermine the walls, although many relied primarily on the slow but effective weapon of starvation. If the besieger believed he could capture the town by an all-out assault, he usually warned of his intentions by a further summons from his heralds. If the city still refused to surrender, the rule was war to the death with no quarter whatsoever for any able-bodied inhabitant. Churches and churchmen were technically exempt, but in many cases they were not spared. Women could be raped and killed out of hand, and spoilation of all the enemy goods was general and acceptable.

The rationalisation behind this ferocity was that the inhabitants had contumaciously disregarded the summons of the prince, and so the forfeiture of their lives and goods was not an act of war, but an act of justice.[9]

It is in the light of these harsh regulations that we must look at the siege of Caen. Henry had followed all the requirements of the law of arms of his day, including a final summons before the last assault. This violent attack, led by Clarence from the river side and the king from the western wall near the abbey, was ultimately successful. One English chronicler ascribed the special ferocity with which the English fought to the painful death of the good-looking and distinguished Sir Edmund Springhouse, who lost his footing while fighting on the wall and fell into one of the breaches. The young man was burnt alive by the defenders who threw burning straw on him as he struggled to extricate himself.[10] Clarence successfully forced the city wall near the river and was able to fight his way through the town to link up with the king's forces on the west. Together they penned the inhabitants into the old market (now the Place St-Sauveur) and killed all in their way. It was a desperate and brutal scene and the chronicler who described the streets as running blood was not indulging in colourful metaphor. Some 2,000 inhabitants of Caen were butchered before the king ordered the massacre to stop, forbade his men to lay hands on clergy, women or children and, on pain of death, forbade the pillaging of churches, although all the other goods to be found in the stormed city were legal prey for the looting soldiers. In these provisos, Henry was more merciful and more correct than the laws actually required. No doubt he was anxious in his treatment of Caen to display a careful mingling of harshness and mercy which might encourage other fortresses of the duchy to surrender without extensive sieges or expensive attacks.

After the king had given thanks at the church of St-Pierre for his victory, he wrote on the same day to the City of London to tell them of his tremendous success and to reassure them that it was "with right litell deth of oure peple", and that he and the army were prosperous and healthy.[11] The castle of Caen, whose garrison had been enlarged by taking in some of the town's defenders and the townspeople, still stood out, but not for long. Shaken by the disastrous effects of the English assault on the town, despairing of any real assistance from the dauphin, and with his walls much weakened by the pounding of the English guns, the captain of the castle took a frequently adopted method of ending a siege with honour. He sent messengers to negotiate with the king and to arrive at an agreement which provided that a truce should suspend all hostilities between the attackers and the besieged for a certain period of days, while the defenders sent to discover if any force was coming to their aid. Once the term was up, the castle was to be surrendered unless a relieving force had arrived. The conditions for surrender were laid down in the solemn agreement worked out between the two sides, hostages were given for its fulfilment, and, if it was broken, they could be put to death. Honour on both sides was satisfied, and wholesale plunder and rape and indiscriminate killing were not allowed.

It was by such an agreement that the captain of Caen castle agreed to surrender by 19 September if no help came – and it did not. The terms were reasonably generous. They ordained that the women could carry away all their clothes and headcoverings, though de Montenay, the captain of the castle, had to swear that they would not carry anything else. The prisoners taken in the town – some of the richest had been spared from the massacre in hopes of fat ransoms – were assured of their lives. All those in the castle not only had their lives spared, but would not be imprisoned. The soldiers among them could take with them their horse, harness and clothes, but no military equipment. In addition, the garrison could take 2,000 crowns of their own goods. The citizens were given the choice of taking their clothing and going where they would, or of staying in Caen under the king's obedience and at his pleasure. The remaining valuables in the castle were to be handed over to the king to do with as he would. During the waiting period there were to be no acts of war, no one was to leave the castle, nor were the soldiers to be allowed to take more than the agreed sum. The castle was not to be damaged in any way nor the goods destined for the English hidden away.[12]

The agreement was signed and sealed 11 September, although most of its conditions had been hammered out the previous day, and the following week the keys of the castle were duly surrendered to the king by de Montenay. His conquest achieved, Henry moved into the castle of Caen and remained there for some two weeks. He issued the necessary safe-conducts so that those inhabitants of Caen who wished to depart could do so, and many seized the opportunity. Apparently the women, to the disgust of the English chronicler who tells the story, managed to smuggle away much of their gold, and the French burnt, before their departure, many of the goods meant to be left in the castle. Nevertheless the king had gained considerable riches from this siege, although it was remarked that instead of keeping it all for himself, as was customary, he turned over to Clarence the piled up goods of the town in recognition of his leading share in the assault. According to the *English Life* all that the king kept for himself from the loot was a "goodlie French booke, of what historie I have not heard".[13]

The king had little time to waste in self-indulgent congratulation after Caen had fallen. The first problem with which he had to deal, and which he discussed with his council, was how to try and reconcile the Normans to the English conquest so that his military successes might not make him lord of "a voyde and desolate countrie". Caen had been seriously depopulated by the end of the siege. It has been estimated that as many as 3,000 merchants and workers had left, as well as the women and children who had all been sent away. Food was short and the king had sent orders to

England that any men who brought over victuals to Caen for the relief of the king and his army might do so without payment of customs dues, though the officials were to be sure that they were destined solely for Caen.[14] Meanwhile, Henry gave away the most valuable houses in the town, and occasionally the heiresses too, to his own supporters. The city itself found it difficult to recover from the drastic damage of the siege. Its walls were in bad shape, and most of the bridges broken. Such repairs were normally the responsibility of the citizens of a town but those of Caen were no longer rich enough to rebuild, and during the remaining years of Henry's reign he allowed the aids on certain categories of merchandise sold in the town to be used for this purpose. It is not surprising that the citizens were crushed by their burdens, since wages in Caen reflected the scarcity of skilled workers. Where, in other parts of Normandy during Henry's reign, a mason or carpenter had a daily wage of 4s 2d, at Caen in 1421 a mason received 16s 8d a day. Henry spent several periods at Caen after its capture, and seems to have enjoyed its castle, improving the garden and constructing a private chapel. It was there that he listened to the preaching of Vincent Ferrer and there, too, that he celebrated with due solemnity the feast of St George in 1418. While the king was in Caen at that time he proclaimed his ownership of the nearby quarries which provided the famous white Caen stone, a highly prized oolitic limestone much used in English and Norman churches. He also ordered that the use of the stone was to be restricted to the repair and building of royal fortresses, churches and buildings in both England and Normandy.[15]

However, apart from the need to reconstitute Caen as a city prosperous enough to serve once again as the base for supplies and administration, Henry's immediate concern was with the next steps to be taken in his plan of conquest. From the military point of view it was urgent that he push on rapidly with the reduction of Normandy's fortresses. Even before the fall of Caen he had sent the Duke of Gloucester to attack Bayeux, which capitulated at about the same time as Caen. From Caen it was Henry's decision to move south: Argentan and Verneuil were besieged and taken, Sées surrendered. Although the strong fortress of Falaise was, for the moment, bypassed, Alençon had fallen to Henry and his army before the end of October. This victory brought the English forces within thirty miles of the capital of Maine and threatened the borders of Anjou. It impelled the Duke of Brittany to come to the king looking for a truce for himself, and for the duchies of Anjou and Maine, presently under the control of Queen Yolande of Jerusalem and Sicily, the widow of Louis II of Anjou. A truce was arranged, to run until 30 September, 1418. With this security for a peaceful interlude along the southern line of conquest, roughly drawn at the base of Normandy, the king could turn his attention first to Falaise, and then to the problems of the north and east.

Falaise was an immensely strong fortress, built in the twelfth century and

best known among the English as the birthplace of William the Conqueror.
When Henry and his army arrived before the gates of the town at the
beginning of December to lay the siege, both sides were optimistic of
success. The French defenders were encouraged by the assistance of
winter, since it was not usual for medieval armies to continue active fighting
during the winter season. Henry however, felt it unwise not to keep his
soldiers fully occupied and he took care of their comfort by having wooden
houses built for them. His biographer probably indulges in some hyperbole
when he insists that the camp of the besiegers with its huts seemed "not a
worse towne than that within the Walls", but the men were at least protected.[16] The season inflicted its hardships on both sides: the water froze,
there were many wind and rainstorms, and Henry had to arrange for provisions from as far away as Holland and Danzig. Nevertheless the French
garrison did its best to repel the English, and even when the town surrendered at the beginning of January 1418, the garrison of the castle maintained its defence with all the ingenious horrors of medieval military
technology. However, despite their resistance, and without outside help,
the castle could not hold out indefinitely. By the beginning of February the
castle sued for surrender and it was granted under reasonable terms of free
passage for all its defenders except only the captain. The unlucky Oliver de
Manny, who had inspired much of the resistance, was ordered by King
Henry to be kept as a prisoner in chains until Falaise castle was fully
repaired and rebuilt at Oliver's own cost.* The king then withdrew to
Bayeux to devote himself to Lenten observances and to enjoy some quiet
and rest.

The period of reflection was all the more necessary, as Henry needed to
ponder his situation and plan his further strategy. News from England
would have told him the results of the November parliament, which had
taken place at Westminster in the presence of the Duke of Bedford. Bishop
Langley as chancellor had again underlined the need of assistance for the
king, and parliament had responded with a further grant of two tenths and
two fifteenths, to be paid on Candlemas (2 February) 1418 and 1419. The
knowledge that these sums would be coming in to assist him in his heavy
expenses must have given Henry much pleasure but he was undoubtedly
even more pleased by the final settlement of the conspiracy of 1414. John
Oldcastle was captured and brought to London at the time of this parliament, and on 14 December was brought before parliament to hear the
petition for his death read before Bedford, the Lords and the Commons.
He was adjudged traitor and heretic and taken briefly to the Tower before
his execution at the gallows in St Giles' Fields. The news from England
was good. The mayor and aldermen of London wrote that London was in

* The work appears to have been done very quickly, as by the end of June
Henry had ordered Oliver to be released from prison if it was true that he had
satisfactorily restored the castle of Falaise.[17]

peace and tranquillity, although their letter was couched in such convoluted and overblown phraseology that it is obvious that the pomposities of local officials have a very long history indeed.[18]

Although matters were moving smoothly enough in England, Henry was regarding with sharp attention and some little apprehension the movements of the Duke of Burgundy. The kaleidoscope of French politics had been given still another turn since Henry's landing in August 1417. Queen Isabel, who had been banished to Blois and then to Tours by the power of Armagnac, had retaliated by forming a new alliance with the Duke of Burgundy. Duke John rescued her from her polite captivity in November 1417, and together they set up a government in Troyes in which Isabel claimed to act as regent of the kingdom. During the autumn of 1417 Duke John had also been improving his military position around Paris, which he hoped to recapture. His forces had ringed Paris to the north and west, capturing Senlis, Beaumont, Pontoise, Meulan and Mantes, as well as Chartres to the southwest. By Lent of 1418 Burgundian garrisons were in charge of Rouen and Caudebec, and were soon to take over Louviers and Evreux. Henry had no desire as yet to face open conflict with the Duke of Burgundy, but there were still strongpoints to be captured to assure his complete control of the lower half of Normandy. While the king rested from his labours and planned the future he sent detachments under his best commanders to complete the task. Clarence was sent to besiege Bec-Hellouin; the Earl of Gloucester to take Cherbourg as well as some of the lesser fortresses of the Cotentin peninsula; the Earl of Warwick besieged Domfront. As one after another of these fortresses fell to the English, holding out for a longer or shorter time – only Mont-St-Michel never fell under English domination – the king saw his road clear to turn to the north and east. His decision was made easier by the Burgundian capture of Paris at the end of May 1418. With the fall of Paris, the seizure of the person of the king, and the destruction of the Armagnac power in the city, it was evident to Henry that any further moves of his in Normandy would inevitably involve collision with Burgundian interests. At least, there would be little difficulty from the Armagnacs who were now reduced to a few strong local positions and whose enmity and struggle for survival must now be primarily directed against the Duke of Burgundy.

CHAPTER XI

The Capture of Rouen

Once the king had estimated the effect of the French political upheavals on his own military activities, he moved to improve his strategic position before turning against his real target – Rouen, the capital and prosperous centre of the duchy of Normandy. Henry moved from Caen to Louviers, a strongpoint on the Eure, which was just south of and protected Pont de l'Arche. Louviers was besieged during June, and fell before the end of the month. While Henry was with his army there Cardinal Orsini came to mediate with the king, hoping to encourage the negotiations for a truce, but although the negotiations went on for some fifteen days, nothing came of them. Henry's temper had begun to show the signs of suspicious inflexibility for which he was often reproached in his last years. During the siege the defending French gunners had scored a chance hit on a tent where the king happened to be. Henry, infuriated at what he apparently considered *lèse-majesté*, had eight of the gunners hanged in revenge after the surrender of the town.[1]

From Louviers Henry turned immediately to the siege of Pont de l'Arche, only some seven miles north. It was still held by an Armagnac garrison, although a truce and alliance had been made between them and the Burgundians in hopes of strengthening the town's defences. Pont de l'Arche was a difficult town to attack. The Seine runs through its middle and the place owes its name to the strong bridge protected by a fortified arch which spans the river. In the fifteenth century it was the only bridge over the Seine between Paris and Rouen, so that Pont de l'Arche controlled the means of sending supplies and troops from Paris to Rouen. The French had improved their defensive position by sinking all the little boats which could be employed for crossing the river, except for a few which they kept under guard in the town for their own use. Under these circumstances, until the English could get a foothold across the river, they could not set a complete siege. Sir John Graville, who commanded the garrison, had asked for more help to watch all the possible fords, but he was remarkably confident of his ability to hold the town.

Some of the peasants from the countryside angered the English army, shattering the quiet of the night with their screams and insults of the besiegers. Henry was so annoyed by the clamour of the peasants which, he felt reflected on his dignity and that of his troops, that he sent Sir John Cornwall to the French commander to urge him to control the rustics. The conversation between the two knights was amicable enough, though Sir John Graville insisted that he could do nothing about the peasants' behaviour and Cornwall replied that the English would soon teach them a lesson. The two captains indulged in a wager on the English crossing of the Seine, Graville pitting his best courser against Cornwall's steel helmet, worth 500 nobles, that the English would fail. Cornwall won the bet, though the English had used guile to effect their crossing. They had had wicker boats, covered with skins, made secretly at the abbey of Bonport, just downstream and out of sight of the defenders. When they were ready for use, Clarence ordered a group of soldiers to swim in the river about a thousand yards from town, meanwhile making a tremendous hubbub. The French immediately hurried off to repel them, while Sir John Cornwall, in a small advance party made up of his young son, a few soldiers, and some small cannon and stores, slipped across the river. He was followed immediately by Clarence with an adequate besieging force. The diversion by the swimmers distracted the French defenders long enough for the English to gain their foothold on the north bank of the Seine before they faced serious opposition. The crossing successfully accomplished, the English disposed themselves for a serious siege of the whole town and the castle. Sir John Graville's early confidence was further undermined when he discovered that the English had even created another bridge downstream by lashing small boats together to provide access. The garrison agreed to surrender both the town and the castle unless help came to them before 20 July.[2]

When the king wrote to the mayor and aldermen of London on 21 July, he not only informed them of the surrender of Pont de l'Arche, but told them that he had sent a pursuivant to the Duke of Burgundy, after the duke's ceremonious entry of Paris which had been taken by his followers. Henry had been anxious to find out whether the duke proposed to keep the truce between them, and the returning pursuivant delivered the uncomprising answer that the duke proposed to give him battle. The king warned the Londoners that "we now hold him our full enemy", suggesting the further difficulties that might arise. He added that he felt it unnecessary to give them any details of the murder of the Count of Armagnac and the slaughter of his supporters at Paris, because they would already have been fully informed.[3] There is little doubt that the general butchery in Paris and the bloody excesses of the Burgundian supporters had strengthened the will of the remaining Armagnacs able to continue the struggle against the harsh Burgundian domination. During the worst of the slaughter, Tanneguy du Chastel, the Armagnac provost of Paris, had saved the terrified dauphin by carrying him in his arms to the Bastille St-Antoine, and then secretly smuggled him away to Melun, where he served as a symbol of the legitimacy of the Armagnac cause.

In reality, Burgundian control of Paris was still very uncertain. On 21 July the Armagnacs seized Compiègne, some fifty miles northeast of Paris, and a vital control point of the trade routes from Burgundy through Picardy. Their forces practically encircled Paris, since the Orleanists held Meaux, thirty miles to the northeast; Melun, thirty miles to the southeast; and Montlhéry, fifteen miles to the south. Compiègne, Meaux and Melun controlled traffic on the Oise, the Marne, and the upper Seine, while Montlhéry sat firmly astride the road to Orleans. To the west lay the menace of the English, operating in force in Normandy. The duke might talk of doing battle with Henry, but Paris was the important thing to him and he was fully occupied maintaining his own rather imperilled position there.

Once Pont de l'Arche had surrendered, the king did not loiter in his march to Rouen, only twenty miles away, for it had now been sealed off from the possibility of reinforcement by boat. Before Henry himself moved against Rouen he sent his heralds and a small advance force under the Duke of Exeter to summon the city to surrender, and incidentally to provide a quick reconnaissance of the best ways in which to attack it. Rouen's defenders not only refused to surrender at such a summons, but opened fire on the duke's company and sallied forth for a short but sharp attack. Exeter had to withdraw, and the citizens immediately put into effect the necessary measures preparing Rouen for the bitter siege they knew was inevitable. Rouen was a valuable prize. It was the capital of the duchy, one of the most important cities of the realm. Henry described it, when writing to the Londoners, as "the most notable place in France save Paris".[4] The French had put a good deal of thought into its defences. Its centre, surrounded by well-built walls, was like a parallelogram attached to the right bank of the Seine. The river protected the south side while the great castle built by Philip Augustus reinforced the wall to the northwest. The stone bridge over the Seine was shielded by a fortified tower known as the Barbacan. The main road from Rouen to Paris, which at this point provided the only route through otherwise marshy ground, was protected by the walled abbey of St-Catherine, built on a hill which overlooked the city to the east. On the south side of the river was the Clos du Galées, the great French naval base built at the end of the thirteenth century where the royal ships were built and repaired, supplied and armed. It also held the warehouses where naval equipment and armament were stored. Less important than in the great days of Charles V, it was still a valuable prize. Although protected by a defensive wall and ditch, it was not really designed to withstand a serious siege.[5]

Rouen too had been torn by the general struggle between the Armagnac and Burgundian factions, and in January 1418 the townspeople had admitted Guy le Bouteiller, the Burgundian captain who succeeded in wresting control of the city from the dauphinist officials. It was obvious to the Duke of Burgundy in the summer of 1418, observing Henry's rapid moves in Normandy, that Rouen's turn was next. About 4,000 men-at-arms were sent to reinforce the citizens, and orders were given that all should prepare for a long siege. Those who wished to stay in the city were commanded to secure enough provisions for ten months, or to leave. According to Monstrelet, many of the poor, the women and the children did leave, but this particular order was almost impossible to enforce. Provisions were scarce, particularly as Henry had carefully laid his siege before the new harvest could be gathered. With so much of Normandy under English rule, where were the refugees to go? Many seem to have remained on the grounds that it was better to trust to the familiar, than attempt to brave the unknown. It is easy to understand their reluctance, since the countryside in those troubled times was overrun by brigands who often claimed to be patriotic guerrillas, operating for one side or the other. In many cases they were merely cut-throat ruffians, like the infamous Tabary. Tabary, a Burgundian adherent "of small stature and lame", collected as many as forty or fifty peasants around him. They had laid hands on an assortment of old weapons and bits of armour and a few had acquired some wretched horses. They set ambushes in the woods, searching particularly for Englishmen and dauphinists, whose throats they cut without mercy.[6] Such lawless men were only better-known examples of a constant hazard to public safety.

At Rouen no sentimental attachments were allowed to slow down the destruction of the flourishing suburbs outside the city walls. Even the Clos du Galées, once the city's pride, was destroyed to prevent it falling into English hands. Churches as well as houses were flattened, the supplies taken away and the earth scorched to make matters more difficult for the attackers. Within the city particular care was taken in the widening of the ditches and strengthening of the walls. Pitfalls were made in the ditches – mantraps the depth of a spear with which to catch the unwary attacker. The inside face of the city wall was strengthened with great piles of earth, which were deep enough and wide enough to carry a cart. This bulwark both helped to counteract the effects of the English guns, and also provided easy access for mending those breaches which were made. According to John Page, the English soldier who wrote from his personal experience the most detailed and lively account of the siege, the defenders also had plenty of artillery at their disposal.[7] He said they had at least three guns in every tower, of which he reckoned there were "many a score" (more prosaically, about sixty) only about thirty yards apart, while each intervening stretch of wall was protected by a cannon and eight small guns. At the gates were the

old-fashioned trebuchets, still useful in slinging heavy missiles to cause disorder in the enemy ranks, and also the "lancets" used to shoot fire at
night. The city and its defenders had done all they could to arm themselves
for the trials to come. They had not long to wait: by the end of July
Henry's army, with the king at its head, had arrived in front of the city.

The siege was set with Henry's usual careful precision. John Page
describes in great detail exactly which commander was placed in front of
each gate or vantage point and praises them all, though with due concern
to maintain the hierarchy of rank. The king's forces were soon strengthened
by the arrival of Warwick, after Domfront surrendered in September, and
of Gloucester, after the capture of Cherbourg in November. Warwick was
sent off to besiege Caudebec, some twenty-two miles downstream, which
was now trapped between the English garrison at Harfleur and the English
army at Rouen. Soon Caudebec, like other similar places in the district,
agreed to abide by what happened to Rouen. If the city finally surrendered,
so would they. King Henry made his headquarters in the Charterhouse of
Notre Dame de la Rose, not far to the east of the Porte St-Hilaire, and
from there he conducted the siege with all the careful attention to detail
which was so characteristic of him.

Because the English army was on both sides of the river the king had
a new timber bridge built on the upstream side, and reinforced it with
a chain some distance away to prevent French ships from trying to attack
the bridge and break the blockade. In addition, as its second line of defence, he made a barrier of small boats, which he had brought overland to
avoid their exposure to fire from the city's defenders. His plans for revic-
tualling his own army were equally carefully made. The king had come to
an agreement with the King of Portugal who provided him with a group
of ships which helped to keep open the mouth of the Seine so that provisions could come from England to Harfleur and then be safely transported up-river to the army. Since it was obvious that the siege was to be
a long-drawn-out affair, Henry also set up a market, protected by armed
guards, to encourage merchants and provisioners to come to it and thus
increase the available supplies for the army. The soldiers found the siege
hot work under the August sun and Henry wrote to the City of London
asking them to send supplies, especially drink, for the army. The city,
which had received his letter on 19 August, only nine days after its dispatch, moved to answer this request with rapidity. By 8 September they
had sent off thirty barrels of sweet wine, 1,000 pipes of ale and beer and
500 cups as a present to the king. Henry's biographer in the *English Life*
in discussing these various arrangements is full of admiration for Henry's
concern about the most minute points of the army's conduct. There was
his insistence, for example, that the tents should not be too widely separa-
ted in case of a surprise attack. When, on one of his visits of inspection, he
found two men outside the specified distance, he immediately had them

hanged for disobedience. Such summary treatment encouraged a prompt attention to royal orders.[8]

The abbey of St-Catherine had to surrender relatively early in the siege. It was too remote from the strength of the city to stand by itself against such a force. The English could then concentrate on the main defences, and for the first three months the siege was the typically monotonous affair of constant watchfulness on the part of the attackers to contain the besieged, and frequent efforts by the defenders to mount vigorous sorties which they hoped might drive off the invader. Both sides, too, indulged in tactics designed to arouse terror among their enemies, and lessen their enthusiasm for the task. The English erected several gibbets, in full view of the city walls, and hanged several captives on them. In retaliation, much to King Henry's displeasure, the citizens built their own gibbet in the ditch just outside the walls and hanged one of their English prisoners. Another Norman blast of defiance came from Robert de Linet, the vicar-general of Rouen and the highest ecclesiastical official remaining in the city. From the vantage-point of the city walls he publicly excommunicated Henry and all his army, an act which the pitiless king would not forget or forgive. When Rouen was finally surrendered Linet was one of the five men specially named to be handed over to the king's mercy. As Monstrelet politely phrases it, the unfortunate vicar-general "during the siege had conducted himself most imprudently". The *English Life* asserts that he paid for his rashness by remaining a prisoner in chains for the rest of his life. It is obvious that, as Henry's reign wore on, he was increasingly sensitive to any breath of criticism of his behaviour, even from the most unimportant. In October 1419 a haberdasher of Southwark was sent before the council for merely speaking disparagingly of the king's conduct at the siege of Rouen.[9]

Both sides waited anxiously for news of a relieving force from the Duke of Burgundy, and inevitably rumours of the imminent arrival of such a force would sweep through the city and the English army, rousing hope and concern. On every occasion the Burgundian army proved a figment of the imagination. In fact, the whole situation in northeast France was so chaotic and torn by faction that the Burgundians in Paris needed all their strength to maintain their precarious hold on the capital. The chief Burgundian financial official in Paris wrote to his colleagues at Lille in the middle of October, giving them a pessimistic view of the state of affairs:

As to the news from here, pestilences of death and of war grieve us. Famine approaches unless God provides. Merchandise ceases by land and water, labour is scarce . . . Treasons and seditions reign, brother against brother, neighbour against neighbour, the son against the father. Justice is moribund. Those in authority prefer their private advantage to the public welfare or the ruler's profit. At Rouen they are eating horseflesh . . . Everything is going to perdition.[10]

The defenders of Rouen were soon reduced to less than horseflesh. Henry's army had been strengthened by a number of reinforcements, including a barefooted Irish contingent armed only with light weapons, whose ability as pillagers struck terror into the surrounding countryside. Bread soared in price and was made of bran not wheat, while it cost a sou for an onion and nine deniers for an egg. By December the besieged were reduced to eating dogs and cats, mice and rats, and even paying high prices for them – a dog went for 10s, a rat for 30d. The famine affected everyone in the city, even parents and children hid food from each other. As Page put it with brisk understanding: "But hunger passyd kynde and love."[11] The poorest ate grass and roots and soon, condemned as "useless mouths", were driven out of the city into the ditches beyond the walls. Despite the pleas of the women with children dying in their arms and old men crying "Have mercy upon us", neither side had compassion on them. The English treated their hunger and their curses against their own "nation" who had forsaken them as still another weapon of their attack, and refused to let them through their lines. The winter cold added to their suffering and many died. Only on Christmas Day was human pity evident. In honour of the feast, Henry ordered a temporary truce for the day and had his men distribute food to the starving souls in the ditches. The tactics, however deplorable, were effective and the pressure of famine grew steadily more oppressive within the city as well, as the attackers' supervision grew even stricter. As Page put it succinctly: "For hunger brekythe the stone wall."[12]

By New Year's Eve the desperate citizens were anxious to bring the siege to an end. At every gate a French knight called out to the attackers but only Sir Gilbert Umfraville, in charge of the English force at the gate leading on to the bridge, heard the call. He listened to their request for a safe-conduct for their negotiators to come out and parley with the king, and went to inform Clarence, his commander, of the good news. On New Year's Day, having gained the king's approval, Umfraville returned to the anxious citizens and told them that he would take twelve of them to see the king the following day. He warned them of the king's firm resolve and suggested that they should consider most carefully the plea they would make. On the following day the delegation – four knights, four clerics, and four burgesses, all soberly dressed in black – came to the king at his headquarters at the Charterhouse. He kept them waiting while he finished his devotions but when he emerged they fell on their knees before him asking for a treaty, and begged too that he should release the poor people in the ditch. This last request angered Henry, who replied sharply that he was not responsible for putting the poor out and that the stubborn obstinacy of the inhabitants had kept "his own city" from him. The citizens reminded him of their duty to their sovereign and the Duke of Burgundy, but the infuriated Henry reiterated again and again that the French king and the

Duke of Burgundy had known of their plight and had not helped them, and that the city had unreasonably held out against its rightful lord, "Rone ys myn herytage".[13] Nevertheless, he was willing to give them a truce and time to treat.

The negotiations were long and at first inconclusive: "They tretyd day, they tretyd nyght, With candelle and torches bryght."[14] At one stage they were broken off by the leaders of the city because they found Henry's terms too hard, but the famished citizens turned on their leaders. They were no longer interested in the details of the terms, they were no longer willing to fight, and they saw only two choices – deliver the city or die. Archbishop Chichele, who had been at the abbey of St-Catherine, came down to add his persuasive powers to the final negotiations, and at last a treaty was arranged. The honour of the defenders was safeguarded by the agreement of an eight-day period to see if help could be obtained from a relieving force, and the other terms, though hard, were not unreasonable for such a long siege of such an important place. If no rescue came, Rouen was to be delivered on 19 January at noon, and was to pay a huge fine of 300,000 crowns. All military supplies of all kinds were to be left in good condition for the king. The soldiers, both French and foreign, were not to bear arms against Henry for another year, but they were allowed to depart freely, though only in their doublets. The king was to have a place of his own choosing within the walls to build a new castle for himself. The dead were to be buried, and those without the walls taken into the city and fed until the day of the city's surrender. In return, the king was willing to accept and maintain in their inheritance and goods those who agreed to swear allegiance to him; the others could leave freely. There were only a few exceptions to the general amnesty: the imprudent vicar-general, the master of the cannon, the bailiff and the mayor, Alain Blanchard (who had been responsible for the hanging of the English prisoner), and "that person who spoke evil and dishonest words, if he can be found without fraud or trickery".[15] Alain Blanchard was beheaded but the others bought their safety, although we do not know if King Henry ever discovered the outspoken opponent who had roused his wrath.

The messengers who had been sent for help brought back the word that there would be no relieving force. On the appointed day, Guy le Bouteiller, as captain of the city, and the burgesses came to the king's lodging and kneeling presented him with the keys of the city. Henry immediately gave the keys to Exeter who led the first triumphant party of English through the Porte Beauvoisine where the duke had been stationed during the siege. John Page writes with enthusiasm of the scene, considering them a goodly company with their fine clothes and flying banners. When the city gates were opened the English trumpets sounded, the pipes and clarions played, and the men on their neighing horses swept through the great gate. As the exulting English paraded into the city they had been besieging for over six months they exclaimed in triumph: "Syn Jorge! Syn Jorge! Welle come Rone, our Kyngs owne ryght!" and proudly raised their banners over the city's strongholds.[16] They were greeted by desolate walking skeletons, for most of the townspeople were on the verge of death by starvation. Although King Henry had food and drink sent into the town in abundance immediately after the surrender, the weakest continued to die faster than the carts could carry them away. After about two weeks, the remaining population began to regain its health.

The king delayed his own entrance into the conquered city until the following day, and took care to ensure discipline by stationing knights in each quarter to guard against looting and violence by the English soldiers. Henry's solemn entrance and procession to the cathedral on Friday 20 January was stage-managed with that almost uncanny theatrical skill which was natural to him. In the midst of all the brilliant banners and colourful clothes the king caught every eye by dressing soberly in black, though with a gold breast-cloth, riding a dark horse, and refusing to have his procession, with its accompanying clergy, played in with the accustomed pipes and clarions. He rode alone, with only an esquire behind him carrying a lance with a fox's brush at the tip.* Having heard mass at the cathedral, Henry went to the castle where he then remained for the rest of the winter.

The departing garrison was searched by the English soldiers to ensure that they took no valuables with them. According to Monstrelet, those at the end of the line, seeing their comrades deprived of their valuables, preferred to throw their gold and silver into the river rather than have them confiscated by the enemy. Some had been more foresighted and had sewn their money into the waistband of their breeches and thus avoided detection.[17] It is impossible to know how great a loss of life was involved in this hard-won siege, but the contemporary estimate that twice as many civilians as soldiers died, and that the total losses came to nearly ten per cent of the population seems consonant with the nature of the campaign.

Bitterness against the English conquerors and the king certainly remained despite Henry's efforts to encourage the Normans to swear allegiance to him, and his relatively mild treatment of them. Within two weeks of the city's surrender, some of the citizens of Rouen had already plotted to seize and kill the king as he went to church to offer his candle on the feast of Candlemas (2 February). The king heard of the plan before it could be carried out, and captured and imprisoned the conspirators. Some fifty of them were sent to England for confinement in various English castles and Strecche, who tells this story, insists that they each had to pay a ransom of 20s a day before they received any food. If the canon of

* The fox's brush was one of Henry's favourite badges, and was inevitably connected by his eulogists with his stays at Kenilworth, his displacement of the foxes there, and their resemblance to the crafty French.

Kenilworth is correct in his statement that these payments went on for thirty-six weeks, it proved an expensive as well as uncomfortable conspiracy for the Norman prisoners.[18] Guy le Bouteiller, the Burgundian captain of Rouen, accepted English rule and found it personally profitable. He is believed to have been the one responsible for betraying the Candlemas conspiracy to the king. He was certainly rewarded by Henry with generous grants of land, and finally with the seigniory and castle of La Roche-Guyon.[19] Perhaps anxious for his own security, Henry also moved quickly to consider plans for building his own castle in accordance with the terms of the surrender. The spot chosen was the southwest corner of the city walls, conveniently near the river. Orders for its building soon began to flow and at least some of its cost was raised in Normandy, for the duchy contributed some £7,000 to the work.[20]

The fortresses, such as Caudebec, which were dependencies of Rouen, submitted to the king after the city's fall. By the end of January all of western Normandy – except for the island stronghold of Mont-St-Michel – stretching as far east as Pont de l'Arche and Louviers, had been subdued by Henry and his captains. The capture of Rouen marked his achievement of the major goal of his second expedition, the conquest of "his own duchy". Now he could take a few months' respite from military activity and plan his future moves, while his commanders mopped up the few remaining centres of resistance.

CHAPTER XII

The Road to Troyes

The continuing success of Henry's military campaign in Normandy did not supersede the king's astute use of diplomatic negotiations to achieve his aims in France. Even during the long-drawn-out and demanding siege of Rouen there was no slackening in such activity. Once again Henry attempted to manipulate the French civil war to his own advantage, warned by the possible dangers of such an abortive agreement as that of St-Maur-des-Fossées which had proposed to unite dauphin and duke against the invader. In October–November of 1418, Henry agreed to negotiate with the dauphin and his party, since the Burgundian possession of Paris was a stumbling-block to both their ambitions, and the usual formalities for setting up such a mission were observed. However, Henry's formal commission to his appointed ambassadors is full of interest as a reflection of the king's mind and as a remarkable insight into his character. The king's instructions are precise and detailed. He laid down specific guidelines on the scope of the first English demands, the ambassadors' possible concessions, and what their reply should be to possible French counter-offers. On the fundamentals Henry was prepared to be absolutely inflexible and to stand on his military achievements. For example, the king brusquely ordered his ambassadors, if the French should offer Normandy or other places he had already conquered, to answer that such an offer was void since God had already given them to him. It is obvious from the tone of his remarks that his claim to the throne of France was, at this time, a bargaining-counter with which to achieve what he considered the essentials – the fulfilment of the terms of the Treaty of Bretigny and Normandy – and, if possible, the sovereignty of Anjou, Maine and Touraine and the county of Flanders. The ambassadors were to be very careful to distinguish between peace and a truce and to make sure that any English concession was made worth the king's while. If the king agreed to a truce, what lands would the dauphin offer in return for his giving up his military efforts for such a term and not making any other alliance? If the dauphin wanted aid against

Burgundy, what would they offer? And so the commission goes on, as Henry endeavoured to provide instructions for any contingency, as well as insisting on being regularly informed on the progress of negotiations. The two embassies met for some two weeks at Alençon, and the proceedings were carefully noted by Richard Coudray, a clerk of the council, whose notarial report of the proceedings survives. The two weeks were spent in a constant squabble between the two parties over every inch of land, every claim to sovereignty, as well as over the choice of language for negotiations. On 23 November the dauphin's ambassadors withdrew, saying that they could offer no more.[1]

Almost immediately upon the failure of these negotiations Henry turned to the other side, to attempt to exploit offers put forward by the Burgundians. All during this period of feverish diplomatic negotiations the documents are often confusing, since it is essential to remember whether it is Armagnac or Burgundian who speaks in the name of the king of France. Charles VI, always weak and often incapacitated by his madness, was the pawn of whichever side managed to seize his person and take over the organised administrative structure of royal government which was established in Paris. The Burgundian capture of Paris in the spring of 1418 had temporarily clarified the situation. The king was under the control of the Burgundians and, for the time being, Queen Isabel was the duke's willing tool. The duke was also in possession of the levers of government while the dauphin and his weak band of supporters, reinforced by a fair number of faithful administrators, gradually withdrew south of the Loire to the centre of Orléans and Armagnac strength, and duplicated royal institutions around Bourges as a capital. During the siege of Rouen, at the beginning of December, Archbishop Chichele and the Earl of Warwick were named to negotiate with the Burgundian ambassadors who included the Bishop of Beauvais and the president of the *Parlement* of Paris. They had persuaded Cardinal Orsini, who had remained in France, to act as mediator. The discussions were almost broken off before they began, as an argument over language bitterly divided the two embassies. Henry absolutely refused to have the business of the embassy carried out in French, and the cardinal's conciliatory tactics finally achieved a compromise allowing for two equally solemn documents – one in Latin, one in French – of which the Latin was to be the final resort in case of questions. Even this much advance required a hurried trip by the cardinal to the king's headquarters outside Rouen, and a four-hour debate with the king. The cardinal's agitated letter to the French ambassadors, dispatched by messenger in the middle of the night, begged them for an immediate reply if the whole mission was not to collapse, and warned them that this was the king's farthest possible concession "on account of the equivocations and synonyms of French words".[2] However, all the flurry over language and the ultimate compromise was in the end immaterial since the opposing embassies at Pont de l'Arche debated for some fifteen days without any result. The French ambassadors had brought a portrait of Catherine, which they presented to Henry "who liked it well".[3] Pleasure, however, was not allowed to interfere with business, for the king still demanded an enormous dowry and such extensive territorial claims that the Burgundians were driven back to the defence that the Duke of Burgundy had no power to surrender so much and that the king could not alienate the heritage of the crown. On this inconclusive note, the embassy broke up.

The king's temper, already short, was not improved by these frustrating negotiations. On 29 November he had written to the Duke of Bedford in England chiding him for the slow repayment and restitution being made when English subjects broke the truce with the Duke of Brittany. He informed his brother that he himself was still getting complaints and pressed John to provide "hasty restitution" so that such complaints would cease and that Henry should not have to waste his time writing about such matters, "considering the great occupation that we have otherwise". The king may have been especially concerned that nothing should upset the truce which was so important for peaceful passage in the Channel, and thus for the reprovisioning of his troops. After Rouen surrendered and Henry's position was strengthened, it seems to have been the Duke of Brittany who was eager to keep the truce in force and armed with gifts he came anxiously to the king to seek a further truce. After some discussion, they agreed on a truce to last seven years, if no war was proclaimed by either party within the next six months.[4]

Although some military operations were continued after Rouen's fall, the king's attention was primarily turned towards diplomatic struggles. Once again the formal pattern of approach first to one side and then to the other, in the effort to squeeze the utmost in concessions, can be traced through the series of safe-conducts, appointments, and commissions. The dauphin's ambassadors suggested a meeting between King Henry and their master, to which Henry agreed, but on the appointed day, the dauphin, after the king had moved to Evreux to meet him, avoided the meeting. Henry then proceeded to consolidate his grasp on eastern Normandy and the approaches to Paris, taking Vernon and Mantes and sending his captains to besiege Ivry, La-Roche-Guyon, and that redoubtable stronghold, Château Gaillard. They all fell, although Château Gaillard held out till September, so that the king's continued successes and his threatening proximity to Paris encouraged the Duke of Burgundy to urge talks between them. Duke John had retreated to the security of Provins, although he had reinforced the city of Paris and assured the inhabitants that he would not withdraw any further, and it was to Provins that the Earl of Warwick led the English embassy. The embassy was imperilled by an Armagnac attempt at an ambush, which was unsuccessful, and the earl's natural annoyance at this insult to their status was smoothed over by the duke when they arrived at

Provins. The soothing appears to have been expensive – the earl and the other ambassadors received 6,000 l.t. for their expenses and presents of jewels and vessels of gold and silver worth more than 2,700 gold crowns.[5] Agreement was finally reached on both sides for a face-to-face meeting of King Henry and the French king and queen and the Duke of Burgundy at the end of May, "to treat of peace and marriage". Early in 1419 Henry had written to his legal officials in Bordeaux asking them to collect any relevant information about the nature of the English rule in Aquitaine. On 4 April the Archbishop of Bordeaux sent the king copies of all the acts which established the sovereignty of the king of England over the duchy. It would appear that Henry was prudently gathering his legal ammunition for the proposed discussions with the French.[6]

The meeting was hedged with remarkable precautions. The English party would be at Mantes, the French and Burgundians at Pontoise and the two should meet at Meulan, at the border between the Norman and the French Vexin. On Tuesday 30 May the queen and Catherine and the Duke of Burgundy came to the field at Meulan, for King Charles was again ill and remained at Pontoise. Tents had been set up on both sides of the field for the opposing parties, with a single pavilion in the centre of the field where the actual conference was to take place. The musicians played, the French party and that of King Henry, with strictly limited retinues, left their separate tents at the same time to arrive simultaneously at the meeting place. Despite the elegance of the two identical thrones draped with cloth of gold for the French queen and King Henry, and the gold and silver garments the English company wore over their armour, the precautions enforced to isolate each side from the other and to control access to the council tent underlined the acute suspicions of both sides. In the end the negotiations broke down – the French and the Duke of Burgundy did not feel they could accede to the English claims, especially as the dauphin, remaining close by at Corbeil, continually encouraged the duke to enter into an alliance with him against the English. The one genuine result of the conference, which was the first occasion on which Henry saw Catherine, was that he seems to have genuinely fallen in love. As the author of the *English Life* puts it, nothing came of this meeting "except the flame of Love some deale fired the hart of this Martiall Kinge to the sight of this younge Virgine Catherine".[7]

The Duke of Burgundy did not delay long in making his change of sides. Clement de Fauquembergue, the *greffier* of the *Parlement* of Paris, wrote in his journal that Duke John went to Corbeil to meet with the dauphin on 7 July, and on 12 July the news came back to Paris of the treaty made between them. The document which was signed on 11 July near Melun was a solemn pact to forget old hatreds and to combine against "the damnable enterprise of our ancient enemies, the English". The news was not slow in reaching the English forces. A private letter, written 14 July from the English headquarters at Mantes to a correspondent in England, recounts how close they felt they had been to a treaty which would have given them all the terms of Bretigny, Normandy and the other conquests in full sovereignty, only at the last moment the French began to hang back. The writer hoped to know in a few days whether it would be war or peace, but he believed that, since the duke and the dauphin had come to an accord and had it proclaimed in Paris, "it is supposed in the King's Host rather war than peace".[8] The unknown letter-writer had justly judged the situation. Henry was angry at the breakdown in the negotiations, and more angry at the peace between the duke and the dauphin which had made nonsense of the elaborate and useless negotiations at Meulan. He turned once more to his most potent weapon – the abilities of his army.

Henry's move was so sudden and so unexpected that he caught his adversaries asleep. On 30 July the king declared that the truce had expired, since no peace could be arranged, and that a state of open war existed as before. His arrangements for attacking Pontoise, the major barrier to Paris, were already complete. On the afternoon of the 30th he sent an advance party from Mantes in the afternoon, under the command of the Captal de Buch. Once they had covered the twenty miles to Pontoise they hid themselves and their horses in a wood near the city, and waited for nightfall. Under the cover of darkness they went on foot to the town's dry ditches where some lay with the scaling ladders they had brought with them while the others hid in the nearby vineyards. When the nightwatch was withdrawn around dawn, the English saw that the walls were left temporarily unguarded. They immediately scaled them, entered the town, broke open the gate for their companions and for the larger body of reinforcements led by the Earl of Huntingdon. The city had been adequately garrisoned and more than adequately provisioned but the startled soldiers fled towards Paris, leaving their food stores for two years to fall into the hands of the attackers. The king was delighted with the success of his stratagem.[9] Within the week Henry had moved to Pontoise himself and sent Clarence and a reconnoitring force to the walls of Paris, to see for themselves its situation and its strength. From 9 to 11 August they probed as far as the northern gates of St-Denis and St-Martin while the citizens of the small garrison debated fearfully the prospects of an immediate attack. But taking Paris by storm was not Henry's intention, and the English force quietly withdrew.

Meanwhile the dauphin's forces had been searching desperately for reinforcements and had turned, in a pattern often to be seen in French history, to enlist the Scots against the English. The mayor of Bayonne wrote hastily to the king on 22 July that the men of Bayonne had captured an armed balinger whose company included a clerk of the King of Castile bearing orders for forty Castilian ships to wait at Belle-Isle (off St-Nazaire) to "take on the men which the French king and the dauphin will send to do mortal war with you". They would then sail to Scotland to transport any men-at-arms willing to fight in France against Henry. Also, the King of Castile intended to besiege Bayonne. The mayor excused the brevity of his letter by his fear that it might be captured by the enemy and explained that he had not sealed it with the town's great seal but only with his privy seal, so that it could be carried more discreetly. The precautions seem to have borne fruit and the letter carried through safely to England, as by 12 August Bedford and the council were ordering ships from Devon and Cornwall to stop any Scots from going to France.[10]

More spectacularly than ever before the events of the autumn of 1419 in France worked to achieve Henry's ends for him without his own intervention. The king had spent the second half of August, after he left Pontoise, in the subduing of various remaining fortresses in the Norman Vexin, and by 31 August had settled to the siege of Gisors, its capital. It was there that the news came to him of the murder of Duke John the Fearless of Burgundy at Montereau during a meeting with the dauphin. The temporary agreement arrived at in July between the dauphin and the duke had needed to be strengthened and further discussions between the principals were required. Montereau, halfway between the dauphinist stronghold of Melun and the Burgundian town of Provins and neatly divided as well by the river Yonne which ran through the middle of the town, was chosen as the meeting-place. The careful preparations against force and treachery – the choice of the bridge itself as the meeting-place and the limitations put on the size of the retinues of the two principals – echo the detailed protocol of the English–French meeting at Meulan. But, on this occasion the force of old enmities was not to be contained, and as the duke made his obeisance to the dauphin he was fatally stabbed. The general modern estimate excuses the dauphin himself of premeditated involvement in the plot, although he was to bear the brunt of the infamy. The finger of guilt is more generally pointed at Tanneguy du Chastel, a fervent supporter of the Count of Armagnac and then of the dauphin, who burned with unslaked wrath against the Burgundians for the massacre in Paris in 1418 and for the unexpiated assassination of Louis of Orléans eleven years before that. He is the most plausible moving force behind the plot, and perhaps even the actual assassin. The duke's body was unceremoniously stripped by the dauphin's servants and thrown dishonourably into a pit without formal burial.

The news of the murder sent shock-waves through France, and confirmed the citizens of Paris and the territories of the north and east in their hatred and distrust of the Armagnacs. Duke John's son and heir, Philip, Count of Charolais, who was to become known as Philip the Good, was bound by all the laws of honour of his day to seek out and do vengeance on the murderers of his father. With King Henry in control of Normandy and practically knocking at the gates of Paris there was little choice for the new duke but to make common cause with Henry against the dauphin as their mutual enemy. Henry knew this. He is reported to have exclaimed when he heard of the murder that he regretted the loss of the duke, that "good and loyal knight and prince of honour", but he recognised at once the valuable lever that events had put into his hands, "by his death, and the help of God and St George, we are at the achievement of our desire". Henry mentioned the appeal of Catherine, but her charms for him were enhanced by the glittering prize she might bring with her – the kingdom of France.[11] It was the prior of the Charterhouse in Dijon a century later who coined the familiar phrase that England had entered France through the hole in the Duke of Burgundy's skull. His statement was more vivid than exact. England was already in France; the Duke of Burgundy's murder merely accelerated and eased Henry's determined course and added the crown of France to the territorial gains upon which he insisted.

The general disgust of the city of Paris with the dauphin's party, and especially with the hated Armagnac upon whom they blamed all their troubles – including the English invasion – was most vividly expressed in the journal of a Parisian bourgeois. The author bewails the ruination of Normandy and the personal tragedies that have flowed from this. He then goes on to lay the blame more specifically:

> Ever since France first heard the names of "Burgundian" and "Armagnac", every crime that can be thought or spoken of has been done in the kingdom of France, so that innocent blood cries for vengeance before God ... I am sure that the King of England would never have dared to set foot in France in the way of war but for the dissensions which sprang from this unhappy name [Armagnac]. Normandy would still have been French, the noble blood of France would not have been spilt nor the lords of the kingdom taken away into exile, nor the battle lost, nor would so many good men have been killed on that frightful day of Agincourt where the king lost so many of his true and loyal friends, had it not been for the pride of this wretched name Armagnac.[12]

Before Henry could give his full attention to the new opportunities for his adroit diplomacy, some matters in England demanded his attention. The king had written to the City of London in August thanking them warmly for their offer of an aid which they had granted of their own initiative.[13] From the terms of this letter, and the warmth and enthusiasm with which Henry greeted this offer, it is obvious that the financial strain of keeping a large army in the field, continuously paid and provisioned, was a continuous drain on his available funds. The process of extracting sufficient resources from Normandy was as yet only in the early stages of organisation, and money from England was sorely needed. The October parliament granted a fifteenth and a tenth, payable in February, and a third of a fifteenth and a tenth for the following November, but the

Commons were not enthusiastic about these continued demands. There was even a very real problem about coins, since so much money was being shipped out of the country to the king in France.[14]

The extraordinary imprisonment in September of Queen Joan, Henry's stepmother, on suspicion of treason by witchcraft must also be judged in the light of the king's acute financial difficulties. The affair was unprecedented and surprising, since Queen Joan had been on good terms with the king. The offence charged against her was that her confessor, Brother John Randolph, a Franciscan from Shrewsbury, accused her of compassing the death of the king by sorcery and necromancy. The friar himself had been speedily clapped into the Tower after having been examined by the king himself at Mantes during the summer. Some ten years later the friar died in the Tower during the course of a quarrel. Despite the very serious charge no formal investigation nor any trial ever took place. The queen was kept a polite prisoner for some three years with a very high standard of living, including the provision of elegant clothes for herself, a new birdcage for her parrot, and the repair of her harp – rather remarkable treatment in view of the seriousness of her alleged offence. The queen was not particularly popular in England, since the English generally disliked Bretons, and the sailors on both sides of the Channel carried on almost continuous hostilities. As well, Joan's father, Charles the Bad of Navarre, had a rather evil reputation for sorcery, which may have helped to lend verisimilitude to the charge. Since Henry on his death-bed restored the queen to complete favour and commanded the return of her lands and rents, it is permissible to presume that her genteel captivity, on a charge which immediately sequestered to the royal treasury all her rents and lands, had more to do with royal finances than royal treason. Joan's dowry was 10,000 marks, and seizing this would add more than 10 per cent to the general revenues of the government. By 1419 Henry's need for money was becoming uncomfortably acute. After his marriage to Catherine, and the resultant need to supply her with a dowry in England of 10,000 marks, the financial strain made the continued detention of Queen Joan's revenues very tempting. The avoidance of any investigation or trial not only set to one side the embarrassing question of penance for her if guilty but also obviated the restoration to her of her lands and rents if innocent. The pretext, although exploited for three years, appears to have lain heavily on Henry's conscience when he was dying and prompted his insistence on her full and unconditional release and restoration.[15]

In France the usually measured pace of diplomacy became almost frenetic. On 20 September Queen Isabel took the initiative and wrote to King Henry from Troyes, where the court then was, hoping to recommence the discussions for peace which had been begun at Meulan in June. She also urged the Duke of Burgundy to do the same. From the end of September on the process of negotiation was almost non-stop, and safe-conducts, commissions, and appointments for ambassadors all proliferate. King Henry wrote hurriedly to Bishop Langley, the current chancellor, to order special custody of the French prisoners from Agincourt still in England. He was particularly concerned at any possibility that the Duke of Orléans might escape, perhaps perverting his keeper Robert Waterton by "trust, fair speeches or promises" so that he relaxed his guard.

Their conditions of imprisonment were tightened as Henry made very sure that the potential leaders of the party in France which opposed the Duke of Burgundy did not escape from their English captivity. In the middle of all this activity, when Henry was driving himself hard in both war and diplomacy, an entry on the Exchequer records suggests that his health was already beginning to feel the strain for Master Peter Henewer, physician, was paid for his expenses in going to Normandy.[16]

Despite the continuing diplomatic activity Henry's army continued to exert pressure on the country around Paris, capturing Meulan and St-Germain-en-Laye. The king himself went to visit Poissy, where one of the French king's older daughters was prioress. He behaved very properly and gave the priory rich presents. On 15 December he returned to Rouen to celebrate Christmas and remained there until the final achievement of the peace treaty with France. Nevertheless, as the author of the *English Life* points out, Henry never let his own religious observances interfere with his military plans.[17] While he rested and attended to his devotions, he sent soldiers under the command of the Earl Marshal and the Earl of Huntingdon to counter the dauphin's army in Maine, and the Earl of Salisbury to take Fresnay-le-Vicomte. The siege there was enlivened by a pitched battle with a French relieving force which had been strengthened by a Scotch contingent under Earl William Douglas. The French were defeated, Marshal de Rous and other nobles were captured, as was Douglas' banner, which Henry was delighted to order hung in Notre Dame, Rouen, as a sign of the English victory.[18]

Meanwhile, the festivities of the season were heightened for the English by the appearance of the ambassadors of the Duke of Burgundy. Led by the Bishop of Arras, they included Ghillebert de Lannoy, later to become so much more intimately involved in the long-range plans of both the king and the duke. A general truce was agreed upon and Henry appointed his own ambassadors to carry on the serious negotiations for a permanent peace. Henry continued his pressure on the city of Paris by a combination of threats and promises. He pledged to maintain the rights and privileges of the city when he obtained the crown of France, but in February he also refused to prolong the truce unless the fortress of Beaumont was handed over to him. Beaumont, which straddles the Oise some twenty-three miles north of Paris, was of vital strategic importance to the city as a distribution point for food and merchandise destined for the capital. After much anguished discussion among the responsible officers in Paris it was decided to accede to Henry's request because of the dangers such a siege would have for the city. They salved their consciences at this ignominious retreat by emphasising that the fortress was "badly fortified, badly equipped, and badly provisioned", and therefore not really defensible.[19]

The focus of the vigorous diplomatic manoeuvring had moved to Troyes, where Duke Philip came to the court of King Charles and Queen Isabel to add his pressure to that already coming from Paris. The queen had believed that it would be possible to arrange a settlement based on the earlier discussions in June of 1419, when Henry had abandoned some of his more extreme claims. She soon came to realise that Henry's ambitions had increased with his cool calculation of his strengthened bargaining power. The queen was greedy and weak, but her final acceptance of Henry's terms was forced by the dreadful state of the royal finances, the unremitting pressure of the Burgundian supporters, especially those in positions of authority in Paris, and the supple diplomacy of Henry and his able ambassadors, including the Earl of Warwick and Louis Robsart. Robsart, who was sent to Troyes at the end of December 1419, after the king's discussions with the Parisians and the Burgundians at Rouen, was originally from Hainault, but he and his father and grandfather had all fought for the English kings. Louis himself had served Henry as an esquire when the king was Prince of Wales. He had fought vigorously in the Norman campaign and been suitably rewarded. He had several advantages: French as a mother tongue, an origin in lands which had belonged to Isabel's family of Bavaria and, above all, Henry's full confidence. He obviously acquitted himself to the king's satisfaction, for after the Treaty of Troyes he was named to the prestigious office of royal standard-bearer.[20]

By 29 April the general outlines of the treaty had been hammered out and letters describing the progress made were submitted to a special gathering at Paris which included representatives of the university and of the bishop, as well as the usual responsible citizens. The Parisians, strongly Burgundian in sympathy, were assured that Duke Philip was not moved by vengeance, but only by the most high-minded desire to avoid the shedding of Christian blood and to arrive at peace, justice and tranquillity. The letters spoke too of the good reports the French king and queen had had of Henry, "that he was said to be prudent and wise, loving God, peace and justice". The dauphin and his party had rendered themselves unworthy of every dignity and honour by their killing of the Duke of Burgundy, disloyally and contrary to their oath. The decision of the Paris gathering was not surprising. The treaty seemed to them *"moult convenable, très prouffitable et nécessaire"*.[21]

Later observers, less prejudiced than the Parisians, were not convinced of Duke Philip's unremitting highmindedness. Philip certainly wanted to avenge his father's murder but he was also goaded by ambition, the urge to play as important a part in the rule and realm of France as his father and grandfather. For him, the English alliance was only a method to achieve his ends, and certainly had no emotional force, either of hatred for France or love for England. The double monarchy, which the Treaty of Troyes was to establish, was seen as a lesser evil. If Henry was allowed to continue his career of conquest, as he seemed most willing and able to do, France – or at least its economic and administrative centre of the Île de France, Normandy and the territories north of the Loire – would be annexed to England, and colonised by Englishmen. Reluctant agreement on the necessity of admitting Henry, while maintaining the separateness of the realm of France, prevailed at Troyes as at Paris. Notice was sent to the English king that the peace treaty which embodied his wildest ambitions was ready for formal ratification.

At the beginning of May Henry left Rouen with a large armed following (the *English Life* puts it as high as 16,000, which is obviously excessive) and set off for Troyes. The impressive cavalcade made a semi-circle around the north of Paris while the devout king stopped at the abbey of St-Denis to pray. As the army, in full battle array, marched past the walls of Paris the curious citizens climbed the towers and steeples and gaped from the walls at the impressive spectacle of English might. Nevertheless, Henry did not allow his satisfaction at the prospects of a favourable peace to cloud his military judgment. He carefully set permanent guards at all the important bridges on his way, particularly at the strategic point of Charenton, which crossed the Seine just south of the Bois de Vincennes and just upstream from the junction of the Marne and the Seine. Henry's estimate of the special importance of this bridge has been underlined by history – it has been rebuilt eighteen times over the centuries. His well-armed company and his careful precautions allowed him to pass unmolested over the wide flat plains of Brie, despite the existence of several dauphinist strongholds there, to the county of Champagne. On 20 May he arrived outside the town of Troyes to be met by the Duke of Burgundy and a distinguished company and led by them into the city. He went first to greet the queen and King Charles, for the time being rational but melancholy, then was conducted to his lodgings. Troyes had been divided in half, undoubtedly to avoid potential conflicts between the French and Burgundian and the English contingents, and the half assigned to Henry's men was not large enough to hold them all within the walls. The king was so displeased at the thought of many of his people being in the suburbs without easy access and concerned, after the events at Montereau, with the possibilities of treachery, that he had the city walls on the side adjoining his lodgings knocked down. At the same time he proclaimed several disciplinary regulations for his troops. The English fondness for wine and tendency to drunkenness were a byword, and Henry firmly ordered his army, "since the wines of this country were so famous and strong", that no one should drink them without adding water, under pain of royal punishment.[22]

On Tuesday 21 May the formal proclamation of the Treaty of Troyes took place in the then unfinished cathedral of St-Pierre. King Henry was accompanied in the church by the Duchess of Clarence and forty lords, knights, and esquires. Queen Isabel, in the illness of the king, came with the Duke of Burgundy and forty members of their council, as well as the Princess Catherine. Together King Henry and Queen Isabel ascended to the high altar and listened to the recital of the articles of peace. These were then sealed, the concord sworn to, and Henry and Catherine betrothed. The Duke of Burgundy was the first to swear publicly that he would be obedient to Henry as regent of France during the life of Charles VI and, after Charles' death, would become Henry's liege man. The peace was proclaimed in both French and English, and then the articles were published throughout the city and the English army.[23]

The treaty so carefully proclaimed was a monument to the disruptive effects of civil war in France and the success of Henry's twin-pronged military and diplomatic attack. Henry was recognised as son and heir of Charles VI and Isabel, because of the enormous crimes and offences of the dauphin, who was thereby rendered incapable of ruling, and was given Catherine as his wife. Although Charles was to retain the crown and royal dignity of France until his death, from that moment on the crown and realm of France should pass to Henry and remain to him and his forever. In the meantime, because of the king's sickness, Henry was to act as regent of France with the counsel of the French nobles. Catherine was to be suitably dowered – at once in England, and later in France. Although the crowns of England and France were to be united in the single person of Henry and his heirs, the two kingdoms themselves were to remain totally separate, each maintaining its own rights, customs, usages, and laws. Normandy and the other places conquered by Henry up to now were to be returned to the crown of France when Henry received that crown. Although no specific provision was made concerning their possession till that moment it is obvious that Henry felt that he had won them, possessed them, and was not going to surrender them until the whole kingdom of France was within his grasp. Henry also committed himself to continuing the war against the dauphin and all the lands and fortresses in France still holding out against King Charles. As well, Henry promised not to style himself King of France at any time before the death of King Charles. In an attempt to provide further safeguards for the treaty King Charles, the Duke of Burgundy, and Henry all promised they would not make peace with the dauphin without the assent of all three of them and also of the three estates of both realms. In token of their agreement the nobles and estates, spiritual and temporal, and the cities and their responsible members were to swear to carry out the provisions of the treaty.

Henry's moment of triumph was sweet. On the day after the formal proclamation he wrote to his brother Humphrey, now warden of England, telling him the news of "a goode Conclusion", and ordering that the peace should be proclaimed in London. The letter enclosed a schedule of his new style as heir and regent of France and ordered that the lettering on all his seals should hastily be amended. Henry could have added that on this same day some 1,500 notables, including the president of the *Parlement* and the Bishop of Troyes, all took the oath upholding the treaty. The news had reached England by 14 June when a solemn procession and a public sermon at St Paul's Cross testified to the solemnity of the occasion.[24]

The final ceremonious touch of the king's stay in Troyes was the celebration of his marriage to Catherine on 2 June. Since Henry and his forces had been lodged in the lower town the wedding took place in the parish church of St-Jean. The present-day church has little to remind the visitor of the occasion, since it has been much rebuilt after a fire at the beginning of the sixteenth century. Even in the still medieval atmosphere which the narrow streets and old crooked houses of Troyes so strongly reinforce it is hard to recreate the pomp and magnificence which Monstrelet assures us were displayed by the self-confident Henry and his princes, "as if he were at that moment king of all the world".[25] Catherine was his, and this was a marriage of desire as well as one of state: the age and weakness of Charles VI implied that the crown of France would soon be in his grasp, and meanwhile he had the right to rule the realm.

Looking back we can see that Henry's day of triumph was only a day, and many of the fair prospects it suggested never came to be. The marriage was achieved, and produced an heir, though he was to inherit the fatal mental weakness of the Valois and later lose the throne he ascended at nine months. The "permanent" treaty was to wither and vanish in less than twenty years under the buffets of unexpected fate. Certainly there was no real enthusiasm for the treaty in France even at the beginning. The queen and the Duke of Burgundy saw it only as a lesser evil, while the dauphin's supporters opposed it vigorously and managed to keep alive French national sentiment south of the Loire until better fortune and the catalyst provided by Joan of Arc helped to spark a return to the offensive. For the time being most of the Burgundian lords upheld the alliance, and those who did not tended to have been influenced by specific local situations or English seizures of their lands.

Although necessity made strange bedfellows their proximity did not warm the relations between them, for the English made few friends among the French. The nobility detested Henry's rigid control of the government, shouldering them from the scene, and all feared his harsh reprisals on anyone who sought relations with the dauphin or even with those parts of France which remained obedient to him. English manners were not French manners. The Earl of Huntingdon, for example, refused to deal with the town's ambassador at the siege of Sens because the man was heavily bearded. The unfortunate envoy had to shave off his beard before negotiations could begin. The king himself bitterly reproached l'Isle-Adam, Marshal of France, for his temerity in looking him in the face when he spoke to him, and when the marshal replied that it was the French custom to do so or be reputed wicked and faithless, Henry answered angrily that it was not the English way. L'Isle-Adam was subsequently imprisoned in the Bastille St-Antoine by the Duke of Exeter for approaches to the dauphin, and remained there during Henry's lifetime. Monstrelet, who tells the whole story, suggests that the king would have had him put to death except for a special plea from the Duke of Burgundy.[26] The Parisians too recorded their disappointment with the behaviour of the English in Paris, but true to their bourgeois background they were more interested in commerce than affairs of honour:

> For, indeed, the English ruled Paris for a very long time, but I do honestly think that never any one of them had any corn or oats sowed or so much as a fireplace built in a house – except the Regent, the Duke of Bedford. He was always building wherever he was; his nature was quite un-English, for he never wanted to make war on anybody, whereas the English, essentially, are always wanting to make war on their neighbours without cause. That is why they all die an evil death.[27]

It is important to remember that the Treaty of Troyes was not a peace treaty between two kings. Rather, it was a triangular agreement between three parties – the English king, the French king, and the Duke of Burgundy – at the expense of the dauphin. In its insistence on the need for continued conquests by Henry, and its careful emphasis on the mutual promises of the signatories that no one of them would make peace with the dauphin without the full consent of the others, it ensured continuing war and civil strife in France. Its force did not lie in the careful legalisms which the French lawyers and propagandists would ultimately tear to shreds in their search for flaws. Its continued existence depended on two things: the concurrence of the Duke of Burgundy, and the strong hand, nimble brain and consummate organising ability of Henry V. Burgundy's concurrence was itself dependent on English strength – it would not be used to prop up any English weakness which might hobble his own ambitions. It is one of the more fascinating of history's unsolved questions to wonder what would have happened if Henry, still a relatively young man at thirty-three, had lived his normal span and been able to devote his formidable talents to the achievement of the total conquest of France he so confidently expected. Even his father, plagued with unexpected illness, had lived to the age of forty-seven, but for Henry the time was still shorter. There were only two years left in which to realise his ambitions, and the weak, mad Charles VI would follow, rather than precede him to the grave.

CHAPTER XIII

Heir and Regent of France

King Henry was never one to linger over formalities. On the day after his wedding the English and French knights had intended to hold a tournament as part of the marriage celebrations, but the king was obsessed with the need to carry on the struggle against the dauphin without delay. His response to the knights' suggestion was to command his own men, and to beg those of the king of France, to be ready to go instead to besiege Sens, still held by dauphinist troops. "There," he said, "we may all tilt and joust and prove our daring and courage, for there is no finer act of courage in the world than to punish evildoers so that poor people can live."[1] Henry's words were persuasive and on Tuesday the army moved off to Sens, some thirty-eight miles away. By Wednesday 4 June siege was being laid to the town. The chroniclers considered it a most "worthy" siege because the attacking army included two kings, two queens and four dukes, as well as many other important nobles. The mere act of setting the siege seemed to have been sufficient to weaken the city, for Sens surrendered after only a few days.

The neighbouring towns were understandably uneasy, wondering what would be the next point of attack for the singleminded English king. The inhabitants of Joigny, only twenty miles south of Sens, wrote nervously to Henry on 5 June. They claimed that they had been about to send their proctor to swear the necessary oath to the treaty recently signed at Troyes when the Count of Joigny arrived and threatened to cut off the heads of any inhabitants who proposed to take the oath. In addition, he seized their proctor and dismissed their captain. The citizens emphasised their loyalty to the Duke of Burgundy and declared that they had closed the gates of the town and were holding the count and his men until they heard from the king or the duke what they should do. They were apprehensive that by the count's actions they were in danger of being taken by their enemies.[2] Fortunately for the nervous citizens the strength of the English and Burgundian armies so near at hand seems to have frightened away any attackers and their hurried apologies saved them from reprisals. Joigny was left in peace as the combined forces moved on to Montereau.

This siege was of particular importance to the Duke of Burgundy, since the capture of the town where his father had been murdered, and the recovery of his father's body for honourable burial, dominated his immediate plans and gave emotional edge to his demands for vengeance. The town on the west bank of the Yonne, and the bridge across that river where Duke John had been cut down fell to the attackers by 24 June, but most of the defenders, led by the Lord of Guitry, fled to the castle, which occupied the point of land between the Seine and the Yonne rivers. Henry had taken a number of prisoners when the town was attacked and he used them as brutal bargaining-counters to encourage the surrender of the castle. The prisoners were made to beseech the defenders of the fortress to surrender, for otherwise King Henry would have them all hanged. The Lord of Guitry, who was the commander of the castle, refused, even when the prisoners begged him on their knees to have pity on them. The inflexible Henry kept his promise: he erected a gibbet in full view of the castle and had all the prisoners hanged upon it. He also hanged his own groom, who ran at his horse's bridle, because the servant in a fit of rage had accidentally killed an English knight. This harshness was acceptable in the light of the standards of the day. What would now be called simple manslaughter was then considered punishable by death because the lower social standing of the groom made his action against the knight a kind of petty treason. It is interesting that the French chroniclers who tell these stories, which seem to indicate a growing brutality on Henry's part, do not condemn him but reserve their particular anger for the Lord of Guitry who surrendered the castle only eight days after allowing the execution of the prisoners.[3] The Duke of Burgundy's body was recovered from its ignominious grave and sent back to Dijon for ceremonious entombment in the Charterhouse, the mausoleum of the house of Burgundy.

From Montereau the Anglo–Burgundian forces went on to Melun, the largest town in southern Brie. In its physical lay-out Melun is reminiscent of Paris. The town had an island in the Seine as its ancient Gallo–Roman core and over the centuries had expanded to both the right and left banks. It was a difficult town to besiege, both because of its location and because it had been very adequately fortified. Each section had its own wall, and the three were linked together by a long bridge from bank to bank. By the middle of July the armies had taken up their positions, with the Burgundians to the north and the English to the south. But Melun, unlike Sens and Montereau, would not surrender without a prolonged struggle. Much of its determination was due to the intransigence of its commander, the Lord of Barbasan, whom even the English chroniclers praised as the "most excellent of deeds of armes of all the knights in those daies". When Henry's herald demanded the surrender of the town, Barbasan stoutly refused, declaring that he had not received his charge over the town and castle from the English king. Henry then had King Charles send his own herald to demand surrender, but Barbasan's second answer was equally defiant. He had received his charge, he said, when King Charles was a free man, but now the king was ruled and governed by the King of England, so that this command came from the great adversary of France and should not be obeyed. However, when King Charles was again at liberty he would most happily obey him.[4]

The siege, begun on this note of defiance, dragged its way through summer and into the autumn. Despite the most vigorous efforts of the besiegers, including the use of a large gun which had been provided by the Londoners and which cast such a huge projectile that it knocked down houses for a quarter of a mile, the defenders held out.[5] They filled up the breaches made by the guns and counter-mined when the English tried to mine the walls. The mining operations on both sides were so extensive and the passages below ground so large that many hand-to-hand battles were fought there. Fighting in the mines of a besieged town had a protocol of its own, and, in this case, appears to have been conducted with much of the punctilio of an underground tournament, with set hours, the use of torches and lights, and the separation of the antagonists by the guards before they were seriously wounded. Juvenal des Ursins, the French chronicler who describes the scene most carefully (because one of his own relatives was involved), emphasises the need for special skills in such fighting and mentions the care which Barbasan showed for those of his men who were not yet experienced.[6]

The fighting in the mines at Melun provided one unusual example of the strict code which governed the law of arms. On one occasion, to settle an argument over precedence, King Henry himself went into the mine and a vigorous hand-to-hand battle ensued between the king and Barbasan, both unaware of the other's identity. At last, convinced of his opponent's ability and courage, each demanded the other's name. When Henry had disclosed himself as the king, Barbasan had the passages closed down and no further passages of arms were allowed. There was an interesting sequel to this combat, for after Melun's surrender Barbasan was claimed as a prisoner liable to death because he had been implicated in the murder of the Duke of Burgundy. The gallant captain denied complicity but was unable to clear himself completely. King Henry wished to put him to death, but Barbasan appealed the sentence to the officer-of-arms, claiming that he was a brother-in-arms to the king because of their hand-to-hand encounter in the mine, and therefore the king could not legally put him to death. The appeal court of the heralds upheld his contention, so Henry committed him to perpetual imprisonment, first at Paris, then at Château Gaillard.*

* Barbasan was gallant to the end. The English captain of Château Gaillard had made him swear to remain a prisoner and not depart without his licence.

Even at such a hard-fought siege the atmosphere retained some incongruous elements of elegance. The newly married Henry, although not willing to put aside his pressing military programme, was anxious to have Queen Catherine near him. He therefore had a house built for her and her damsels near his tents, which had been placed at some distance from the town so that the cannon might not disturb them. Every day at sunrise and nightfall the king and queen were serenaded for an hour by a group of English musicians playing clarions and other instruments. Incidentally, the king's tents may not have been disturbed by the cannon but they seem to have suffered from natural disasters. Another house had to be built for Arthur of Brittany who had been occupying the king's tent when it blew down with Arthur inside it.[8] During this siege Henry and Duke Philip of Burgundy came closer to genuine understanding and co-operation than at any other time. The long days of relative inactivity allowed them to discuss their dreams of a future crusade. Both promised to go to the Holy Land and decided on the dispatch to the Near East of a mission of exploration, headed by the duke's standard-bearer, Ghillebert de Lannoy.[9]

But despite such unexpected sidelights the siege was a slow and brutal affair, relying on hunger and disease to do the attackers' work. Henry's army was bolstered by the arrival of the Duke of Bedford with new reinforcements from England, and by a company of some 700 horsemen led by his brother-in-law, Louis of Bavaria. Louis had never received the dowry he had been promised with Blanche, the king's sister. Although she had died in 1406 the duke continued to press for the arrears and an annuity of 1,000 marks seems to have been arranged about the same time as the treaty with Sigismund in 1416. It was probably in fulfilment of the terms of this agreement that Louis brought his contingent to Melun. Henry was glad of this support. On the other hand, he was angered by the Prince of Orange who came to support the Duke of Burgundy but refused categorically to swear to the Treaty of Troyes, saying it put the kingdom of France in the hands of "its ancient and capital enemy".[10]

When the town and the castle finally surrendered on 18 November the siege had lasted over four months. The besieged had been forced out by hunger but there had also been serious fighting for much of this time and the losses, both from combat and siege-related disease, were heavy on both sides. As the chronicler from St Albans gloomily commented, it was a "victory as destructive as glorious".[11] Henry's increasing harshness and severity show up clearly in his actions after Melun's capture. The terms of the surrender called for the sparing of the lives of all in the town who were not implicated in the murder at Montereau, but they were to lay down

---

When the French recovered Château Gaillard some years later they were overjoyed to discover Barbasan locked in an iron cage and hastened to free him. The emaciated prisoner refused to leave until the English captain was brought back to relieve him from his promise.[7]

their arms and to be held as prisoners until ransom was paid. About 400 were held and sent to various castles under Henry's control, where some French chroniclers claimed that they were ill-treated. More unfortunate were the group of Scots mercenaries in the town, who had been specifically excluded from the general terms of the agreement. Henry had arranged for James of Scotland to be brought specially from England so that he might order his subjects to surrender. They refused, and after the town fell they were immediately hanged for disobedience to their king. Henry was always totally unforgiving to those who disobeyed the letter of the law or any of his strict orders. On this occasion, Bertrand de Chaumont, who had fought with Henry at Agincourt and was a member of the king's household, was accused and executed for having illicitly allowed a prisoner to get away. It mattered not at all that Henry had been fond of the knight and that many of the great lords pleaded for him. The king declared that he wanted his orders obeyed – and showed he meant it.[12]

Once Melun had surrendered the road lay open to Paris. The Treaty of Troyes had already been proclaimed there on 28 May, and a solemn mass and procession of thanksgiving had taken place the following day. The townspeople, who were strongly Burgundian in sentiment, were pleased with the settlement and easily swore the oath to obey King Henry. Although individual Englishmen had been moving in and out of the city since the end of May without difficulty, the formal entrance of both kings had to be marked by the appropriate ceremonial. Henry joined Charles VI at Corbeil until the arrangements were made. On 1 December, the two kings, accompanied by the Duke of Burgundy and their retinues of nobles, entered Paris by the Grande Rue St-Denis, the traditional cere-monial route of French kings on their solemn entry into the city. The people of Paris, no doubt encouraged by the wine running through all the conduits in honour of the occasion, threw aside their worries for the moment and did their utmost to make it a festive occasion. The streets through which the cavalcade passed were decorated gaily and carols were sung by the inhabitants, many of whom were wearing red as a sign of rejoicing. While processions of priests in copes and surplices sang Te Deums in the streets, a magnificent living representation of the Mystery of the Passion, as it appeared around the choir of Notre Dame, was staged in the Rue de la Calandre.[13] Henry and his brothers lodged in the palace of the Louvre and on the following day the two queens joined their husbands in Paris. Queen Catherine had not been left unaccompanied, for the English party included the noble ladies whom Henry had ordered to come overseas to attend her.

Charles and Isabel went to their usual residence, the Hôtel St-Pol in the east end of the city near the Rue St-Antoine, the old Roman road which led southeastward beyond the walls to Vincennes and Melun. The Hôtel St-Pol had been built by Charles V in the preceding century and was most luxuriously and spaciously designed. No trace remains of the sprawling palace which stretched from the Rue St-Antoine to the Seine, but in the fifteenth century it was famous for its elegant painted chambers, its richly decorated chapels, and the luxurious baths where the great wooden tubs were adorned with gilt bosses. The aviaries and gardens have disappeared without trace but the cherry orchard and the king's famous menagerie of lions are still recalled by the local street names.

As usual, the king did not allow elegant formalities to delay him for long. The three estates of France were convoked on 6 December by King Charles to hear the reasons for the peace treaty and why they should swear to uphold it. Four days later Charles fulfilled one of the requirements laid down at Troyes by solemnly promulgating the treaty with the consent of the three estates. He decreed that it should be observed in all the realm of France as public law and those who refused to swear to it or keep it were to be regarded and punished as rebels. As well, two days before Christmas, a *lit de justice* presided over by both kings was called in judgment on the murderers of Duke John of Burgundy. The judgment gave Duke Philip more emotional satisfaction than actual revenge. The dauphin was condemned *in absentia* and solemnly declared incapable of succeeding his father as king because of his crimes. Only those captured in battles or sieges were to be put to death; for the others the penance was public humiliation but no more.[14]

The Christmas festivities of 1420 in Paris celebrated for Henry the formal achievement of his ambitions. The prize for which he had fought and manoeuvred so tenaciously since the beginning of his reign was officially his, although he would have to wait to sit on the throne of France until the death of Charles VI. But Charles was fifty-two and mad, and his death could not be long delayed. However, Charles' physical vigour seems to have remained high. Perhaps as a Christmas present, Henry had ordered a special consignment of bows, arrows, and bow-strings to be sent to his father-in-law.[15] The English king recognised the considerable military effort that lay ahead of him if he was to fulfil the terms of the treaty and reduce the dauphinist strongholds, some of which were dangerously close to Paris. It is interesting to speculate whether Henry had ever really faced the immensity of the task which lay ahead of him if he was to attempt to extend his power south of the Loire. His reasonable expectations could easily foresee the subduing of the northern half of France, so much more important to him because of Normandy, the commercial and prestigious value of Paris, and the maintenance of the continuing English interest in Flanders. His actions over the next year and a half – all that remained to him – show a vigilant and careful extension of his forces in the north and the continued containment of the dauphin's main forces behind the line of the Loire. There certainly was no time for a campaign to the south, but there seems to have been no real advance planning for one either.

The contrast between the English and French establishments in Paris during the Christmas season was very marked, and bitterly underlined by French chroniclers. Chastellain, the Burgundian who was a warm admirer of the duke and less than lukewarm about the English, puts the more chauvinist French feeling most vividly:

> It was the city of Paris, ancient seat of the French royal majesty, which now seemed to have changed name and situation, because this king and his numerous English people had made of it a new London, as much in language as in their rude and proud manner of conversation and behaviour. And they went with their heads high, like a stag, looking to their sides and to the rear.

Monstrelet too lashes out at the magnificence of the state surrounding King Henry and Queen Catherine at the Louvre, while at the Hôtel St-Pol the king of France was "poorly and meanly served", attended only by his old servants and persons of low degree.[16] The crowd of courtiers had abandoned poor King Charles and had flocked like vultures to the court of the English king where power now rested and favour could be won.

Henry had obviously taken the reins of government in charge. He had previously arranged to hold the Louvre, the castle of Vincennes, the palace of Nesle, and the Bastille St-Antoine in his own hands as the essential strongpoints within the city. Of all these, the Bastille, the massive fortification which protected the eastern flank of the Hôtel St-Pol and stood just within the Porte St-Antoine, was the most important and Henry wished to be completely sure of its loyalty. According to one of his biographers the English had to take the place by guile as it was in the hands of Burgundians who were not committed to Henry. The English company charged with the ruse hid most of its men in small groups nearby, while the knight in command and three of his companions sought a peaceful talk with the constable. The unsuspecting castellan opened the gate and let down the drawbridge to talk with the English commander while the knight's companions stood on the end of the drawbridge so that it could not be raised quickly. After much casual conversation the English knight approached the gate and suddenly entered it, while his hidden supporters rushed to join him. They seized the keys from the outwitted castellan and held the fortress, though they let the humiliated constable and his men go free.[17]

Henry did not linger in Paris. Soon after Christmas the king and queen moved on to Rouen, on their way to England, leaving the Duke of Exeter in command in Paris. They left behind a city gripped by cold and famine, for it was an excessively hard, long winter. Natural hardships added to the misery brought on by rising prices and the difficulties of supply from lands devastated by almost continuous fighting. The bourgeois of Paris wrote sadly that by spring the people were eating what the pigs refused, and that the wolves had reappeared in the city, often swimming across the Seine to dig up and worry the newly buried corpses.[18]

Henry and Catherine celebrated Epiphany at Rouen, where still another magnificent feast was held in the castle, but the king was more concerned with the necessary orders for the government of his conquest than with these required functions. He called together the three estates of the duchy, and of the conquered country beyond Normandy, to deal with the most urgent problems. When Henry had conquered Normandy he had not tried to change its government, but merely took over the existing local administration. He carefully put his own men in the key positions, but Norman officials were allowed to continue below them. The *baillis*, for example, in charge of the eight main units of civil administration, were all English by 1421 but the officials below them were natives. There were three principal civil officials: the chancellor, with his chancery established at Rouen; the seneschal, whose office had been revived to serve as an overseer of all officers, civil and military, but with no control over finances; and the treasurer, whose treasury was established at Caen, and who was responsible for the collection and receipt of all revenues. On the military side, a lieutenant was head of the organisation of the troops, and the admiral of Normandy was responsible for the safeguarding of the coasts. All these officials answered to the king's council at Rouen, presided over by the chancellor. In 1421 John Kemp, the Bishop of Rochester, served as chancellor, Richard Wydeville as seneschal, and William Alington as treasurer. The Earl of Salisbury, probably Henry's most able commander, was the lieutenant, but his duties included more than mere defence. With the army under his command he continued to wage offensive war against dauphinist enclaves, and made sorties into Maine and Anjou. Suffolk, as admiral, had a less arduous post.

The number of soldiers, including castle garrisons, in continuous service in Normandy during these last years of Henry's reign was relatively high – close to 5,000 men, most of them English. They had to be paid with some regularity if they were to be kept in service, and restrained from harassing the local citizens whose loyalty was sufficiently tenuous in any case. The problem was acute. The soldiers, unless actively engaged in campaigning were often bored, and frequently without money. They turned naturally to lawlessness and many preyed upon the inhabitants, since the king's strict regulations, constantly reiterated, made desertion and escape to England very difficult. They thus helped to aggravate the problem of brigandage in Normandy, which though less acute during Henry V's own reign than later on, was nevertheless troubling. On this question the natural reactions of French and English writers are diametrically opposed. For most of the French, all brigands were patriots, fighting a noble guerrilla war against the invaders of their land. For most English, the brigands were merely thieves with no political sense, taking advantage of the disorder in the countryside. The truth appears to lie somewhere between the two extremes. There were both brigand-partisans and brigand-thieves, both of whom were encouraged in their activities by the continued indiscipline and exactions of the English soldiers. Desperate bands of dispossessed men hid in the woods and caves, controlled many of the roads, and attacked solitary travellers. Their membership sprang almost completely from the lower peasant class whose security and livelihood were most cruelly affected. The nobles had too much to lose to join in this kind of resistance. Indeed, both in Normandy and Aquitaine, most prudent families with extensive lands arranged to have members on each of the opposing sides, as useful insurance against any of the twists of fate. The Norman clergy were mollified by Henry's strict regard for the rights of the church and, in general, officially took the English side, although the ecclesiastical courts exercised remarkable clemency towards those brigands who came within their jurisdiction. The general disruption characteristic of the duchy during these years of continued fighting with its concomitant of ravaging and looting, was made worse in 1421 by desperate weather conditions, and was underlined by the enormous increase in wolves throughout the district. It was necessary to appoint a large number of *louvetiers*, i.e., officers to capture and kill wolves. One such appointment speaks of the multitude of wolves in many places in Normandy, who attack and devour human beings, cattle and sheep. The officials were to be paid a bounty for each capture, but the money was to be raised from the already burdened inhabitants. The matter-of-fact order that executed criminals should be cut down and buried rather than left hanging to be devoured by wild beasts was inspired by the need to discourage the hungry wolves from entering inhabited places.[19]

The deliberations of the estates of Normandy in January 1421 make it clear that the king's primary concern was financial. Although the estates were urged to observe the Treaty of Troyes, it had little immediate effect for Normandy since the lands of the conquest were already completely under Henry's rule. The Norman coinage had been much debased and plans for a new coinage were put in hand, but they were never completely successful, and devalued coins continued to circulate. The effort to reform the currency led naturally enough to a request by Henry for a grant, since the estates themselves had complained about the disturbed state of the duchy. Henry had been careful in imposing taxes on Normandy. Soon after he captured Caen he had decreed the removal of the hated *gabelle*, or salt tax, which was one of the most unpopular of the taxes imposed by the French king, but he had gradually had to return to the earlier French taxes and to demands for money. On this occasion the clergy offered two tenths, and the towns agreed to bring this amount to 400,000 *livres tournois*. Henry's policy was to attempt to make Normandy not only pay for itself but also carry a share of the financial burden of the war. This was difficult to achieve. Although the accounts are confused and difficult to interpret, it would appear that during Henry V's reign Normandy supported itself but gave little real assistance to the English king.[20] It is certainly a fact that one of Henry's most urgent items of business during his short stay in England in the spring of 1421 was to tap new sources for loans with which to finance the prolonged war, for he was not getting extensive sums in France.

It was necessary for the king to return to England – he had been away for three and a half years and the autumn parliament had expressed its anxiety at his continued absence – but he does not seem to have contemplated a long stay. The Treaty of Troyes obligated him to continue the fight against the dauphin, and this inevitably meant a need to raise both troops and money with which to pay them, and then to make a speedy return to France. In addition, until Queen Catherine was crowned the king could not gain possession of her dowry. During his absence many of his experienced commanders remained in France with the Duke of Clarence at their head. The king and queen were accompanied only by the Duke of Bedford, the King of Scots, whose long term of imprisonment was at last coming to an end, and the earls of Warwick and March. They travelled through Picardy to Calais and reached Dover on 1 February to a tumultuous welcome. The dignified barons of the Cinque Ports carried the royal pair to shore on their own shoulders and large numbers of enthusiastic citizens accompanied them to Canterbury where they were formally welcomed by Archbishop Chichele. They rested there for a few days before moving on to Eltham. Arrangements were made for the celebrations in London and for the necessary splendours of the queen's coronation. In the usual pattern of medieval pageantry the king and queen were met at Blackheath by the mayor and aldermen and a large crowd of London citizens, dressed for the festive occasion in white trimmed with red. They accompanied the royal couple through streets, decorated as they had been after Agincourt, to the Tower where they spent the night. On Sunday 23 February the queen was ceremoniously conducted to Westminster where she was crowned by Archbishop Chichele. Afterwards a splendid coronation feast was held in Westminster Palace over which the queen presided – the king did not attend since on this day the queen was to be the centre of all attention. The *Brut* describes with loving care the detail of the placement of the guests and the complete menu of the feast which, handicapped by the prohibition of meat during Lent, called on an incredible range of fish, from such continuing delicacies as salmon, sole, sturgeon, and crayfish to such things as porpoises, whelks, lampreys and tench which no longer appear on our banquet tables. Between each of the three courses the pastry cooks presented a "subtlety", climaxing their work with a magnificent creation of a tiger led by St George.[21] It was an impressive occasion, marked by the pageantry and symbolism so very dear to medieval men and consciously used by medieval monarchs to reinforce the majesty and superiority of the royal estate.

Not much time could be wasted, however, on ceremonies, no matter how satisfying or impressive. Henry was anxious to get down to business and the king and queen's quick tour of England in the two months after Catherine's coronation had a serious double purpose, camouflaged by the ceremonial processions and the pious visits to shrines. The king visited a large number of towns, including several where Lollard sentiment had been very strong in the beginning of the reign. Undoubtedly he was anxious to see for himself whether the climate was one of loyalty and acceptance. As well, and of even more immediate importance, he needed money quickly and that meant he must encourage loans, since any grants conceded by parliament would inevitably be slow in collection. Of course, the journey made useful propaganda, a matter in which Henry was remarkably astute. He visited St Albans, Bristol, Shrewsbury, his favourite palace of Kenilworth, and the midland towns of Coventry, Leicester, and Nottingham. From there he turned north to Pontefract and York, paid flying visits to the shrines at Bridlington and Beverly, returning to Lincoln for the installation of the new bishop, Richard Fleming. During this swing to the north he received news of the English defeat at Baugé and of the death in the struggle of his brother Clarence – bad news which added urgency to his journey. Despite this, however, he continued his planned tour, going to Lynn, the famous shrine at Walsingham, and on to Norwich before returning to London. According to Monstrelet he everywhere "explained with great elegance what great deeds he had performed through his prowess in France, and what yet remained to be done for the complete conquest of that kingdom". The chronicler adds that Henry underlined his need for men and money and received both in abundance.[22]

Parliament opened at Westminster on 2 May 1421 in the king's presence. Two matters were of outstanding importance. It was essential that parliament should ratify the Treaty of Troyes. Henry had Bishop Langley, the chancellor, explain the terms to them and parliament then solemnly "agreed, approved, praised, and authorized the peace", accepting its obligations as well as its gains.[23] The previous parliament had requested, and the king had granted, that the two realms of England and France would always remain separate, each ruled according to its own laws and customs, though the same king might occupy both thrones. The May parliament, secure in this decision, may have been more willing to give its formal approbation to the treaty and shoulder its obligations.

Then too, as always, the king needed money. By 13 May he had already received over £38,000 in loans brought in by judicious pressure on both individuals and towns. Of this sum Bishop Beaufort contributed almost forty-five per cent, £17,666, and thus bought a remission of the king's wrath over his injudicious acceptance of a cardinal's hat without royal permission. Despite these sums new money was needed in the exchequer so that at least a start could be made on repayment. The king got a grant of a tenth from the clergy and a fifteenth from the laity which, although they would come in slowly, would provide a useful margin with which to meet the ever-rising costs. The financial documents of Henry's reign, though incomplete and excessively difficult to interpret, illustrate clearly the very narrow financial base from which Henry operated. Costs were high, and the enormous expenditures for the king's campaigns required every possible manoeuvre. Ransoms helped, as did other windfall profits of war, but by Henry's death the exchequer had a deficit of some £30,000 for the years 1416–22, as well as expenses left over from the Agincourt campaign and debts of over £25,000.[24] Henry had the prestige and the force to be able to carry this fragile structure and maintain his credit. His death struck it a toppling blow.

The king did not restrict himself to the French war and his finances in this last parliament over which he would preside. Preoccupied as he was with other matters, he insisted on calling together the Black Monks to insist on their reforming monastic practice.[25] He also ordered during this parliament that every third benefice which pertained to monasteries or prelates should be presented to a clerk of Oxford or Cambridge. Here the king was attempting to redress a balance, for the Statute of Provisors, in barring provision to English benefices by the pope, had also cut off an avenue by which educated clerics were usually included among such provisions. Benefices to such recipients helped to finance the cost of studies and encouraged the flow of educated and able men into the service of the church.

The spring parliament did not dally about its business. Walsingham cheerfully remarks that it was "happily concluded within a month".[26] Apart from the usual affairs of state the king also had certain diplomatic moves in mind. At the end of May a treaty of alliance was made with Genoa, in which the English promised not to give aid to the Aragonese and the Catalonians while, more importantly, the Genoese promised not to aid the dauphin. There was to be a mutual right of free entry for trade.[27] Also, the current diplomatic situation encouraged further negotiations concerning some of the king's most valuable prisoners. King James of Scotland, who had been a prisoner at the English court since 1405, provided a useful bargaining-counter with the Scots, who at Melun and Baugé had been providing active support to the dauphin. The Earl of Douglas came to the May parliament with full power to treat. A two-year truce was achieved and a settlement arrived at by which the Earl of Douglas promised 200 Scottish knights and 200 mounted archers to serve in Henry's forces in France. In exchange, within three months from Henry's return from this expedition, James would be restored to Scotland, though to maintain a certain English influence he was to give hostages for his loyalty and marry Joan Beaufort, the niece of the Bishop of Winchester. The bishop was considered to be the principal advocate of both the marriage and the freeing of James.[28] In any case, Henry's death delayed the carrying out of the agreement and it was 1424 before James again set foot in his northern kingdom.

In Rouen during March, after the king had crossed to England, an agreement was finally made with the Duke of Bourbon, one of the most important of the prisoners of Agincourt. The matter had been in train for a long time. Second only in rank to Charles of Orléans, the Duke of Bourbon had been unable to adjust to his captivity in England. His efforts to obtain his freedom went as far back as 1416, though nothing had come of them at that time. The French prisoners had remained valuable pawns in Henry's continual diplomatic negotiations and Bourbon was the most willing to make major concessions as he was the most anxious to regain his freedom at whatever cost in money and prestige. After the Treaty of Troyes had been signed Bourbon was brought over to Normandy and in March 1421 the conditions for his release were agreed upon at Rouen castle. Undoubtedly they were drawn up along the lines determined by King Henry before he returned to England, and they displayed an abject acceptance of the English proposals. Bourbon promised to accept and keep the Treaty of Troyes, to hand over the county of Clermont to King Charles (in other words, to Henry's rule), and to pay a ransom of 100,000 gold crowns – 60,000 by 8 August, at which time he could be released. In addition, he was to leave his younger son and ten other notables as hostages, and six major castles as surety for the payment of the rest of the ransom.[29] On this pledge he was temporarily released. The details are admirably clear, but the arrangement came to nothing, although the duke spent some time in France trying to fulfil its terms. He could not raise the ransom or provide the hostages and, soon after Henry's death, he was returned to England a sick and broken man, to die in captivity.

A surprising visitor to England just before Henry's departure illustrates once again how strongly personal relationships influenced, and some times dictated, matters of policy. Jacqueline of Hainault ran away from her husband, John of Brabant, and came to England to seek asylum. Her arrival not only caused immediate problems, it opened a dangerous rift between King Henry and the Duke of Burgundy. Jacqueline was attractive, gay and unconventional but her importance lay in her position as heir of the Count of Holland and ruler in her own right of Holland, Hainault, Friesland and Zeeland. The Duke of Burgundy, who was her overlord, saw a useful buttress to his own possessions in the Netherlands in arranging her marriage to her cousin John of Brabant. John was not an attractive husband for a vivacious and self-willed woman and, more gallingly, was complaisantly willing to surrender his wife's ancestral rights. Jacqueline determined to break away. She vainly petitioned for a dissolution of her marriage and when this failed she determined to seek asylum in England, hoping to gain Henry's assistance in dissolving her marriage. In March 1421 she left

Valenciennes and waited in Calais for permission to enter England. Permission finally came, and Jacqueline landed in Dover near the end of May to be greeted by the Duke of Gloucester and other English lords. The runaway wife further complicated matters by falling in love with the gay and attractive Duke Humphrey. King Henry treated her most generously. He paid the expenses of her journey and of her stay at Calais, and allowed her an annuity in London.[30] It is difficult to discover the reasoning behind Henry's actions, since such generosity to a recalcitrant vassal was bound to inflame the temper of the Duke of Burgundy, and a good relationship with the duke was still basic to his success in France. It seems totally unlikely that the coldly calculating Henry would have countenanced Humphrey's marriage to Jacqueline, which was forced through after his death, but it is difficult to see what he hoped to gain by his modified espousal of her cause. In reality it cost him heavily, by rousing at a most unfortunate time all the suspicions of the Duke of Burgundy about English aims in the Netherlands. The whole affair, with its unfortunate consequences, seems somehow out of character for the astute, controlled and methodical monarch, but the king, as always, kept his own counsel and any judgment of his motives and aims is purely conjectural.

By the beginning of June Henry had achieved the purposes which had brought him to England, and the military situation in France, disturbed by the defeat of Baugé, once more demanded his presence in France. On 10 June, fortified by new supplies of money and a further contingent of troops, he sailed from Dover to Calais on his last voyage.

CHAPTER XIV

The Last Campaign

When Henry and Catherine had returned to England at the end of January the king had left the Duke of Clarence in charge in Normandy. It undoubtedly suited both Clarence's restless and warlike temperament and Henry's desire for continued pressure against the dauphin for the duke to decide on an aggressive testing of the borders of Maine and Anjou. In March, when the weather was again more suitable for campaigning in the open country, Clarence set off on his expedition. The duke and his army moved southwestward to Alençon, skirted Le Mans, and crossed the Loir, a tributary of the Sarthe. Passing through Baugé they came to the outskirts of Angers, but that city, protected by its magnificent castle built by Blanche of Castile in the thirteenth century as a frontier bastion of French power, closed its gates against them. Clarence did not have the force to attempt a siege of such a formidable stronghold, and withdrew to the castle of Beaufort, some fifteen miles east.

Meanwhile a French army of 4,000 to 5,000 men, including a sizeable contingent of Scottish allies, had gathered at Tours. They had begun a march towards La Flèche, but, hearing of the English forces at Beaufort, turned aside to Baugé, where they arrived on Good Friday 21 March. On Saturday both armies got news of each other's positions as their respective scouts and foragers met and took the occasional prisoner. When some of the French captives were brought to Clarence, the duke, whose intelligence system had not been well informed, learned for the first time of the nearness of the French. Clarence was by nature impulsive, and he had always regretted that his illness at Harfleur had driven him home to England and deprived him of the glory of having fought at Agincourt. He saw in this encounter with a larger French army a chance to heighten his own prestige, perhaps he even dreamt of another Agincourt. However, his generalship was not as careful as that of his brother. Without pausing to collect his dispersed troops or the archers, he insisted on setting off at once for battle, accompanied by a force of only 1,000–1,500. Beaufort was some ten miles southwest of Baugé, and to reach the French army the English had to fight their way through a boggy valley and across a small stream where the French, warned of the English approach, were already protecting the bridge. Even when they had succeeded in crossing the stream, the terrain still favoured the French and Clarence had to try to reorganise his men on a slope leading up to the ridge on which Viel Baugé was situated. The French and Scottish descended on them from above, and in the resulting mêlée Clarence, Umfraville, and several other nobles were killed. The earls of Huntingdon and Somerset, as well as a number of less important men, were captured before the conflict was ended by the lateness of the hour.

When the Earl of Salisbury and Clarence's bastard son rode up, having paused to marshal the archers and the remaining troops, Clarence's body had already been bundled into a cart to be taken in triumph to the dauphin. The bastard managed to retrieve his father's body, and sent it back to the duchess at Rouen. Salisbury took over command of the disheartened army and skilfully led the retreat into the safety of Normandy, though his task was made easier by the unwillingness, or inability, of the French forces to follow up their initial success.

The battle of Baugé was a serious blow to the myth of English invincibility, remarkably powerful in France after Henry's incredible success at Agincourt and his well-planned and executed series of sieges in Normandy. Baugé made it obvious that the English were not invincible – a dangerous piece of knowledge when a small army was attempting to retain control of a wide territory. Popular opinion in England blamed Clarence for his mismanagement of the battle, and especially for his neglect of the archers. They argued that the battle was lost

... by cause they wolde nott take with hem archers, but thought to have doo with the ffrenshmen them selff wythoute hem. And yet whan he was slayne the archers come and rescued the body of the Duke, which they wold have carried with hem.

Despite the criticism the popular epitaph was a just one: "God have mercy a pon his soule, he was a valyant man."[1] The Duke of Clarence's body was returned to England in April and buried in Canterbury Cathedral near that of his father.

The news of the defeat, and of his brother's death, had reached Henry in the north of England. Although the king quickly realised the serious blow it inflicted on his position in France, he did not deviate from his already carefully planned programme. His feelings of loss at Clarence's death were probably embittered by the damage which Clarence's impetuous attack had done to the English cause. There seems to have been no real sympathy between the two older brothers – it is interesting to note that only Clarence, of all the brothers, was not mentioned in Henry's will of 1415 – and during their early years there had been undisguised rivalry between them. Nevertheless, Henry respected his brother as a brave soldier and a vigorous captain whose death deprived the English army of a notable leader.

While the king was busy in London with parliament and with his further preparations for his return to France, the dauphin, encouraged by the success at Baugé, besieged Alençon. Salisbury, firmly in charge of the English forces in Normandy, marched immediately to its relief. The dauphin raised the siege without attempting battle, and Salisbury took his force on an expedition through Maine and Anjou, as far south as Angers, endeavouring to bolster the English prestige which the defeat had undermined. In a letter to the king Salisbury assured him of the ease with which many of the French strongholds could be assaulted, for the earl was convinced that most of them would not be able to stand against him. He also announced proudly that "we broughten Hom the fareste and gretteste Prey of Bestes", professed himself well rested, and ready to follow whatever orders the king might have.*[2]

Henry had returned to France at the beginning of June, but had chosen to cross to Calais and march down through Picardy rather than to return directly to Normandy. There seem to have been two reasons for this: the king had great confidence in Salisbury's ability to maintain the English position in Normandy, and Henry was also anxious, as he put it in a letter to the mayor and aldermen of London, to set Picardy in better governance.[3] The reality behind the noncommittal phrase was the king's desire to counter the vigorous activity of Jacques d'Harcourt, Count of Tancarville, who, although a Burgundian follower, had refused to accept the Treaty of Troyes and was busy attacking English outposts. However, new word of the dauphin's advance in force on Chartres brought the king hastily south. He reached Paris by way of Gisors on 4 July, anxious to reassure himself that the Duke of Exeter was in full control. He had reason for concern as the sudden resurgence of the dauphin after the disaster of Baugé had encouraged wavering even in Paris among those less committed to the English cause. As well, there was much public displeasure at this time over the English arrest of de l'Isle-Adam. The king remained in the capital only a few days, although he found time to go to Notre Dame and make the customary offering. By 8 July he was off again to Mantes, to rally his men to fight the dauphin. The Duke of Burgundy also came to Mantes, intending to go from there to the support of Chartres, and Henry reassured the Londoners (and perhaps himself) that he found him "a trusty, loving, and faithful brother to us in all things".[4] As the threat to Chartres weakened,

---

* The disorderly state of Normandy is illustrated by Salisbury's statement that he had previously sent his pursuivant to the king but that he had been informed that the man had been killed by brigands on his return journey. The earl was not sure whether the luckless official had been carrying word from the king, so informed Henry in case he had further instructions.

Henry turned instead to the siege of Dreux, held by the dauphin's men and of vital strategic importance, situated as it was on the frontier between Normandy and the Île-de-France. Dreux surrendered early in August and, as the rumour again circulated that the dauphin was willing to do battle, Henry set out once more towards Chartres.*

The dauphin was not anxious to risk battle with the English army and once more slipped away to his strongholds on the Loire. Henry marched down through the Beauce country, accepting the surrender of Bonneval and of the town of Beaugency. He could not cross the river for Beaugency's bridge over the Loire was held securely against him, so the king and his army turned to march east along the right bank. At Orléans, a strong dauphinist centre, they encamped before the town for three days, but the city was so strongly guarded and he and his men were so short of provisions that he was obliged to withdraw without attempting to lay a siege. The chroniclers emphasise the real scarcity of provisions for the army in this expedition, and comment that both men and horses perished from hunger. Nevertheless, despite the inconclusive nature of his raid, for Henry had not succeeded in tempting the dauphin to battle, the king had demonstrated the feasibility of English campaigns as far south as the Loire. From Orléans, the king turned north to Villeneuve-le-Roi, a few miles south of Sens on the Yonne river, since that town had been intercepting goods being sent by river from Dijon to Paris. After a siege of only a few days it surrendered to him at the end of September.

True to the pattern which he had consistently followed from the beginning of his second expedition to France Henry decided to disregard the usual winter break in campaigning and devote his energies to reducing one of the most recalcitrant of the dauphinist outposts in the north. His immediate target was the town of Meaux, some twenty-five miles northeast of Paris on the Marne river and the most important Armagnac stronghold near Paris. The garrison there, led by the brutal Bastard of Vaurus, had tyrannised the surrounding countryside and served as a continuing threat to the safety of Paris itself. The siege of Meaux required all Henry's military skills and ingenuity. The town was ideally located strategically in a great bend of the river Marne. The old ramparts, which still exist in part, are further delineated by a modern boulevard which clearly illustrates the small size of the fifteenth-century town. Its central core rises from the river to the cathedral of St Stephen, which crowns a slight hill near the walls. Across the river – now placidly bordered by lines of poplars and formal public gardens – lay the fortified suburb known as the Market. The Market, which still serves its original function, was established during the

---

* Although Henry never fought at Chartres, he did take advantage of his proximity to the famous cathedral and shrine to make a pilgrimage. He had already demonstrated his generosity to the cathedral, having in 1420 presented it with a portable altar, which was probably the work of a Burgundian craftsman.[5]

Norse invasions of the tenth century and served as a secure last resort for
defence, since it was protected on three sides by the river and on the fourth
by a canal. As well as the defences already provided by nature the Market
had been reinforced with strong walls and deep ditches.

The siege of Meaux was marked by Henry's most intensive employment
of artillery, and some of the guns used there still survive.[6] The constant
sieges in which Henry had been involved since 1400, from his early efforts
against the Welsh castles to the series of struggles in France, had encouraged the king to search out any possible technical improvements.
When Henry ascended the throne his inheritance of artillery seems to have
consisted chiefly of cannon which had broken during the attacks on the
great Welsh castles and Henry quickly ordered new guns for his projected
expedition to France. The accounts mention such types as bombards,
veuglaires, ribaudequins,* culverins, and serpentines – names which were
usually, though not always, indicative of size but which were rarely
applied with technical precision. Most of these early-fifteenth century
guns were heavy-barrelled and small calibred, and made of iron bars
assembled and then soldered together. They were further strengthened by
being bound with iron rings, in order to lessen the ever-present danger of
the barrel exploding from too heavy a charge of gunpowder, or some
unknown impurity in the iron.

The early gunners had difficulty estimating the amount of gunpowder
needed for a charge though a practical rule of thumb had gradually been
evolved. The skilled gunner of this time used one pound of powder to
nine pounds of stone, and only loaded the chamber to three-fifths of its
capacity. The fifth immediately beyond the charge was left as an air-space,
and the remaining fifth for the wad. Loading these guns was a tedious
operation since many of the first cannon were filled from the mouth,
rather than having an accessible firing-chamber, and the barrel had to be
cleaned after every shot. Because no convenient gun-carriage had yet been
devised the gunners found it hard to keep up with an army on the march
for their cannon had to be dragged in rude carts and then transferred to
some makeshift firing frame. It was also impossible to get the barrels of
the early cannon absolutely smooth and straight so their inevitable defects
slowed the velocity of the shot, lowered the range and made real accuracy
impossible. All these natural crudities of technology in a developing field
made the fifteenth-century cannon less useful in pitched battles but did
not affect their value in sieges where the target was stationary and the whole
approach leisurely. The English attackers found their cannon a tremendous
aid for the very persistence of their battering and the ability of the heavy

---

* The term "ribaudequin" was applied to a certain size of gun and also to a
kind of cart, armed with several small guns shooting heavy bolts. It had a protective
screen for the gunners and was drawn first by men, and later by horses. It bristled
with fixed spears and later was further protected by scythes attached to the axles.

gunstones to break down walls and houses. The descriptive phrases of the chroniclers show how effective the noise, the fire, and the general dislocation caused by the guns were in harassing and terrifying the defenders.[7]

The siege of Meaux was set at the beginning of October and dragged on for seven months. Conditions were made more uncomfortable by lack of food and bad weather, for it was more than usually cold and rainy. The bourgeois of Paris wrote in his journal that the snow and rain in December were so heavy that the Seine overflowed its banks and flooded much of Paris. The ensuing misery was increased by a heavy frost which held Paris ice-bound for a time and also stopped the water-mills that ground the greater part of the city's corn.[8] During the winter months Henry remained with his army, seconded by Exeter, Warwick, and the Earl of March. The attackers kept Christmas and Epiphany entrenched before Meaux where their gloomy discomfort was only lightened by the news of the birth of the king's son and heir at Windsor on 6 December. The news reached Paris on 22 December and the bells of the city pealed, the citizens dutifully joined processions to thank God for the news, and lit great bonfires in celebration.

At the beginning of March a bold attempt was made to bring reinforcements to the Armagnacs within the town. One night Guy de Nesle, Lord of Offemont, at the head of a small company, picked his way secretly through the English host and was almost at the city walls when the plank by which Offemont was crossing the ditch broke, and he tumbled in. Dressed in full armour he was so heavy that his companions found it almost impossible to pull him out, and the noise they made in the attempt roused the sleeping English who easily captured most of the party. The besieged lost heart at this mischance and decided to abandon the town itself and cross over to the more easily defensible Market, taking with them the town's food and riches. The poor people and the less warlike who were thus abandoned had no stomach to continue the resistance and quickly surrendered. King Henry made his official entrance into the town on 9 March, but two further months of struggle were to ensue before the determined defenders of the Market were willing to capitulate. Henry took every possible advantage of his strategic position. The walls and houses of the Market were heavily bombarded by his cannon, which he had succeeded in placing on a little island in the river. The English captured the water-mills on the bridge, seriously hindering the grinding of corn for the besieged. Just before the final surrender Henry had been experimenting with the design of a strong high tower which was to be floated down stream and grappled to the walls to provide the attackers with a further point of attack. Always concerned with widening the range of military techniques, Henry made the experiment, even though the Market had surrendered. St-Rémy, who commented from the professional point of view of a herald, approved the king's operations saying "it was a pretty thing to see its siege".[9]

But for the soldiers who laboured in the mud and the damp and the cold it was a long and desperate struggle, and the armies in both camps suffered from fevers and dysentery. It was probably at Meaux that the king himself contracted the dysentery which was to end his life that summer. Tempers had run short, too, as the besieged relieved the tension with ingenious insults against their attackers. A Burgundian chronicler tells of an ass being led onto the walls and beaten until it brayed, while the mocking defenders shouted at the English that their King Henry was calling and they ought to come and help him.[10] One Orace, a cornet-player who particularly mocked the English force, so infuriated the king that he was specifically named in the terms of surrender and was promptly beheaded. When the Market of Meaux finally capitulated at the beginning of May 1422, the terms for its surrender were generally harsh. Any former subjects of the English king were reserved to his judgment. Beside the unfortunate Orace, the Bastard of Vaurus, a captain of the garrison, and several others were handed over to Henry for judgment. No tears were shed over the fate of the Bastard of Vaurus for he had a cruel and tyrannical reputation among the common people. King Henry had him beheaded and his body hung from the tree where he had been accustomed to hang his numerous victims, with his head at the foot of his standard – a medieval symbol of the utmost shame. The remaining defenders were treated as prisoners and the most important of them were sent to England to be redeemed by high ransoms. The group included the Bishop of Meaux among some 150 others, and careful provisions were made for their guard and transportation. The booty, including victuals, armaments, gold, silver, jewels, and books were all to be gathered together in specific places in the Market for the king's final decision about their disposition.[11]

The fall of Meaux encouraged the capitulation of many of the surrounding strongpoints and Henry felt free to return to Paris to rest from his labours and to greet Queen Catherine, who had returned from England after the birth of their child. On Saturday 30 May, the eve of Pentecost, King Henry and Queen Catherine came from Vincennes to Paris to the palace of the Louvre to celebrate the feast. The author of the *English Life* describes the splendour of their state as they sat crowned at table in the open hall, and he emphasises the richness and abundance of the dishes and the drinks. The contrast with the poverty-stricken surroundings of the French king and queen at the Hôtel St-Pol was accentuated by the flocking of the Parisians to the court of the English king. On 2 and 3 June the whole glittering retinue crossed to the Hôtel de Nesle (on the Left Bank where the Institut de France now stands) to see a play of the life of St George. The complete cycle of this mystery was put on by some of the inhabitants of Paris who hoped to flatter King Henry by this representation of his favourite saint.[12]

Pleasant as these festivities must have been, Henry could pause for only a brief interlude. In these last few months of his life the king was more then ever driven by the urgency and immensity of the task which still lay ahead of him, and he forced himself to struggle on against his growing weakness. Following the entertainment, Henry held a council at the Hôtel de Nesle with both English and French lords in attendance. Bedford had accompanied the queen from England, leaving the Duke of Gloucester as guardian of the realm. The king had already learned of the proceedings of the December parliament, which had granted him a fifteenth but allowed the first half to be paid in light-weight old coins. England was beginning to grumble over the weight of the war and the constant drain of men and supplies to France. The brewers, for example, complained before the mayor of London in 1422 of the high price of malt. They argued that their present customers did not pay well and that the absence of the lords and so many of the people to whom they normally sold made it difficult for them to make a living.[13]

Diplomatic activity also continued unabated, as it was necessary for the king to bend every effort to achieving the acceptance of the Treaty of Troyes throughout those parts of France where his armies did not operate. The difficulties he faced are well illustrated by a sheaf of communications with the Count of Foix during the first half of 1422. The Count of Foix, whose lands in the central Pyrénées adjoined the English lands in Gascony, exemplified the common habit of the Gascon nobles to play both sides of any controversy. His younger brother, the Captal de Buch, vigorously supported the English and even fought for Henry, while the count himself supported the dauphin. In the negotiations to gain the count's agreement to the Treaty of Troyes, King Henry was pushed into providing the funds for the force which the count promised to raise in order to fight the dauphin and persuade the people of Languedoc and Bigorre to swear the oath to the treaty. The money was duly paid in April to the count's ambassadors in England, but at the end of July the count was still writing from his court at Orthez, insisting on modifications of the treaty to his own advantage and putting off for another year any expedition in the field.[14] Negotiations with the Duke of Brittany, who had also been delaying his adherence to the treaty, had succeeded in moving the duke to send his senior officials to swear the oath. However, by the time they finally arrived Henry was so ill that they could not carry out their mission, and the oath was finally taken by the duke himself some time after Henry's death.

At the same time the king was endeavouring to keep the emperor informed and enthusiastic about his plans, for Henry continued to hope that Sigismund would send him the troops he felt were implied in their original alliance. Sir Hartonk von Clux, the knight who was continually used as a go-between by the two monarchs, wrote to King Henry at the end of April. He informed him of Sigismund's complete absorption in the Hussite uprising in Bohemia, the kingdom which he had inherited after the death of his brother. Von Clux reported regretfully that the troubles there would require all the emperor's forces and that he could not be counted on for help in France.[15]

The situation, even in the north of France, was by no means settled. The dauphin's forces, although dislodged from Meaux and its immediate surroundings, were active in many places near Paris. During the siege of Meaux, for example, they had taken for a brief period the town of Meulan, a vital supply link on the Seine just west of Paris. It had been recovered in ten days but its loss illustrated the tenuous nature of King Henry's hold. In Picardy, Amiens and Abbeville were troubled and wanted help but Henry warned them that, although he was willing to send forces to aid them, he must be assured of sufficient provisions at reasonable prices. The famine his men had suffered at Meaux was a constant concern. Compiègne had been besieged by the Burgundians and Henry turned north to see if his help was needed there. The town had already surrendered and Henry was at Senlis when Burgundian messengers notified him that the Armagnac forces were besieging Cosne-sur-Loire. The town was running short of supplies and needed assistance. Cosne, on the right bank of the Loire some fifteen miles upstream from Orléans, lay on the direct route to Dijon, the capital of Burgundy, and its safety was obviously of crucial importance to Duke Philip. Henry, although already seriously ill, heeded the call and set out with his army. At Corbeil it became obvious that the king himself could go no further. He ordered his troops, under the Duke of Bedford and the Earl of Warwick, to join the Duke of Burgundy and counter the dauphin's threat while he remained for a time at Corbeil, hoping to regain his strength.

Prayers and processions for the king's health had been publicly instituted in Paris as early as 8 July. The weather had been excessively hot in both June and July, and Fauquembergue remarks that it had brought on an epidemic of smallpox. The bourgeois of Paris, commenting on the unusual weather, bewailed the crops which were burnt in the fields, and claimed that the smallpox was particularly prevalent among the English, and that King Henry had caught it as well.[16] Despite these statements from local Parisians there is fairly general agreement among the king's biographers and the contemporary chroniclers that Henry suffered from fever and acute dysentery, a most wasting disease for one whose constitution does not appear to have been particularly strong. Although there were other more dramatic suggestions such as St Anthony's fire, i.e. erysipelas, and even one rumour of leprosy, most of the French chroniclers agree with the diagnosis of dysentery. Some of them go further and call the king's illness the "sickness of St-Fiacre", a raging dysentery complicated by various intestinal growths. They claim that the royal malady was caused by Henry's plan to move the relics of St-Fiacre from his oratory near Meaux to England. St-Fiacre was one of the peripatetic Celtic saints of the seventh century who emigrated to Gaul and set up a hermitage a few miles east of Meaux, where a village grew up named after its holy but difficult patron. Highly esteemed in the Middle Ages, St-Fiacre would seem to have been as irascible as St-Jerome and was reputed to heap misfortunes on anyone who profaned his sanctuary. The pious pundits naturally regarded as an obvious sign of divine retribution the fact that St-Fiacre's feast day was celebrated in Brie on 30 August, and King Henry died just after midnight on 21 August.*

In any case, the stay at Corbeil did not improve King Henry, for after rallying briefly he again grew worse. He decided to return to Vincennes where the castle, set in its surrounding forest, was reputed to be "one of the most agreeable residences of the king of France".[18] The king was taken by barge from Corbeil to Charenton where he made one final effort to ride the short distance to Vincennes, but his weakness was too great and he had to be carried to the castle where he arrived on 13 August, almost at the end of his strength. The royal apartments at Vincennes were in the massive donjon tower which had been built by Charles V. The great hall was on the first floor, connected by a wide spiral staircase to the king's chamber on the floor above. Each of these two main rooms had four small chambers opening off them, space made by the use of the small flanking towers which protected each angle of the keep and which provided some privacy. The royal chamber itself was a handsome room with a decorated chimney and a high, vaulted ceiling rising from a central pillar. Here Henry spent his last days, surrounded by his brother Bedford, his uncle Exeter, and his closest companions. It is interesting to note that, although the Duke of Burgundy never appeared in person, he did send Sir Hugh de Lannoy, the elder brother of Ghillebert and, like him, one of Duke Philip's trusted officers, to the dying king.†[19] Queen Catherine did not come to

---

* St-Fiacre was a noted patron of the sick and his intercession was especially sought by those suffering from haemorrhoids. On a more cheerful note, he became the patron saint of gardeners because of the magnificent vegetables he was reputed to have grown around his hermitage on the land which he had ploughed by merely tracing the furrows with his staff. A delightful story in the *Scotichronicon* makes St-Fiacre into the son of an early Scottish king and underlines Henry's supposed fear of the malevolence of the Scots. When the king was informed on the night of his death of the nature of his illness and that it may have been due to St-Fiacre's rage at the king's insults to the relics, the patriotic Scots chronicler has the English king exclaim: "Everywhere I have put my foot, living or dead, I find some Scotsman opposing me."[17]

† Chastellain, the Burgundian chronicler who has a rather full account of Henry's deathbed counsels, may well have gained his information from this knight who was like himself, a respected member of the duke's household.

Vincennes – she remained in Paris with her mother and father – and she had no place in any of Henry's last words, nor apparently of his thoughts.

These last weeks of the king's life, as reported by his biographers and the chroniclers, were marked by a rigid adherence to the pattern considered suitable for medieval kings. Nevertheless, Henry's own nature suggests that his conventional acceptance of the customs of his time mirrored his own deepest concerns and beliefs. His thoughts were first of his duties towards his kingdoms – England, and the France he had nearly conquered but never really grasped. By his dispositions he hoped to provide safety and continuity for his nine-month-old heir during the long period of his minority. He appointed Gloucester as regent of England, while his uncles, Exeter and Bishop Beaufort, aided by the Earl of Warwick, were to have the personal rule of his young son. In regard to France, he warned Bedford not to give up Normandy but to offer the government of France to the Duke of Burgundy first. Only if Duke Philip refused the office was Bedford to act as regent. He warned Bedford, too, not to argue with the duke, and especially not to let the impetuous Duke Humphrey do so. Looking worriedly into the future Henry saw very clearly how any division between the English and Burgundy would cause all the advantages they had won to turn against them. In the interests of his infant son, he ordered them not to release the most important French prisoners who could bolster the French strength. Such leaders as Orléans, the Count of Eu, and Gaucourt were to be held in England until the little king was of age to rule competently, although the other prisoners could be let go. Henry gave Lannoy a special message for the Duke of Burgundy. He recommended his son and the kingdom of France to the duke as the one who "most in the world could bring advancement or grief".[20]

Once these specific appointments had been made, he begged pardon for any injustices he might have done, thanked his soldiers for their valour, and exhorted them to continue until peace could be achieved. Solemnly he claimed that he had not been led by ambition or worldly desires, but only by his wish to obtain both peace and his own rights. In a moment of uncharacteristic self-doubt, he added that he had been assured by holy men that he could and should take these actions without danger to his soul. Finally he gave a long speech to the lords in attendance on the sober political realities which lay ahead, informing them "with marvellous prudence of the just and right ways which they should follow and the political regimen they should observe".[21] From affairs of state the king turned to his own dispositions, showing the lords who attended him his will, with its codicils which provided for the payment of his father's still remaining debts as well as his own. It allowed too for suitable sums for his faithful servants. During his last illness Henry repented his treatment of his stepmother and urged her immediate restoration to her freedom and dignities.[22]

Once these things had been done and his final advice given, the king demanded from his physicians how much time remained to him. They attempted to evade the question, but finally admitted that death was inevitable in some two hours. The moment had come for concern with his own soul. The king received the last sacraments and joined in saying the penitential psalms with his confessor and the accompanying chaplains. At this solemn moment his dream of the crusade – a long-held dream and not merely a pious thought in his final hours – rose again to his mind. When the psalm *Miserere* spoke of rebuilding the walls of Jerusalem, the dying king broke in on the prayer to sum up his own unfulfilled hopes:

> O good Lord, thou knowest that if thie pleasure had been to have suffered me to live my natural age my firme purpose and intent was, after I had established this Realme of France in sure peace, to have gon and visited Iherusalem, to have reedified the walls thereof, and to have expulsed from it the Miscreants thine adversaries.[23]

At one moment during those last hours a cry broke from him: "You lie, you lie, my portion is with the Lord Jesus Christ," as if, says the biographer reporting it, he was addressed boldly by an evil spirit. At the last, between two and three in the morning of 31 August, the thirty-five-year-old King Henry slipped away clutching the crucifix and with a final prayer of acceptance: "In thy hands, O Lord, thou hast redeemed my end," while those around him "would rather have thought that he fell asleep than died".[24]

The shock and sorrow which marked his passing were echoed in the respectful eulogies of the chroniclers, but the requirements of royal protocol determined the activities of the next few weeks. In his will, Henry had specified that he was to be buried at Westminster and the body had to be prepared for the long trip home.* While these preparations were being made, the Duke of Burgundy came to Vincennes and Bedford, in accordance with Henry's last wishes, offered him the government of the realm of France. Duke Philip weighed the case and then refused so that Bedford took the title as of regent.[26] It would appear that the Duke of Burgundy saw more scope for his ambition in remaining a free agent, not officially bound to the day-to-day upholding of the Treaty of Troyes. The fragile unity between English and Burgundian interests, which was the essential prop of the English position in France, had already begun to disintegrate.

---

* There is some disagreement about the preparing of the king's body for burial. The greater number of the accounts state that the king's entrails were buried in the church of St-Maur-des-Fossées near Vincennes, and the body boiled, according to medieval practice, to separate the flesh from the bones so that the remains could withstand the long trip home. The "Pseudo-Elmham", which is particularly full on Henry's death, states that the king was so wasted by his illness that there was no need to remove the entrails, and that the body was merely embalmed, wrapped, and put in a leaden coffin.[25]

On 14 September the king's funeral cortège began its long, pageant-encrusted trip to Westminster. The king's coffin was laid in a chariot drawn by four great horses, and above the coffin a bed held a figure of boiled leather made in his likeness, complete even to hair. This effigy of the living king was wrapped in a state mantle of purple bordered with ermine, its feet shod in royal sandals. It wore a diadem of gold and precious stones and carried in its right hand a sceptre, in its left the golden cross and ball. The awe-inspiring figure was so elevated that, as the procession passed by, it was visible to all. The first stop for the cortège was at St-Denis, where the first of an incredible number of masses were said. From there it moved by slow stages to Rouen, Abbeville, Hesdin and Calais on the journey home to England. The pomp and ceremony were extreme. Whenever the procession passed through a town, the important citizens carried a rich canopy to shelter the chariot. The accompanying priests sang masses at each stopping-place, while men clothed in white and carrying burning torches surrounded the bier. The household servants, gowned in black, followed behind the corpse and behind them came the great lords, including the King of Scotland. Queen Catherine travelled a mile or two behind the elaborate procession.[27]

As the magnificent cortège took its solemn way across the plains of northern France, where Henry had won his most famous victory, Frenchmen gazed at its passing. They regarded the final disappearance of that intrepid soldier with mixed feelings. Monstrelet tells the delightful story of Sir Sarrasin d'Arly, an elderly Picard knight, who was laid up with the gout but still interested in all the news. His pursuivant returned from Abbeville with an account of his view of King Henry's funeral procession. The knight immediately asked if the king had his boots on. When the pursuivant answered no, the knight – unable to believe that Henry was really leaving France never to return – cried out in disbelief: "Never believe me if he has not left them in France."[28]

In England the loss of the king, of whom they had seen so little but who had achieved so many successes, evoked more genuine feeling. But even in London mourning was not left to the hazards of genuine feeling. All the panoply which the resources of royalty could command was lavished on these final ceremonies. An interesting extract from the book of the brewers' guild shows how far-reaching and precise the instructions were. Every householder of every craft was to wear a black or russet gown with a black hood, and to be present at the burial. Each craft was to find its share of the torches for the procession, though the chamberlain paid for the white gowns the torchbearers were to wear. For one last time the mayor, aldermen and citizens went out to meet their king at Blackheath and to follow him in procession across London Bridge and through the streets of the city to St Paul's. Every householder on the route of the procession, from London Bridge to Temple Bar, was ordered to have a servant at his door holding a burning torch to light the procession on its way. After the sung masses in St Paul's on Friday 6 November the lords were given the opportunity to eat their dinner and then, in the short November afternoon, the procession with all the lords and the officers and people of London made their way to Westminster Abbey. Finally on Saturday 7 November, after a funeral procession which had lasted for almost two months, the last requiem was sung at Westminster and the king buried with great solemnity. The offerings included not only the customary cloths of gold, but four magnificently caparisoned horses, one of which was ridden by a fully armed knight, clad in the king's coat armour and crowned.[29]

While Henry's body was making its slow way home to Westminster, Charles VI died in Paris on 21 October. His funeral, though staged with the expected elaborate pageantry, was a sad affair. Not one French prince rode as a mourner in the procession: the king's servants, the dignitaries and people of Paris were followed only by the Duke of Bedford. On his return from the burial at St-Denis the duke had the sword of the king of France carried before him in token of his position as regent. The bourgeois of Paris who records the scene suggests the unhappy days to come: "The people murmured very much, but had to endure it for the time being."[30]

Henry V had been balked of his ambition to wear the crowns of both England and France by less than two months. His son was to be the only English king ever to wear those two crowns – and to lose them both.

Epilogue

The life and character of Henry V were soon transformed into the stuff of legend, and the colourful elaborations of the sixteenth-century historians were made unforgettable by Shakespeare's imperishable genius. This accidental combination of factors makes it extraordinarily difficult to go back to the truly historical Henry, to understand and appreciate the real nature of the man and the accomplishments of his reign in the terms of the century in which he lived. This already awkward problem is further complicated by the existence of a number of contemporary ballads and verse eulogies, inspired by the lustre of his victories, and especially by that of Agincourt. The *Agincourt Carol*[1] is probably the best known, as well as the most poetic. Even its opening verse:

> Our King went forth to Normandy
> With grace and might of chivalry;
> Ther God for him wrought mervelusly;
> Wherfore England may call and cry
> > *Deo gracias, Anglia,*
> > *Redde pro victoria*

suggests the extraordinary English pride in their king's achievements, and the conviction they shared with him that God was on their side. The estimates of his more sober contemporaries are perhaps the most reliable witness to Henry's reputation. It is revealing that the French chroniclers, even Juvenal des Ursins, the most prejudiced supporter of the dauphin, speak well of him. They all underline his unflinching justice, without respect for the social status of the evil-doers, or his previous friendship with them. They laud his courage, his wisdom and his success in conquest, though the French point out, reasonably enough, that his task was made much easier by the fortunate chance of French divisions. The monk of St-Denis, the official chronicler of the French monarchy, provides the most balanced and temperate of the French estimates:

No prince of his time appeared more capable than he to subdue and conquer a country, by the wisdom of his government, by his prudence and by the other qualities with which he was endowed, although the dissensions and discords which reigned among the French princes had powerfully assisted him in realising his projects of conquest.[2]

Others spoke with more passion. Alain Chartier, the clerk from Bayeux who became a canon of Paris and served as secretary for the dauphin Charles for some years, wrote bitterly in his *Quadrilogus Invectif* of the sad state of the kingdom in 1422. His allegorical figure of France accused the knights, the clergy and the people – despite their energetic attempts to put the blame on someone else – of all being responsible for the desperate state in which the country found itself. His gloomy conclusion was that "the hand of God was on us and that his anger had put in train this flail of persecution".[3] Henry never went so far as to compare himself to a flail, but one of the attitudes which made him so effective in his campaigns was his singleminded conviction that he was God's chosen instrument to punish the sinful French.

Naturally the English were more enthusiastic in their praises of their masterful king. Although they too emphasised Henry's courage and impartial justice, his wisdom and his conquests, they frequently expressed a genuine sense of loss which was founded on their fear for the stability of the social order – fears which proved only too prophetic. The chronicler John Hardyng perhaps puts it as well as any when in his rough verse he berates God for having taken away so suddenly "this noble prince, peerlesse of Regyment", who had ensured peace and law in England even when he was busiest in France.[4] It is indicative of the medieval outlook of the early fifteenth century that both French and English writers emphasise Henry's justice. Justice was the prime virtue of a medieval king, for the solid base of all government was the strength and even-handedness of his personal royal rule.

Henry inspired awed respect, even among his closest advisers, and he was mourned in his public image as king. Indeed, his headlong career of conquest and consolidation gave him little time to practise the graces of living or to devote much energy to other matters than those of state. King Henry was an intensely private and complex man who intelligently manipulated the formal image of the medieval monarch to suit his own well-defined aims. He certainly gave the impression of sublime self-confidence. His ambitions had always been high: no thought of any cloud upon his title to the English throne or of any possible defect in his claims to France ever seem to have crossed his mind. Only on his deathbed did he feel the need to reassure himself of the righteousness of his demands and remind himself of the support they had been given by his spiritual advisers. Although it is hard to disentangle his carefully assumed negotiating position from his real convictions, the evidence for his emotional belief in his right to the possession of Normandy is overwhelming. The reasons for that blind faith do not emerge, but it is impossible to deny the strength of the king's conviction.

The king was intelligently conscious of the value of planned propaganda and was always particularly careful to create a favourable climate of opinion for his actions. Besides his well-planned use of diplomatic documents to convince the princes of Europe of the legitimacy of his claims, he employed all the ceremonial and pomp which surrounded a medieval monarch to influence both great and small in his own realm. Such formalities served to reinforce his strategic decisions and overawe any questioners. Henry felt the king held a quasi-religious position. He would not tolerate any opposition, or even the breath of criticism, because he saw such disagreement as undermining the orthodoxy of the realm which should be of one mind with its king. No one, not even his rich and powerful uncle Bishop Beaufort, who had loyally bolstered the throne during his reign and that of his father, could run counter to his will without calling down immediate and severe punishment.

Henry's plans for his tomb and chantry chapel, which were specified in his will and carefully carried out after his death, suggest the pre-eminent position he felt he should occupy among the kings of England. The spot he chose for his chapel dwarfed the shrine of Edward the Confessor, and its height made it an eye-compelling focus for any congregation in the nave. Although Henry stated that this was so the people would follow with greater devotion the masses celebrated in the chapel for his soul, the nagging conviction remains that the king was also anxious to ensure his continuing glorification, not only in the people's prayers, but in their recognition of his deeds. Westminster has continued to remember its royal benefactor. Each year on the feasts of Saints Crispin and Crispinian, the anniversary of Agincourt, the morning communion service is held in his tiny chantry chapel, although the procession no longer carries the sword Henry was reputed to have used in the battle. Soon after the king's death his executors saw to the setting up of his tomb, but it appears to have been Queen Catherine who arranged for the effigy on it. The figure was made with a wooden core, the body covered with plates of silver-gilt, and the head, hands and royal regalia made of solid silver.* The tomb was complete by 1431, but the elaborate chantry chapel was not even started until 1438 and must have taken at least ten years to complete.[5]

* The valuable silver was soon stolen – some of the plates had been removed as early as 1467, and the whole head had disappeared by 1546. In October 1971 Westminster commemorated Agincourt day by unveiling a new head and hands for the mutilated effigy. The artist's work in bronze is based on the familiar portrait of the king, and on the verbal description of his appearance given in the contemporary *Versus Rythmici*.

Before it was even begun Queen Catherine herself had died, and was brought to Westminster for burial. After his marriage King Henry had never amplified his instructions for his burial to provide a place for his wife, and the mother of his heir. Catherine was buried in the old Lady Chapel, and her handsome funeral effigy can still be seen in the Abbey museum, but her corpse was displaced during the reign of Henry VII, when a new foundation had to be laid for that king's magnificent new chapel. The antiquarian Stow writing in his survey of London almost a century later, remarked that she had never been reburied, but rested in a coffin of boards behind the east end of the presbytery.[6] The treatment of her remains was extraordinarily casual, for in 1669 Pepys could write, with ill-concealed pride, that he had handled the body of Queen Catherine and kissed her lips – a rather macabre way of celebrating his birthday. It is the more startling that Henry VII paid so little attention to a decent burial for Catherine since she was his grandmother. When Catherine disappeared from court soon after the king's death she was a gay and irresponsible young woman of twenty-one. She had little serious influence on her son, and none on the conduct of English affairs. She was, in fact, seldom heard of, though that indefatigable traveller, Ghillebert de Lannoy, recorded a visit to her at Pleshy in 1431, on his return from a trip through England and a pilgrimage to St Patrick's Purgatory in Ireland.[7] The astute Lannoy makes no mention of Queen Catherine's domestic arrangements which were indeed unusual for a dowager queen. Within a few years after Henry's death the queen had been conquered by the charms of the young and attractive Owen Tudor, a Welsh clerk in her household, and had three sons and a daughter by him. It is a sign of the absorption of the factions at court in their deadly rivalry that so little attention was ever paid to this extraordinary mésalliance. It seems to have been blessed by some form of ecclesiastical ceremony, but it could never have been condoned by the secular authorities.

Our judgment of the victor of Agincourt is inevitably influenced by the years of trouble and strife, both internal and external, which followed his death. Henry himself cannot be blamed for all of these, nor expected to foresee that he would be cut off at the age of thirty-five, leaving an infant as heir. His hope of unifying the kingdoms of France and England under his own strong government, and then turning their mutual energies against the Turks rather than against each other, seems to have been a genuine and carefully pursued ideal. His dream of subduing all of France seems chimerical to us, and full of menace for England, since we look at the scheme from the experience of a France that has been a strongly unitary state for several centuries. But in Henry's day France was not a unified state and gave little promise of soon reaching that situation. Nationalism, in our sense of the word, was beginning to develop, but it was stronger among the common people, whose interests were rooted in their own soil, than

among the great. Joan of Arc was, in a sense, part of the wave of the future.
The ideas of power current among the kings and great nobles during the
fifteenth century continued to be based on old feudal principles and useful
marriage alliances. Kingdoms were still the private property of kings – and
the king was answerable only to God, not to his subjects. Their only
sanction was to rise in violence against him when misgovernment became
shockingly bad.

The efforts of the House of Burgundy to establish its own state during
this century show how close France came to splitting into a loose grouping
of local princedoms. If this tendency had been successful, Henry could
most reasonably have hoped to dominate France north of the Loire, from
Paris west. This was the part of the country in which he was most interested. The English foothold in Gascony would have been sufficient to give it
the leadership in the shifting alliances of the southern lords, and would
have given him some security against a unified opposition there. In such
a climate Henry's dream of occupying the thrones of both England and
France, and the careful efforts to trace his heredity, as well as that of his
young son, back to Saint Louis, takes on a different aspect. We tend to
regard such moves as hypocritical attempts to provide the colour of a legal
title to a conquest won only by the sword, and see them as part of a mis-
leading and impossible fantasy. But, at that time, it was not impossible of
conception and perhaps – given a few more years of health and strength –
not impossible of achievement to a man who looked at the situation from
the preconceptions of the fifteenth, not the twentieth, century. Henry had
none of the more attractive virtues – he had little charm, although a real
concern for his soldiers; no sense of humour, and a truly terrifying conviction of his own position as the instrument of God. But, in the light of
his own day, he was an outstandingly efficient, able, and above all just king.
He provided strength and good government for England during his short
reign and achieved a position in France never equalled by any other English
king. No wonder the shock of his sudden death elicited the desolate cry:

"King Henry died, once the glory, now the grief of the world!"[8]

The Narrative Sources

Those interested in the life of Henry V may wish a guiding thread through the maze of contemporary lives, chronicles, and eulogies of the warlike king. There is, of course, a great deal available even before the end of the fifteenth century, since Henry's activities in France meant that he was of passionate interest to the French as well as the English chroniclers. Some works are devoted exclusively to Henry's life and achievements. Of these the most immediate and the most informative is the *Gesta Henrici Quinti* (ed. B. Williams, English Historical Society, 1850) which is without question the best contemporary narrative. It covers the first three-and-a-half years of Henry's reign and was completed before July 1417. Its most recent editors argue cogently that it was specifically designed as propaganda to encourage English enthusiasm for their king's second campaign of 1417, and as reinforcement for the English delegation at the Council of Constance.[1] It was certainly written by a cleric, a yet unidentified chaplain of the king's household, who was present during many of the events he describes, and who provides an eye-witness account of Agincourt. Two Latin lives cover the king's whole reign. The *Vita Henrici Quinti* (edited by Thomas Hearne in 1716) was written by an Italian, Titus Livius of Forli, a humanist and classical scholar in the household of Duke Humphrey of Gloucester. Commissioned by his patron to write the official life of Henry in 1437–8, Livius took much of his material from the English chroniclers known as the *Brut*, but also benefited from further information given him by Duke Humphrey, whose share in his brother's campaigns he tactfully inflates. This Latin work was translated into English at the beginning of the sixteenth century (*First English Life of Henry V*, ed by C. L. Kingsford, Oxford, 1911). The unknown translator added to his main source some material derived from Monstrelet and some stories – many of them exaggerated – which he had learned from the earls of Ormonde. The second Latin life of Henry, the *Vita et Gesta Henrici Quinti Anglorum Regis* (also edited by Thomas Hearne, 1727, and ascribed by him to Thomas of Elmham) is a somewhat later compilation of 1447–48. It is now known that Thomas of Elmham, the Cluniac prior of Henry's reign, was not its author, though the true author is still unknown. Nevertheless, Hearne's attribution has made it the usual practice to refer to this work as the "Pseudo-Elmham". It is a useful source for the last three years of Henry's reign for which it provides material not mentioned elsewhere. Written in a verbose classical style, its dates are generally more accurate than those of Titus Livius.

There are two outstanding chronicle sources in England – those emanating from St Albans and from London. Thomas Walsingham, monk of St Albans, wrote his chronicle of England for more than forty years. He was a conscientious and contemporary compiler, particularly interested in the Lollards and other clerical matters, and his accurate, if somewhat dull, work is basic to any discussion of the period. Although his chronicles have been edited in various recensions and under different titles, the essential matter appears in either the *Historia Anglicana* (ed. H. T. Riley, Rolls Series, 1863–64) or the *St Albans Chronicle, 1406–20* (ed. V. H. Galbraith, Oxford, 1937). The chronicles of London, originally in Latin and then later in English, are many and varied and their relationships are a matter for specialists. The most famous of all the vernacular chronicles is the *Brut* (ed. by F. W. Brie for the Early English Text Society, 1908), which with its various additions was later published by Caxton. It is rich in stories of the time and in matter particularly relating to London.

On the French side, the abbey of St-Denis was the centre for some centuries of the official chronicle of the French monarchy. The material dealing with Henry IV and V is included in the text known as the *Chronique d'un religieux de St-Denis* (ed. by L. Bellaguet in the Collection de Documents Inédits, 1852–54). The monk of St-Denis provides a generally judicious and full account of events in France, and Henry's activities as they related to France. Juvenal des Ursins, who was also contemporary with the period he described, wrote a prejudiced *Histoire de Charles VI*, from the most extreme Orléanist position (2nd ed. by Denis Godeffroy, Paris, 1653). The most interesting of the French accounts were written by Burgundian supporters, working more or less consciously in the pattern of Froissart. The best known is Enguerrand de Monstrelet, who was born near Agincourt and gives a very full account of the battle. Although he did not fight there, his account was written within twenty-five years. Because of his dislike for the Armagnacs he often favours the English, especially during the reign of Henry V (*The Chronicles*, trans. by Thomas Johnes, London, 1809). Two other Burgundian chroniclers, Jean Waurin (*Recueil des croniques*, ed. William Hardy, Rolls Series, 1864) and Le Fèvre de St-Rémy (*Chronique*, ed. by Francois Morand, Société pour l'histoire de France, Paris, 1876) were both actually present at Agincourt. Waurin, born in Flanders, fought on the French side, St-Rémy was an officer-at-arms in the English army. Both are very full on the battle, and though their chronicles appeared later than that of Monstrelet and borrowed considerably from him, they also provided considerable independent material. Georges Chastellain was born in the year of Agincourt and his chronicle, especially favourable to Duke Philip of Burgundy, covers the years 1419–75 (*Oeuvres*, ed. Kervyn de Lettenhove, Brussels 1883–84). He was official chronicler of the court of Burgundy and a councillor of the duke, a position he shared with Le Fèvre de St-Rémy, who had become King-of-Arms of the Golden Fleece, the Burgundian order of chivalry.

As well as the full-scale contemporary lives and the works of the major chroniclers there are also a number of miscellaneous works dealing particularly with Henry, or with some aspect of his reign. Thomas of Elmham, the Cluniac prior, wrote a eulogistic and rather impressionistic biography of the king in Latin verse known as the *Liber Metricus*. Much of the material in this is also be to found – and more accurately – in the *Gesta*, but there are interesting variations. Another, even more blatantly flattering poem, is that known as the *Versus Rythmici* (both this and the *Liber Metricus* are printed in the *Memorials of Henry the Fifth*, ed. by C. A. Cole, Rolls Series, 1858), which was written by a monk of Westminster Abbey who seems to have been intimately connected with the royal chapel. John Page, an otherwise unknown English soldier, wrote a rough but vivid poem on the siege of Rouen, where he himself served (included in J. Gairdner's *Historical Collections of a Citizen of London*, Camden Society, 1876). There are several other partial and rather personal chronicles which cast light on certain aspects of Henry's reign. The *Chronicle* of John Strecche (ed. by F. Taylor in the *Bulletin* of the John Rylands Library, vol. 16, 1932) is full of gossip and lively stories which Strecche, as a canon of Kenilworth, was able to collect because of his occasional proximity to the royal household. John Hardyng (the first version of whose chronicle is printed by C. L. Kingsford in the *English Historical Review*, vol. 27, 1912) was a member of Percy's household until Shrewsbury and then served with Umfraville and fought at Agincourt. Both Lancastrian and Yorkist versions of his chronicle exist, but he is often of considerable interest for matters which touched northern interests. Another local man, who spoke vigorously for local interests, was Adam of Usk, the Welsh ecclesiastical lawyer whose *Chronicon* (ed. by E. M. Thompson, London, 1904) is particularly vivid on Welsh affairs. Adam was attached to Archbishop Arundel in 1399, but he was out of England between 1400 and 1408, having had to flee the country for his theft of a horse and its harness. He returned to Wales in time to report on the gradual disintegration of Glendower's campaign and continued his chronicle to 1421, when almost his last sentences dealt with the dissatisfaction in England over the continued taxation for Henry's war in France.

Although not strictly one of the sources, Sir Harris Nicolas' *History of the Battle of Agincourt* (2nd ed., 1832, facsimile reprint, 1970) is a most generous compilation of all the material pertaining to the whole of Henry's first expedition. Besides a translation of the relevant chronicles it includes indentures, diplomatic documents, lists of members of the expedition, and various other pertinent items. It is a mine of useful material, conveniently gathered in one place.

Abbreviations Used in Notes

Anglo-Norman Letters: *Anglo-Norman Letters and Petitions*, ed. M. D. Legge (Anglo-Norman Texts, III), Oxford, 1941.

Brut: *The Brut or the Chronicles of England*, ed. F. W. D. Brie (Early English Text Society, Original Series 136), II, London, 1908.

CCR: *Calendar of Close Rolls*, Public Record Office Publications.

CPR: *Calendar of Patent Rolls*, Public Record Office Publications.

Chambers and Daunt: R. W. Chambers and M. Daunt, *A Book of London English 1384–1425*, Oxford, 1931.

Chastellain: G. Chastellain, *Oeuvres*, ed. Kervyn de Lettenhove (Académie Royale de Belgique) I, Brussels, 1883.

De Reg. Princ.: Thomas Hoccleve, *De Regimine Principum*, ed. T. Wright, Roxburghe Club, London, 1860.

EHR: *English Historical Review*.

Ellis: *Original Letters*, ed. H. Ellis. 1st, 2nd, and 3rd series, London, 1824–46.

Emden: A. B. Emden, *A Biographical Register of Members of the University of Oxford from A.D. 1176 to 1500*. 3 vols, Oxford, 1957–59.

English Life: *The First English Life of Henry V*, ed. C. L. Kingsford, Oxford, 1911.

Froissart: *The Chronicles of England, France, and Spain*, trans. T. Johnes, adapted H. P. Dunster, London, 1906.

Gesta: *Gesta Henrici Quinti*, ed. B. Williams (English Historical Society), London, 1850.

Hardyng: "The First Version of Hardyng's Chronicle", ed. C. L. Kingsford, *EHR* 27 (L912).

Historia Anglicana: Thomas Walsingham, *Historia Anglicana*, ed. H. T. Riley (Rolls Series), II, London, 1864.

Issues: *Issues of the Exchequer from King Henry III to King Henry VI inclusive*, extracted and trans. Frederick Devon, Record Commission Publication, London, 1837.

Juvenal des Ursins: Jean Juvenal des Ursins, *Histoire de Charles VI roy de France*, 2nd ed. Denis Godefroy, Paris, 1653.

King's Works: *The History of the King's Works*, ed. H. M. Colvin. Vols I and II: *The Middle Ages*, London, 1963.

Lannoy: Ghillebert de Lannoy, *Oeuvres*, ed. Charles Potvin, Louvain, 1878.

Liber Metricus: *Elmhami liber metricus de Henrico quinto*, in *Memorials of Henry the Fifth, king of England*, ed. C. A. Cole (Rolls Series), London, 1858.

Monstrelet: Enguerrand de Monstrelet, *The Chronicles*, trans. T. Johnes, I and II, London, 1809.

Page: John Page, "Siege of Rouen", in *The Historical Collections of a Citizen of London in the Fifteenth Century*, ed. J. Gairdner (Camden Society, New Series 17), London, 1876.

Parisian Journal: *A Parisian Journal 1405–1449*, trans. from the anon. *Journal d'un bourgeois de Paris* by J. Shirley, Oxford, 1968.

Privy Council: *Proceedings and Ordinances of the Privy Council of England*, ed. H. Nicolas, I and II, Record Commission Publication, London, 1834.

Pseudo-Elmham: *Thoma de Elmham Vita et Gesta Henrici Quinti Anglorum Regis*, ed. T. Hearne, London, 1727.

Rot. Parl.: *Rotuli Parliamentorum; ut et petitiones et placita in parliamento*, III and IV, Record Commission Publication, London, 1832.

Rymer: *Foedera, conventiones, litterae, etc.*, ed. T. Rymer, 3rd ed., revised G. Holmes, IV, 1740 (reprint ed., New York, 1967).

St Albans: *The St Albans Chronicle, 1406–20*, ed. V. H. Galbraith, Oxford, 1937.

St-Denis: *Chronique d'un religieux de St-Denys*, ed. L. Bellaguet (Collection des Documents Inédits), V and VI, Paris, 1852–54.

St-Rémy: *Chronique de Jean Le Fèvre, seigneur de Saint-Rémy*, ed. F. Morand (Société de l'Histoire de France), 2 vols, Paris, 1876–81.

Strecche: "The Chronicle of John Strecche for the Reign of Henry V (1414–22)", *Bulletin of the John Rylands Library* 16 (1932).

Titus Livius: Titus Livius of Forli, *Vita Henrici Quinti*, ed. T. Hearne, London, 1716.

Usk: *Chronicon Adae de Usk*, ed. with trans. and notes by E. M. Thompson, 2nd ed., London, 1904.

Versus Rythmici: *Versus Rythmici in laudem regis Henrici quinti*, in *Memorials of Henry the Fifth, king of England*, ed. C. A. Cole (Rolls Series), London, 1858.

Waurin: *Recueil des croniques et anciennes istories de la Grant Bretaigne par Jehan de Waurin*, ed. W. Hardy (Rolls Series), II, London, 1868.

Notes

INTRODUCTION

1   Monstrelet I, 1.
2   R. Vaughan, *John the Fearless* (London, 1966), 205. E. Perroy, *The Hundred Years War* (London, 1965), intro. D. C. Douglas, xviii. C. L. Kingsford, *Henry V* (New York, 1903), 402. E. F. Jacob, *Henry V and the Invasion of France* (London, 1947), 188.

CHAPTER I   COUSIN TO THE KING

1   J. H. Wylie, *History of England under Henry the Fourth* (reprint ed. New York, 1969), III, 327; IV, 170.
2   *Versus Rythmici*, 64.
3   A. R. Myers ed., *English Historical Documents, 1327–1485* (London, 1969), 1157–58. *Issues*, 368.
4   *Issues*, 407.
5   K. B. McFarlane, *Lancastrian Kings and Lollard Knights* (Oxford, 1972), 116–17; appendix C, 233–38. *Issues*, 372.
6   A. Thomas, *Jean de Gerson et l'éducation des dauphins de France* (Paris, 1930), 48–51.
7   *English Life*, 17.
8   "A French Metrical History of the Deposition of King Richard the Second", ed. and trans. by J. Webb, *Archaelogia* 20 (1824), 299.
9   *Brut*, 545.
10 The most recent work on the life and reign of Henry IV is J. L. Kirby, *Henry IV of England* (London, 1970). The life by J. H. Wylie is a mine of often incoherent facts.

CHAPTER II   PRINCE OF WALES

1   *CCR 1399–1402*, 320–21; *CCR 1402–5*, 222.
2   J. E. Lloyd, *Owen Glendower* (Oxford, 1931), 26–7.
3   *Anglo-Norman Letters*, 373–74.
4   *CPR 1399–1401*, 451.
5   Usk, 224–25.
6   Kirby, *Henry IV*, 117. *Statutes of the Realm*, 2 Henry IV (1401), cc. 12, 16–20.

7   Usk, 226.
8   *Anglo–Norman Letters*, 292.
9   *Ibid.*, 301–2, 299–300.
10 Usk, 237.
11 *Anglo–Norman Letters*, 312–13.
12 *Ibid.*, 290, 296.
13 *Privy Conncil* I, 177–78.
14 *Historia Anglicana*, 253.
15 *Ibid.*, 250–51.
16 *Privy Council* II, 61–3; I, 199–200.
17 Titus Livius, 3.
18 Ellis, 2nd ser., I, 35–7.
19 *Ibid.*, 14, 31–4.
20 Rymer IV, i, 65.
21 *Privy Council* I, 229–35.
22 Rymer IV, i, 79. *Privy Council* I, 248–50.
23 Usk, 282–83.
24 *Historia Anglicana*, 271–72.
25 R. Griffiths, "Some Secret Supporters of Owain Glyn Dŵr?", *Bulletin of the Institute of Historical Research* 37 (1964), 77–85.
26 *Rot. Parl.* III, 569. Kirby, *Henry IV*, 197.
27 *CPR 1405–8*, 362.
28 *Ibid.*, 361–62.
29 Emden III, 1928–29.
30 Usk, 313. Lloyd, *Glendower*, 144–45. *CPR 1417–22*, 335.

CHAPTER III   APPRENTICESHIP TO POWER

1   *Privy Council* I, 295.
2   *King's Works* II, 930–37.
3   *CCR 1405–9*, 250. *CPR 1405–8*, 284.
4   Emden I, 51–3. Kirby, *Henry IV*, 208–25 and "The Council of 1407 and the Problem of Calais", *History Today* 5 (1955), 44–52.
5   *Privy Council* I, 319–20.
6   *St Albans*, 52–5.
7   *Ibid.*, 51–2.
8   Emden I, 500–2. "The Old University Library at Oxford", *Times Literary Supplement* (1973), 400.
9   *Snappe's Formulary and Other Records*, ed. H. E. Salter (Oxford Historical Society 80, 1924), 101–14; 156–75. *Munimenta Academica*, ed. H. Anstey (Rolls Series, 1868), I, 251–52.
10 *Brut*, 372.
11 *Privy Council* II, 34–5.
12 C. E. Mallet, *A History of the University of Oxford* (New York, 1924), I, 273–74.
13 *English Life*, 11–13.
14 *De Reg. Princ.*, 17–18, 37.
15 *Ibid.*, 191.
16 *Brut*, 494. Pseudo-Elmham, 12–13. *English Life*, 17.
17 R. L. Storey, "Liveries and Commissions of the Peace 1388–90", *The Reign of Richard II : Essays in Honour of May McKisack*, ed. F. R. H. Du Boulay and C. M. Barron (London, 1971), 135.
18 Monstrelet I, 451–52.

19 John Capgrave, *The Chronicle of England*, ed. F. C. Hingeston (Rolls Series, London, 1858), 303.
20 *English Life*, 13–16.

CHAPTER IV   CROWNED KING: REBELLION AND HERESY

1 *Versus Rythmici*, 65–6. Titus Livius, 4. Pseudo-Elmham, 12.
2 Roy Strong, *Tudor and Jacobean Portraits* (London, 1969), I, 144–45.
3 *English Life*, 17. *St Albans*, 69.
4 Titus Livius, 5.
5 *Issues*, 329.
6 *Rot. Parl.* IV, 3–14.
7 Rymer IV, i, 31. *Privy Council* II, 125–35.
8 *Issues*, 321.
9 *Brut*, 494–95. C. L. Kingsford, *English Historical Literature in the Fifteenth Century* (Oxford, 1913), 292. *St Albans*, 77. *Issues*, 327–28.
10 *CCR 1413–19*, 86.
11 The most convenient summary of the whole background of the Lollard movement and of the Oldcastle rising is K. B. McFarlane, *Wycliffe and the Beginnings of English Non-Conformity* (London, 1952). There are full accounts in *St Albans*, 70–9, and *Gesta*, 3–7.
12 *Issues*, 333.
13 *Ibid.*, 330.
14 *CCR 1413–19*, 109–10.
15 Rymer IV, ii, 92.
16 *Gesta*, 11–13. *St Albans*, 87–8. *Liber Metricus*, 105–6.
17 *St Albans*, 88.
18 *Ibid.*, 89.
19 M. E. Aston, "Lollardy and Sedition, 1381–1431", *Past and Present* 17 (1960), 21.
20 *Liber Metricus*, 156. Kingsford, *English Historical Literature*, 294.
21 *St Albans*, 116.

CHAPTER V   PREPARATIONS FOR WAR: DIPLOMATIC MANOEUVRES

1 Froissart, 517.
2 P. S. Lewis, *Later Medieval France; the Polity* (London, 1968), xi–xii.
3 Rymer IV, i, 106–9.
4 *Liber Metricus*, 153–54.
5 Juvenal des Ursins, 289.
6 *Twenty-six Political and Other Poems*, ed. J. Kail (Early English Text Society 124, 1904), 59.
7 St-Rémy I, 261.
8 *Issues*, 331.
9 *King's Works* II, 685; I, 245. *Liber Metricus*, 100–1.
10 Strecche, 147.
11 *Rot. Parl.* IV, 15–26.
12 M. M. Morgan, "The Suppression of the Alien Priories", *History* 26 (1941), 204–12.
13 Vaughan, *John the Fearless*, 205–8.
14 *St Albans*, 81–2.
15 Strecche, 150–51.
16 *Rot. Parl.* IV, 34.
17 *Privy Council* II, 150–51, 142.

18 Lannoy, 471.
19 *De Reg. Princ.*, 193.
20 *Choix de pièces inédites relatives au règne de Charles VI*, ed. Douet d'Arcq (Société de l'Histoire de France, Paris, 1863), I, 59 (trans. in Lewis, *Later Medieval France*, 92).
21 A. Coville, *Gontier et Pierre Col et l'humanisme en France au temps de Charles VI* (Paris, 1934), 51–2.
22 St-Rémy I, 211–12.
23 J. Le Laboureur, *Histoire de Charles VI roy de France* (Paris, 1663), II, 993–95. (Trans. H. Nicolas, *The History of the Battle of Agincourt*, 2nd ed., London, 1832, appendix, 1–4.)
24 G. Besse, *Recueil de diverses pièces servant à l'histoire de Charles VI* (Paris, 1660), 94–111.
25 Rymer IV, ii, 111.
26 Archives Nationales, J646/14.
27 *Gesta*, 1.
28 Le Laboureur, *Charles VI*, II, 1001.
29 Le Laboureur, *Charles VI*, II, 1000. Juvenal des Ursins, 291. (Both trans. Nicolas, *Battle of Agincourt*, appendix, 5–7.)

CHAPTER VI   PREPARATIONS FOR WAR: MILITARY ORGANISATION

1   H. A. Dillon, "On a MS Collection of Ordinances of Chivalry of the fifteenth century", *Archaeologia* 57 (1900), 30–1.
2   Christine de Pisan, *Book of Fayttes of Armes and of Chyvalrye*, ed. A. T. P. Byles (Early English Text Society 189, London, 1932). S. Solente, "Un traité inédit de Christine de Pisan", *Bibliothèque de l'école des Chartes* 85 (1924), 264.
3   Conrad Kyeser of Eichstatt, *Bellifortis* (Dusseldorf, 1967), v. I, facsimile; v. II, transcription, translation and notes by Gotz Quarg.
4   M. H. Keen, *The Laws of War in the Late Middle Ages* (London, 1965) provides the essential background on this subject.
5   *Black Book of the Admiralty*, ed. T. Twiss (Rolls Series, London, 1871), I, 459–72. *English Life*, 44.
6   K. B. McFarlane, "A Business Partnership in War and Administration, 1421–45", *EHR* 78 (1963), 290.
7   Honoré de Bonet, *The Tree of Battles*, trans. and intro. by G. W. Coopland. Liverpool, 1949.
8   G. Chaucer, House of Fame (*Complete Works*, ed. F. N. Robinson, Boston, 1933), ll. 1320–23.
9   *Le Débat des Hérauts d'Armes de France et d'Angleterre*, ed. J. Pannier and P. Meyer (Société des Anciens Textes Français, Paris, 1877), 19.
10 Lannoy, 52–62. *Privy Council* II, 192.
11 Dillon, "Ordinances", 70.
12 Anthony Wagner, *Heralds of England* (London, 1967), 40–3.
13 *Ibid.*, 40, 48–9, 58–62.
14 R. B. Pugh, "Some Mediaeval Moneylenders", *Speculum* 43 (1968), 288.
15 *Privy Council* II, 165–66.
16 *CPR 1416–22*, 47–8; *CPR 1413–16*, 350.
17 *Privy Council* II, 155–58.
18 Nicolas, *Battle of Agincourt*, 373–89.
19 Froissart, 346.
20 *CCR 1413–19*, 214, 218, 223.

21 *Issues*, 338–39.
22 C. F. Richmond, "The War at Sea", *The Hundred Years War*, ed. K. Fowler (London, 1971), 121, n. 62. *Issues*, 356. Chambers and Daunt, 297.
23 *CCR 1413–19*, 162.
24 Chambers and Daunt, 295–96.
25 Froissart, 492.
26 *King's Works* I, 423–30. J. L. Kirby, "The Financing of Calais under Henry V", *Bulletin of the Institute of Historical Research* 23 (1950), 165–77.
27 *St Albans*, 57.

CHAPTER VII   FIRST EXPEDITION TO FRANCE

1 *English Life*, 30–2. Le Laboureur, *Charles VI* II, 1000.
2 St-Rémy I, 224. *Gesta*, 13.
3 *Gesta*, 13–15.
4 L. Mirot and E. Deprez, "Les Ambassades Anglaises pendant la guerre du Cent Ans", *Bibliothèque de l'école des Chartes* 61 (1900), 26–7.
5 *English Life*, 36.
6 St-Denis V, 537.
7 J. Delpit, *Collection générale des documents français qui se trouvent en Angleterre* (Paris, 1847), 217.
8 Juvenal des Ursins, 292.
9 *Calendar of the French Rolls* (Annual Report of the Deputy Keeper of the Public Records, 1884), 576.
10 Rymer IV, ii, 147.
11 *English Life*, 42.
12 Most of the narrative material for the march to Calais and the battle of Agincourt is collected in Nicolas, *Battle of Agincourt*. Christopher Hibbert, *Agincourt* (London, 1964) and A. H. Burne, *The Agincourt War* (London, 1956) provide modern summaries and discuss the military details.
13 *Parisian Journal*, 94.
14 St-Denis V, 555.
15 St-Rémy I, 247.
16 *English Life*, 56–7.
17 *Brut*, 378.
18 Le Laboureur, *Charles VI* II, 1008.
19 *Brut*, 596, 378.
20 *English Life*, 60.
21 St-Rémy I, 256.
22 *English Life*, 57–8.
23 Lannoy, 49–50. Le Laboureur, *Charles VI* II, 1010.
24 St-Rémy I, 260. Monstrelet II, 89.
25 St-Rémy I, 261. *Brut*, 596.
26 Solente, "Un traité inédit", 268–75.
27 *Rot. Parl.* IV, 62–4.
28 *Issues*, 342.
29 *Liber Metricus*, 125–29. *Gesta*, 61 ff.

CHAPTER VIII   THE KING, THE ENGLISH CHURCH, AND THE COUNCIL OF CONSTANCE

1 *Historia Anglicana*, 344. *Versus Rythmici*, 70.
2 R. M. Haines, "'Wild Wittes and Wilfulness': John Swetstock's Attack on

those 'Poyswun mongeres', the Lollards'', *Studies in Church History* 8 (1971), 146.

3 G. R. Owst, *Literature and Pulpit in Medieval England*, 2nd ed. (Oxford, 1966), 72, 74–5.

4 *The Book of Margery Kempe*, a modern version by W. Butler-Bowdon. London, 1936.

5 Rymer IV, ii, 138–39. *Versus Rythmici*, 71–2. *CPR 1413–16*, 146.

6 *St Albans*, 82–3. *Calendar of Charter Rolls 1341–1417*, 469–70, 479–80. M. D. Knowles, *The Religious Orders in England* (Cambridge, 1955), II, 181.

7 *Documents illustrating the activities of the General and Provincial Chapters of the English Black Monks, 1215–1540*, ed. W. A. Pantin (Camden Third Series 47, 1933), II, 98–134. Knowles, *Religious Orders* II, 182–84.

8 *CPR 1413–16*, 142. Emden III, 1435–36.

9 Ellis, 1st ser. I, 3–5.

10 Emden II, 1343–44.

11 *English Life*, 130–32. *St Albans*, 118–19.

12 Chastellain, 554.

13 Lannoy, 67, 161–62.

14 *St Albans*, 70, 100. C. L. Kingsford, "A Legend of Sigismund's Visit to England", *EHR* 26 (1911), 751.

15 *Issues*, 361–62. F. L. Harrison, *Music in Medieval Britain* (London, 1958), 20–22. M. Bent, "Sources of the Old Hall Music", *Proceedings, The Royal Music Association* 94 (1967–68), 33–5.

16 Rymer IV, ii, 138–39.

17 E. F. Jacob, *Essays in the Conciliar Epoch* (Manchester, 2nd ed., 1953), 82–4.

18 *The Council of Constance*, trans. L. R. Loomis, ed. and annotated by J. H. Mundy and K. M. Woods (Columbia Records of Civilization 63, New York, 1961), 159.

19 Hardt, *Magnum Oecumenicum Constantiense Concilium* I, 499. (trans. in L. R. Loomis, "Nationality at the Council of Constance: an Anglo-French dispute", *Change in Medieval Society*, ed. S. L. Thrupp, New York, 1964, 293).

20 C. M. D. Crowder, "Henry V, Sigismund, and the Council of Constance", *Historical Studies* IV (Fifth Irish Conference of Historians, London, 1963), 93–110.

21 Rymer IV, iii, 163.

22 Rymer IV, iii, 136–7.

23 K. B. McFarlane, "Bishop Beaufort and the Red Hat", *EHR* 60 (1945), 316–48.

24 E. F. Jacob, *Essays in Later Medieval History* (Manchester, 1968), 65–6.

25 J. Ferguson, *English Diplomacy 1422–1461* (Oxford, 1972), 150–51.

26 Rymer IV, iii, 88–9.

CHAPTER IX   ONCE MORE TO FRANCE

1 *Privy Council* II, 184–85.

2 *Ibid.*, 196–97.

3 *Gesta*, 74.

4 *Privy Council* II, 350–58.

5 Monstrelet II, 105.

6 *Privy Council* II, 193–94. *English Life*, 67.

7 *Brut*, 558–59. *The Historical Collections of a Citizen of London in the Fifteenth Century* (Camden Society, New Series 17, 1876), ed. J. Gairdner, 113–14. *CPR 1416–22*, 11.

8 *English Life*, 70.
9 *Gesta*, 88.
10 Rymer IV, ii, 171–72.
11 *Gesta*, 89.
12 *Issues*, 347, 348.
13 Monstrelet II, 119–20.
14 Rymer IV, ii, 177–78. Vaughan, *John the Fearless*, 214–15.
15 *Gesta*, 103–4.
16 Waurin, 237.
17 *Gesta*, 105.
18 *Council of Constance*, 149–50. C. L. Kingsford, "An Historical Collection of the Fifteenth Century", *EHR* 29 (1914), 512.
19 *Rot. Parl.* IV, 94–9.
20 *Gesta*, 105–7.
21 Rymer IV, ii, 190–91.
22 Kingsford, "Historical Collection", 512.
23 *CCR 1413–19*, 397.
24 C. F. Richmond, "The Keeping of the Seas during the Hundred Years War: 1422–40", *History* 49 (1964), 283–98. Ellis, 3rd ser., I, 72–4.
25 Charles de La Roncière, *Histoire de la Marine Française*, 2nd ed. (Paris, 1909), I, 256.
26 *Brut*, 382.

CHAPTER X   THE CONQUEST OF LOWER NORMANDY

1 Monstrelet II, 143.
2 *St Albans*, 110.
3 *Parisian Journal*, 107.
4 *Brut*, 385.
5 Kingsford, *English Historical Literature*, 304.
6 L. Puiseux, *Siège et prise de Caen par les Anglais en 1417* (Caen, 1858) is a local historian's painstaking study of the episode, and also includes some useful documents.
7 *Historia Anglicana*, 322–23. *St Albans*, 111–12. Kingsford, "Historical Collection", 512.
8 Froissart, 41.
9 Keen, *Laws of War*, 119–33.
10 *St Albans*, 112–13.
11 Chambers and Daunt, 67–8.
12 Puiseux, *Siège et prise*, Pièces justificatives, ii, 85–9.
13 *St Albans*, 113. *English Life*, 92.
14 *CCR 1413–19*, 438–39.
15 L. Puiseux, *Caen en 1421* (Caen, 1860), 5–14. *Calendar of Norman Rolls* I (41st Report of the Deputy Keeper of the Public Records, 1880), 691.
16 *English Life*, 102.
17 *Calendar of Norman Rolls* I, 692.
18 Chambers and Daunt, 68–70.

CHAPTER XI   THE CAPTURE OF ROUEN

1 Chambers and Daunt, 71. Strecche, 163.
2 *English Life*, 119–21. Monstrelet II, 202–4. Strecche, 164–65.
3 Chambers and Daunt, 71–2.

4 *Ibid.*, 74.
5 L. Puiseux, *Siège et prise de Rouen par les Anglais* (1418–19) (Caen, 1866), 1–12. Richmond, "War at Sea", 104–5.
6 Monstrelet II, 206–7.
7 Page, 1–46.
8 Chambers and Daunt, 73–6. *English Life*, 126–27.
9 Monstrelet II, 221. *English Life*, 128. J. G. Bellamy, *The Law of Treason in England in the Later Middle Ages* (Cambridge, 1970), 153 n.1.
10 Vaughan, *John the Fearless*, 270 (quoting Arch. Dept. du Nord, Lille B17624).
11 Page, 19.
12 Page, 22.
13 Page, 32.
14 *Ibid.*
15 Rymer IV, iii, 82–3.
16 Page, 42.
17 Monstrelet II, 223.
18 Strecche, 176–77.
19 G. Lefèvre-Pontalis, "Episodes de l'invasion anglaise: La Guerre des Partisans dans la Haute-Normandie", *Bibliothèque de l'école des Chartes* 54 (1893), 478–79.
20 *Calendar of Norman Rolls* II (42nd Report of the Deputy Keeper of the Public Records, 1881) 357. J. H. Wylie and W. T. Waugh, *The Reign of Henry the Fifth* III (London, 1929), 259.

CHAPTER XII THE ROAD TO TROYES

1 Rymer IV, iii, 68–9; 70–5.
2 Rymer IV, iii, 79–80.
3 Monstrelet II, 216.
4 *Privy Council* II, 243–44. *English Life*, 139.
5 Pocquet du Haut-Jussé, *La France gouvernée par Jean sans Peur* (Mémoires et documents publiés par la Société de l'école des Chartes 13, Paris, 1959), nos. 645, 1106.
6 Delpit, *Collection Générale*, 226.
7 *English Life*, 145.
8 C. de Fauquembergue, *Journal, 1417–35*, ed. A. Tuetey (Société de l'Histoire de France, Paris, 1903–6), I, 306. Rymer IV, iii, 125; 126–7.
9 *Historia Anglicana*, 329–30. *English Life*, 147–48.
10 Rymer IV, 128, 131.
11 Waurin, 286.
12 *Parisian Journal*, 146.
13 Chambers and Daunt, 82–3.
14 *Rot. Parl.* IV, 117–18.
15 A. R. Myers, "The Captivity of a Royal Witch", *Bulletin of the John Rylands Library* 24 (1940), 263–84.
16 Rymer IV, iii, 135. *Issues*, 361.
17 *Gesta*, 248. *English Life*, 155.
18 *Historia Anglicana*, 331.
19 Fauquembergue I, 352.
20 P. Bonenfant, *Du Meutre de Montereau au Traité de Troyes* (Brussels, 1958), 120–25, 180–83.
21 Fauquembergue I, 361.
22 *English Life*, 158–59.

23 Rymer IV, iii, 171–74.
24 Rymer IV, iii, 175. *Historia Anglicana*, 335.
25 Monstrelet II, 277.
26 Monstrelet II, 297; 314–15.
27 *Parisian Journal*, 307.

CHAPTER XIII   HEIR AND REGENT OF FRANCE

 1 *Parisian Journal*, 151.
 2 J. J. Champollion-Figeach, *Lettres des rois, reines, et autres personages des cours de France et d'Angleterre* (Collection des documents inédits, Paris, 1847), II, 379–80.
 3 Waurin, 321–22. St-Rémy II, 11–12. Pierre de Fenin, *Mémoires*, ed. L. M. E. Dupont (Société de l'Histoire de France, Paris, 1837), 141.
 4 *English Life*, 167–68.
 5 Strecche, 183.
 6 Juvenal des Ursins, 381–82.
 7 *English Life*, 168–71.
 8 Waurin, 329–30. *Privy Council* II, 278–79.
 9 Chastellain, 554. Supra, p. 100.
10 Juvenal des Ursins, 382.
11 *Historia Anglicana*, 335.
12 Waurin, 341–42. Monstrelet II, 295–300. Fenin, 147.
13 *Parisian Journal*, 153–54.
14 Rymer IV, iii, 192–93; 194.
15 *Issues*, 364.
16 Chastellain, 198. Monstrelet II, 305.
17 Pseudo-Elmham, 282–84.
18 *Parisian Journal*, 158, 162.
19 M. R. Jouet, *La Résistance à l'occupation anglaise en basse-Normande 1418–50* (Cahiers des Annales de Normandie 5, Caen, 1967) 15–28, 39–54. Rymer IV, iii, 158. *Calendar Norman Rolls* II, 356.
20 E. F. Jacob, *The Fifteenth Century, 1399–1485* (Oxford, 1969), 202–10.
21 *Brut*, 447.
22 Monstrelet II, 307.
23 *Rot. Parl.* IV, 135.
24 Jacob, *Fifteenth Century*, 204–5.
25 Supra, p. 98.
26 *Historia Anglicana*, 337–38.
27 Rymer IV, iv, 28–30
28 Rymer IV, iv, 30–31. Kingsford, *English Historical Literature*, 290. *English Life*, 174.
29 Rymer IV, iv, 15–16.
30 Monstrelet II, 307–8. Chastellain, 210–17. *Issues*, 368.

CHAPTER XIV   THE LAST CAMPAIGN

 1 R. A. Newhall, *The English Conquest of Normandy 1416–24* (New Haven, 1928), 276 n. 35 (quoting BM Cottonian MSS Claudius A VIII, f. 10v.).
 2 Rymer IV, iv, 33.
 3 Chambers and Daunt, 83.
 4 Chambers and Daunt, 83–4.
 5 J. Evans, *English Art, 1307–1461* (Oxford, 1949), 110.

6 Musée de l'Armée, Paris.
7 R. C. Clephan, "The Ordnance of the Fourteenth and Fifteenth Centuries", *Archaeological Journal*, 2nd ser. 18 (1911), 49–84.
8 *Parisian Journal*, 166.
9 St-Rémy II, 45.
10 Waurin, 404.
11 Waurin, 392–93; 404–7. *English Life*, 175–78. Rymer IV, iv, 64–6, 70.
12 *English Life*, 178–79. Fauquembergue II, 50–1.
13 Chambers and Daunt, 144.
14 Rymer IV, iv, 51–8; 62; 72.
15 Rymer IV, iv, 63.
16 Fauquembergue II, 56. *Parisian Journal*, 173.
17 A. Morosini, *Chronique*, ed. G. Lefèvre-Pontalis and L. Dorez (Société de l'Histoire de France, 1902), IV, 297.
18 St-Denis VI, 481.
19 Chastellain, 528.
20 Chastellain, 529.
21 Pseudo-Elmham, 333.
22 *Rot. Parl.* IV, 248.
23 *English Life*, 182.
24 Pseudo-Elmham, 334.
25 *English Life*, 183. Chastellain, 531. Pseudo-Elmham, 336.
26 Chastellain, 532.
27 *English Life*, 183–85. *Historia Anglicana*, 345–46.
28 Monstrelet II, 375.
29 Chambers and Daunt, 144–46. *Brut*, 430, 493.
30 *Parisian Journal*, 183.

EPILOGUE

1 *Oxford Book of Medieval English Verse*, ed. C. and K. Sisam (Oxford, 1970), 381–82.
2 St-Denis VI, 481.
3 Alain Chartier, *Le Quadrilogus Invectif*, ed. E. Droz (Paris, 1923), 4.
4 Hardyng, 744.
5 *King's Works* I, 488–89.
6 John Stow, *Survey of London*, ed. C. L. Kingsford (Oxford, 1908), 419.
7 Lannoy, 173.
8 *An English Chronicle from 1377–1461*, ed. J. S. Davies (Camden Society, Old Series 64, 1856), 52.

THE NARRATIVE SOURCES

1 J. S. Roskell and F. Taylor, "The Authorship and Purpose of the *Gesta Henrici Quinti*", *Bulletin of the John Rylands Library* 53 (1971), 428–64; 54 (1972), 223–40. The full text has not yet been published.

Bibliography

Full bibliographies of this period are easily available in such standard works as
E. F. Jacob, *The Fifteenth Century* (Oxford, 1969); M. H. Keen, *England in the
Later Middle Ages* (London, 1973); and K. Fowler, *The Age of Plantagenet and
Valois* (London, 1967) that it has seemed superfluous to repeat them. The following
brief list suggests a few particularly interesting general works on the period, as
well as some especially relevant to a further exploration of King Henry and his
time. In addition, the Notes contain complete bibliographical references to all
works cited.

Allmand, C. T., ed. *Society at War*. Edinburgh, 1973.
Aston, Margaret. *The Fifteenth Century: The Prospect of Europe*. London, 1968.
Burne, A. H. *The Agincourt War*. London, 1956.
Calmette, Joseph. *Chute et Relèvement de la France sous Charles VI et Charles VII*.
   Paris, 1945.
Contamine, Philippe. *Azincourt*. Paris, 1964.
Du Boulay, F. R. H. *An Age of Ambition: English Society in the Late Middle Ages*.
   London, 1970.
Fowler, K., ed. *The Hundred Years War*. London, 1971.
Jacob, E. F. *Henry V and the Invasion of France*. London, 1947.
Keen, M. H. *The Laws of War in the Late Middle Ages*. London, 1965.
Lander, J. R. *Conflict and Stability in Fifteenth-Century England*. London, 1969.
Mathew, Gervase. *The Court of Richard II*. London, 1968.
McFarlane, K. B. *John Wycliffe and the Beginnings of English Non-Conformity*.
   London, 1952.
   Lancastrian Kings and Lollard Knights. Oxford, 1972.
Newhall, R. A. *The English Conquest of Normandy 1416–24*. New Haven, 1929.
Perroy, Edouard. *The Hundred Years War*. Intro. to the English edition by D. C.
   Douglas. London, 1965.
Scattergood, V. J. *Politics and Poetry in the Fifteenth Century*. London, 1971.
Vaughan, Richard. *John the Fearless*. London, 1966.
   Philip the Good. London, 1970.

Index

Index

Abbeville (Somme), 84, 85, 180, 184

Aberystwyth (Card.), 19, 22, 23, 25

Agincourt (Pas-de-Calais), xi, 55, 59, 68, 69, 73, 85, 86, 87, 90, 91n, 92, 93, 101, 108, 110, 111, 113, 117, 119, 150, 152, 162, 169, 170, 172, 173, 186, 188, 189, 191, 192, 193

Albret, Charles d', Constable of France, 35, 83, 84, 85, 87, 90, 108

Alençon (Orne), 123, 131, 145, 172, 174

Alençon, John, Duke of, 36, 87, 89, 90, 110

Alexander V, "Pisan" pope, 102

Alington, William, 165

Almeley (Hereford), 50

Amiens (Somme), 84, 85, 180

André, Master Jean, 61

Angers (Maine-et-Loire), 172, 174

Anjou, county of, 53, 123, 131, 144, 165, 172, 174

Anjou, Duke of, 110

Anvin (Pas-de-Calais), 85

Aquitaine, duchy of, xi, 29, 30, 32, 36, 54, 55, 76, 77, 147, 166

Argentan (Orne), 131

Arly, Sir Sarrasin d', 184

Armagnac, Bernard, Count of, 35, 36, 108, 109, 110, 111, 113, 124, 133, 135, 149

Arques (Pas-de-Calais), 84

Arras, Bishop of, 152

Artois, 113

Arundel, Richard, Earl of (d. 1397), 5

Arundel, Thomas, Archbishop of Canterbury, 3, 5, 8, 23, 28, 29, 31, 32, 33, 34, 35, 41, 44, 45, 46, 47, 193

Arundel, Thomas, Earl of, 8, 14, 35, 42, 82

Avignon (Vaucluse), 102

Badby, John, 33, 44

Bangor (Caern.), 14

Bangor, Bishop of, 75

Bar, Edward, Duke of, 87, 90

Barbasan, Lord of, 159, 160, 161

Baugé (Maine-et-Loire), 168, 169, 171, 172, 173, 174

Bavaria, Louis, Duke of, 17, 161

Bayeux (Calvados), 123, 125, 131, 132, 187

Bayonne (Pyr.-Atl.), 148, 149

Beaufort (Maine-et-Loire), 172

Beaufort, Henry, Bishop of Winchester, 28, 29, 32, 42, 45, 58, 62, 72, 92, 95, 105, 106, 109, 168, 169, 182, 188

Beaufort, Joan, 169

Beaufort, John, Earl of Somerset, 28, 31, 173

Beaufort, Thomas, Earl of Dorset, then Duke of Exeter, 71, 75, 82, 108, 109, 114, 118, 136, 141, 157, 164, 174, 177, 181, 182
Beaugency (Loiret), 175
Beaumont (Val-d'Oise), 133, 152
Beauvais (Oise), 111, 115
Beauvais, Bishop of, 145
Bec-Hellouin (Eure), 133
Bedford, John, Duke of, brother of Henry V, 2, 32, 50, 57, 113, 114, 119, 121, 132, 146, 149, 157, 167, 179, 180, 181, 182, 183, 185
Bellême (Orne), 123
Benedict XIII, "Avignonese" pope, 102, 105
Benham, Master Robert, 92
Berkeley, Thomas, Lord, 24, 25, 65
Berkhamsted (Herts.), 32
Berry, Jean, Duke of, 7, 35, 36, 61n, 110, 111
Berry, Marie de, 7, 91
Berwick (Salop.), 20
Bethencourt (Aisne), 84
Beverley (Yorks.), 168
Blackheath (London), 92, 111, 167, 184
Blanchard, Alain, 141
Blanche, daughter of Henry IV, 2, 17, 161
Blangy (Pas-de-Calais), 85
Blois (Loire-et-Cher), 133
Bohemia, Anne of, Queen, wife of Richard II, 1, 6, 43
Bohemia, Wenceslas, King of, 44
Bohun, Mary de, 1st wife of Henry IV when Earl of Derby, 1, 2, 18, 43
Bokelond, Richard, 82
Bonet, Master Honoré de, 69
Bonneval (Eure-et-Loire), 175
Bordeaux (Gironde), 29, 30, 32, 36, 54, 77, 147
Bordeaux, Archbishop of, 147
Boucicaut, Jean de, Marshal of France, 5, 83, 87, 90, 100
Bourg (Gironde), 29
Bourbon, Bastard of, 120
Bourbon, John, Duke of, 35, 36, 84, 87, 90, 91, 110, 118, 119, 120, 170

Bourges (Cher), 36, 145
Bourges, Archbishop of, 55, 61
Bouteiller, Guy le, 137, 141, 143
Boves (Somme), 84
Brabant, Anthony, Duke of, 89, 90
Brabant, John, Duke of, 170
Bradwardyn, William, 73
Bramham Moor (Yorks.), 30
Braquemont, Lord of, 61
Bretigny, Treaty of, xi, 53, 54, 110, 112, 144, 148
Bridlington (Yorks.), 168
Bristol, 23, 119, 168
Brittany, duchy of, 53, 99, 123
Brittany, Arthur of, 161
Brittany, John, Duke of, 131, 146, 179
Bruges (Flanders), 73
Bruges, Richard, 70
Bruges, William, 70–71
Bubwith, Nicholas, Bishop of Bath and Wells, 103
Burgundy, duchy of, 136
Burgundy, John the Fearless, Duke of, 35, 44, 52, 60, 66, 77, 90, 100, 105, 110, 112, 113, 115, 116, 117, 124, 133, 135, 137, 139, 140, 141, 146, 147, 149, 150, 159, 163
Burgundy, Philip the Bold, Duke of, 8, 100
Burgundy, Philip the Good, Duke of, 59n., 70, 90, 91, 100, 101, 116, 149, 151, 152, 153, 154, 155, 156, 157, 158, 159, 161, 162, 163, 170, 171, 174, 180, 181, 182, 183, 193
Burton, Thomas, 46
Bury St Edmunds, Abbot of, 24

Caen (Calvados), 3, 99, 123, 125, 126, 127, 128, 129, 130, 131, 134, 166
Caen, castle of, 127, 129, 130, 131
Caernarvon, 14, 16, 22
Calais (Pas-de-Calais), 7, 30, 31, 36, 54, 62, 67, 76, 77, 82, 83, 84, 85, 86, 91, 92, 109, 111, 112, 113, 115, 116, 117, 167, 171, 174, 184
Cambridge, 3, 38, 99, 169
Cambridge, Richard, Earl of, 48, 49, 78
Canterbury (Kent), 29, 92, 114, 167

Canterbury, Archbishops of, *see* Arundel, Thomas; Chichele, Henry
Canterbury, cathedral of, 18, 43, 173
Canterbury, Christchurch, 3
Canterbury, Treaty of, 114, 117, 118
Cany (Seine-Mar.), 108
Capgrave, John, 39
Captal de Buch, brother of the Count of Foix, 148, 179
Carmarthen, 22, 23, 24
Castile, 4, 53, 148, 149
Castile, Constance of, 2nd wife of John of Gaunt, 1
Catherine of France, Queen of Henry V, 53, 54, 61, 62, 78, 146, 147, 150, 151, 155, 156, 161, 162, 164, 165, 167, 168, 172, 178, 181, 184, 188, 189
Catterick, John, Bishop of St David's, then Lichfield, then Exeter, 43, 103, 107
Caudebec (Seine-Mar.), 133, 138, 143
Charenton (Paris), 154, 181
Charles V, King of France, 7, 54, 66, 136, 162, 181
Charles VI, King of France, 4, 7, 8, 9, 35, 55, 60, 61, 63, 78, 83, 90, 103, 105, 124, 145, 147, 153, 154, 155, 156, 157, 160, 162, 163, 164, 170, 185
Charles, dauphin of France, later Charles VII, 110, 124, 146, 147, 149, 155, 157, 163, 174, 175, 179
Charles the Bad, King of Navarre, 151
Charlton, John, Lord Powys, 15, 16
Charolais, Count of, *see* Burgundy, Duke Philip the Good
Chartier, Alain, 187
Chartres (Eure-et-Loire), 124, 133, 174, 175
Chastellain, Georges, 164, 181n, 193
Château Gaillard, 146, 160, 161
Chaucer, Geoffrey, 3, 37, 69, 75
Chaucer, Thomas, 32
Chaumont, Bertrand de, 162
Chef de Caux (Seine-Mar.), 79
Cherbourg (Manche), 120, 133, 138
Chester (Ches.), 9, 11, 12, 14, 15, 20, 22
Chester, earldom of, 11

Chesterton (Warw.), 49
Chichele, Henry, Archbishop of Canterbury, 62, 99, 103, 106, 107, 141, 145, 167
Clarence, Thomas, Duke of, brother of Henry V, 2, 31, 36, 39, 68, 81, 82, 126, 129, 130, 133, 135, 140, 148, 167, 168, 172, 173
Clarence, Duchess of, 155, 173
Clermont, county of, 170
Clux, Sir Hartonk von, 180
Col, Gontier, 61, 62
Colnet, Master Nicholas, 73
Compiègne (Oise), 136, 180
Constance (Baden), 70, 103, 104, 117
Constance, Council of, 63, 99, 103, 104, 107, 111, 191
Constantinople, 100
Conway (Caern.), 15
Corbeil (Essonne), 147, 162, 180, 181
Corbie (Somme), 85
Corfu, 5
Cornwall, Sir John, 89, 135
Cosne-sur-Loire (Nièvre), 180
Coucy, Enguerrand de, 100
Coudray, Richard, 145
Courtenay, Master Richard, Bishop of Norwich, 25, 26, 34, 60n, 62, 82, 97
Coventry (Warw.), 36, 168
Crécy (Somme), 54, 84, 88
Croprede, prebend of, 106
Cynllaith Owain, lordship of, 13, 19

Dartmouth (Devon), 115
Dauphin of France, Charles, *see* Charles, dauphin of France
Dauphin, John (d. 1417), 110, 112, 124
Dauphin, Louis (d. 1415), 81, 83, 110
Despenser, Edward, Lord, 12
Despenser, Hugh, Lord, 16
Dijon (Côte-d'or), 150, 159, 175, 180
Domfront (Oise), 123, 133, 138
Dordrecht (Low Countries), 117
Dorset, Earl of, *see* Beaufort, Thomas
Douglas, Earl William, 152, 169
Dover (Kent), 92, 111, 167, 171
Dreux (Eure-et-Loire), 175
Dublin, 9

Du Guesclin, Bertrand, 54, 83
Dyss, Friar Thomas, 99

Edward III, King of England, xi, 52, 54, 76, 84, 127
Elmham, Thomas of, x, 54, 56, 58, 192, 193
Eltham, manor of, 18, 28, 39, 46, 47, 92, 93, 167
Eric, King of Denmark, 17, 26, 97
Erpingham, Sir Thomas, 31, 46, 88, 113
Eu (Seine-Mar.), 84
Eu, Charles d', Artois, Count of, 87, 90, 91, 182
Evreux (Eure), 133, 146
Exeter, Bishop of (Edmund Lacy), 98
Exeter, Duke of, see Beaufort, Thomas

Falaise (Calvados), 98, 123, 131–32
Fauquembergue, Clement de, 147, 180
Ferrer, St Vincent, 99–100, 131
Fitzhugh, Lord, 103
Flanders, county of, 8, 30, 52, 53, 113, 117, 144, 163, 192
Fleming, Richard, Bishop of Lincoln, 168
Flint, 12
Foix, Gaston Phébus, Count of, 3, 116, 179
Forster, Master John, 106
Fresnay-le-Vicomte (Sarthe), 152
Froissart, Jean, ix, 5, 53, 73, 76, 127
Fusoris, Master John, 60n

Gamme, Davy, 90
Gaucourt, Ralph, Sire de, 81, 118, 119, 182
Gaunt, John of, Duke of Lancaster, xi, 1, 2, 3, 4, 5, 6, 28, 29, 38, 56, 70, 72, 98
Genoa, 169
Gerson, Jean, 4
Giles of Rome, 37, 65
Gisors (Eure), 149, 174
Glamorgan, 18, 23
Glendower, Griffith, son of Owen, 24
Glendower, Meredith, son of Owen, 26

Glendower, Owen, 13, 15, 16, 17, 18, 19, 20, 21, 22, 23, 24, 25, 26, 30, 48, 193
Glendower, Tudor, brother of Owen, 24
Gloucester, Humphrey, Duke of, brother of Henry V, 2, 3n, 57, 89, 111, 116, 117, 131, 133, 138, 155, 171, 179, 182, 191
Gloucester, Humphrey (d. 1399), son of Duke Thomas, 7, 9
Gloucester, Thomas of Woodstock, Duke of, son of Edward III, 1, 5, 6
Glyndyfrdwy (Merion.), 13, 14, 19
Graville, Sir John, 134, 135
Gray, Sir Thomas (of Heton), 48, 49, 78
Gregory XII, "Roman" pope, 102, 105
Grey, Reginald, Lord, of Ruthin, 13, 14, 18
Grey, Richard, Lord, of Codnor, 79
Greyndon, Sir John, 73
Griffith, Llewellyn ap, of Cayo, 16
Grosmont (Mon.), 23
Guines (Pas-de-Calais), 91
Guitry, Lord of, 159
Gwent, 18, 23, 24

Hainault, county of, 153
Hainault, Jacqueline, Countess of, 170–71
Hainault, Philippa, Queen of Edward III, xi
Hallum, Robert, Bishop of Salisbury, 26n, 103, 104, 105
Hanmer, Sir David, 13
Harcourt, Jacques d', Count of Tancarville, 174
Hardyng, John, 187, 193
Harfleur (Seine-Mar.), 22, 63, 73, 77, 79, 81, 82, 83, 85, 92, 108, 109, 111, 112, 113, 114, 115, 118, 119, 120, 122, 123, 138, 172
Harlech (Merion.), 16, 19, 22, 23, 25, 26
Heilly, Lord Jacques de, 89
Henewer, Master Peter, 152

Henry IV, of Bolingbroke, King of England: 10, 11, 12, 13, 14, 16, 18, 19, 20, 21, 23, 24, 28, 29–31, 35, 36, 39–40, 41, 43, 46, 48, 54, 63, 66, 76, 103, 121; as Earl of Derby, 2, 4, 5, 6, 7, 8, 9, 29, 70; as Duke of Lancaster, 9, 10, 22

Henry V, of Monmouth, King of England: appearance and character, x–xii, 16–17, 22, 38–40, 41, 43, 55, 94, 187–88, 189, 190; birth and early years, 1, 2–4, 7, 8–9; Welsh campaign, 12, 15–16, 18–21, 22–24, 25–26; attendance at council, 28, 31–32; coronation, 41–42; plots against, 11–12, 46–48, 48–49, 142–43; marriage negotiations, 17–18, 53–54, 62, 63, 78, 146, 147, 155, 156; relations with church, 57, 96–97, 98, 98–100, 101, 103, 105–7; diplomacy, 35, 52–54, 57–59, 60, 61–63, 78, 112, 113, 114, 115–17, 121, 144–45, 145–46, 146–47, 151–52, 153–54, 156, 169, 179–80; military and naval preparations, 67, 71–73, 74–76, 118–19, 119–20, 163, 168–69, 176–77; Harfleur and Agincourt, 79, 81–82, 84–91; campaign in Normandy, 123, 125–26, 129–30, 131–32, 133, 134–35, 136–42, 148; administration of Normandy, 130, 143, 165–67; campaign in France, 158, 159–62, 172–73, 175–76, 178; last days and burial, 180–81, 182–83, 184–85

Henry VI, King of England, 99, 177
Henry VII, King of England, 189
Hereford, 16, 18
Hereford, earldom of, 1, 17
Hesdin (Pas-de-Calais), 91, 184
Hoccleve, Thomas, 37, 38, 59
Holland, William, Count of, 112
Homildon Hill, 19, 21, 30
Honfleur (Calvados), 123
Honyngham, John, 103
Hungerford, Sir Walter, 56, 103
Huntingdon, 24
Huntingdon, John Holand, Earl of (d. 1400), 12

Huntingdon, John Holand, Earl of (d. 1447), 120, 121, 148, 152, 156, 173
Hus, John, 44, 45, 104, 105

Île-de-France, 154, 175
Isabel of Bavaria, Queen, wife of Charles VI, 124, 133, 145, 151, 153, 155
Isabella of France, Queen, 2nd wife of Richard II, 6
Ivry (Eure), 146

James I, King of the Scots, 30, 162, 167, 169, 170, 184
Jerusalem, 3, 5, 105, 183
Joan of Arc, 156, 190
Joan of Navarre, Queen, 2nd wife of Henry IV, 18, 38, 91, 151, 182
John II, the Good, King of France, 53, 54
John XXIII, "Pisan" pope, 102, 103, 104, 105
Joigny (Yonne), 158, 159
Joigny, Count of, 158
Juvenal des Ursins, 160, 186, 192

Kemp, John, Bishop of Rochester, 165
Kempe, Margery, 96
Kenilworth (Warw.), 56, 58, 142n, 168, 193
Kennington (Kent), 16, 45
Kent, Thomas Holland, Earl of (d. 1400), 12
King's Langley (Herts.), 43
Kyeser, Conrad, of Eichstatt, 66, 76

La Flèche (Sarthe), 172
La Marche, John, Count of, 22
Lancaster, duchy of, 6, 11, 56
Lancaster, Blanche, Duchess of, wife of John of Gaunt, 1
Langley, Thomas, Bishop of Durham, 28, 60n, 72, 97, 120, 132, 152, 168
Lannoy, Ghillebert de, 59, 70, 89, 100, 101, 152, 161, 181, 189
Lannoy, Hugh de, 181, 182

La Roche-Guyon (Val-d'Oise), 143, 146

Lay, John, 45

Leeds (Kent), 15

Leicester, 2, 43, 56, 58, 168

Le Mans (Sarthe), 172

Lichfield (Staffs.), 20, 23

Lille (Nord), 44, 113, 139

Lincoln, 168

Lincoln, diocese of, 106

Linet, Robert de, 139

Lisieux (Calvados), 106, 123, 125

Lisieux, Bishop of, 61

L'Isle-Adam, Marshal of France, 157, 174

Livius, Titus, of Forli, x, 42, 191, 192

Llandovery (Carm.), 16

London: 2, 15, 17, 37, 39, 43, 47, 56, 58, 62, 68, 72, 91, 92, 113, 115, 156, 167, 168, 171, 174, 184, 185; City of, 72, 81, 129, 138, 150; mayor of, 46, 72, 91, 92, 132, 135, 167, 179, 184; Tower of, 10, 42, 45, 46, 151, 167

Louviers (Eure), 133, 134, 143

Lucas, Thomas, 49, 50

Lynn (King's Lynn, Norf.), 96, 168

Machynlleth (Mont.), 23

Maine, county of, 53, 123, 131, 144, 152, 165, 172, 174

Maisoncelles (Pas-de-Calais), 85, 86, 91

Manny, Sir Oliver de, 132

Mantes (Yvelines), 106, 133, 146, 147, 148, 151, 174

March, Edmund Mortimer, Earl of, 48, 195, 167, 177

March, Roger Mortimer, Earl of (d. 1398), 6, 7

Martin V, pope, 105, 106, 107

Meaux (Seine-et-Marne), 3, 136, 175, 176, 177, 178, 180, 181

Meaux, Bishop of, 178

Meaux, Market of, 175, 176, 177, 178

Melun (Seine-et-Marne), 100, 136, 147, 149, 151, 159, 160, 161, 162, 169

Merstede, Thomas, 73

Meulan (Yvelines), 133, 147, 148, 149, 151, 152, 180

Molyneux, Nicholas, 68

Monmouth, 1, 42

Monmouth, Henry of, see Henry V

Monstrelet, Enguerrand de, ix, 39, 124, 137, 139, 142, 156, 157, 164, 168, 184, 191, 192

Montereau (Seine-et-Marne), 149, 154, 159, 161

Montivilliers (Seine-Mar.), 81

Montlhéry (Essonne), 124, 136

Mont-St-Michel (Manche), 123, 133, 143

Morgan, Master Philip, 106

Mortimer, Edmund (d. 1409), brother of Roger, Earl of March, 18, 23, 26

Mowbray, John, Earl Marshal of Norfolk (d. 1432), 82, 152

Mowbray, Thomas, Earl of Norfolk (d. 1399), 6

Mowbray, Thomas, Earl of Norfolk (d. 1405), 24, 30

Nesle (Somme), 84

Nesle, Guy de, Lord of Offemont, 177

Netter, Thomas, 99

Nevers, John of, see Burgundy, John the Fearless

Nevers, Philip, Count of, brother of Duke John of Burgundy, 90, 91

Nicolas, Sir Harris, 193

Nicopolis, battle of, 100

Normandy, Duchy, of, xi, 53, 54, 55, 75, 77, 79, 102, 122, 123, 124, 125, 131, 133, 134, 143, 144, 146, 148, 149, 150, 152, 154, 155, 163, 165, 167, 170, 173, 174, 175, 182, 188

Northampton, 14

Norwich (Norfolk): 168; Bishops of, see Courtenay Master Richard; Wakeryng, John

Nottingham, 168

Oke, John, 24

Oldcastle, Sir John, Lord Cobham, 32, 35, 44, 45, 46, 47, 48, 49, 50, 93, 99, 132

Oldcastle, Joan, wife of John and grand-daughter of Lord Cobham, 44
Orace, 178
Orange, Prince of, 161
Orléans (Loiret), 60, 175, 180
Orléans, Charles, Duke of, 35, 36, 68, 87, 90, 91, 110, 118, 152, 170, 182
Orléans, Louis, Duke of (d. 1407), 8, 30, 35, 68, 149
Orsini, Cardinal, 134, 145
Orthez (Pyr.-Atl.), 179
Oxford, 3n, 29, 33, 34, 51, 98, 169

Page, John, 137, 138, 140, 141, 193
Parcheminer, William, 46
Paris: 7, 8, 22, 29, 44, 56, 60, 61, 63, 97, 110, 111, 112, 124, 133, 135, 136, 144, 145, 146, 147, 148, 150, 152, 153, 154, 160, 162, 163, 164, 174, 175, 177, 178, 179, 180, 182, 185; Bastille St-Antoine, 136, 157, 164; Hôtel St-Pol, 60, 162, 164, 178; Louvre, 111, 162, 164, 178; bourgeois of (chronicler), 84, 125, 150, 164, 180, 185
Patrington, Stephen, Bishop of St David's, 98, 99
Pelham, Sir John, 38
Percy, Henry, Earl of Northumberland (d. 1408), 12, 17, 19, 20, 21, 23, 24, 30
Percy, Henry (Hotspur), (d. 1403), 11, 12, 15, 16, 18, 19, 20, 21, 22, 40, 193
Percy, Thomas, Earl of Worcester (d. 1403), 17, 20, 21
Péronne (Somme), 85
Philippa, daughter of Henry IV, 2, 17, 26, 97
Picardy, 52, 136, 167, 174, 180
Pisa, Council of, 26n, 102, 103, 104
Pisan, Christine de, 65, 66, 91
Pleshy (Essex), 189
Poissy (Yvelines), 152
Poitiers (Vienne), 53, 54, 88
Polton, Master Thomas, 107
Pont de l'Arche (Eure), 134, 135, 136, 143, 146
Pontefract (Yorks.), 168

Pontoise (Val-d'Oise), 124, 133, 147, 148, 149
Portsmouth (Hants.), 18
Provins (Seine-et-Marne), 146, 147, 149
"Pseudo-Elmham", 183n, 192

Randolph, Brother John, 151
Ravenspur (Yorks.), 9, 29
Rhodes, 5, 100
Richard I, the Lionhearted, King of England, x–xi
Richard II, King of England, 1, 4, 6, 7, 8, 9, 10, 11, 12, 20, 22, 25, 28, 29, 40, 41, 43, 48, 50, 54, 55, 56, 96, 97
Richental, 104
Richmond, Arthur, Count of, 90
Robsart, Sir Louis, 153
Rochester (Kent), 92, 111
Rolle, Richard, 95
Rome, 8, 102
Rouen (Seine-Mar.): 19, 83, 84, 85, 109, 123, 133, 134, 136, 137, 143, 145, 152, 154, 164, 165, 170, 173, 184; siege of, 137–42, 145
Rous, Marshal de, 152
Ruisseauville (Pas-de-Calais), 85, 91
Ruthin (Denb.), 13, 14, 16, 18
Rutland, Edward, Earl of, 12

St Albans (Herts.): 168, 192; abbot of, 98; chronicler of, *see* Walsingham, Thomas
St-Denis, abbey of, 154, 184, 185, 192
St-Germain-en-Laye (Yvelines), 152
St-Maur-des-Fossées (Val-de-Marne), 144, 183n
St-Omer (Pas-de-Calais), 76, 116, 117
St-Quentin (Aisne), 84
St-Rémy, Jean Le Fèvre de, 60, 85, 177, 192, 193
St Vaast-La-Hougue (Manche), 125
Salisbury, John Montague, Earl of (d. 1400), 12
Salisbury, Thomas Montague, Earl of (d. 1428), 116, 125, 152, 165, 173, 174
Sandwich (Kent), 115

Scrope, Henry, Lord of Masham (d. 1415), 32, 48, 49, 78

Scrope, Richard, Archbishop of York (d. 1405), 24, 30, 32, 39, 49, 97

Scudamore, Sir John, 24, 25, 26

Sées (Orne), 131

Senlis (Oise), 133, 180

Sens (Yonne), 156, 158, 159, 175

Sens, Archbishop of, 90

Sheen: manor of, 56, 97; monastery of, 3, 97, 113

Shrewsbury (Salop.): 14, 19, 20, 21, 22, 30, 151, 168, 193; battle of, 20–21

Sigismund, King of Hungary, Bohemia, and Holy Roman Emperor, 49, 63, 71, 100, 101, 102, 103, 104, 105, 111, 112, 113, 114, 115, 117, 118, 161, 179, 180

Sluys, 73, 100

Smallhithe (Kent), 114, 120

Somerset, Earl of, see Beaufort, John

Soper, William, 74

Southampton, 49, 62, 63, 74, 75, 78, 120, 124, 125

Springhouse, Sir Edmund, 129

Stafford, Edmund, Earl of (d. 1403), 20

Strata Florida, abbey of, 16

Strecche, John, canon of Kenilworth, 58, 142–43, 193

Suffolk, Michael de la Pole, Earl of Suffolk (d. Sept., 1415), 82

Suffolk, Michael de la Pole, Earl of Suffolk (d. Oct., 1415), 90

Suffolk, William de la Pole, Earl of Suffolk, 165

Swan, William, 106, 107

Swineshead, John, 25

Sycharth (Denb.), 13

Thomas, Rhys ap, 42

Tichfield, abbey of, 63

Tiptoft, Sir John, 32, 117, 118

Touques (Calvados), 123, 124, 125

Touraine, county of, 53, 144

Tours (Indre-et-Loire), 133, 172

Tramecourt (Pas-de-Calais), 86, 87, 91n

Troyes (Aube), 133, 151, 153, 154, 156, 163

Troyes, Treaty of, xi, 153, 155, 157, 161, 162, 166, 167, 168, 170, 174, 179, 183

Troyes, Bishop of, 156

Tudor, Owen, 189

Tudor, Rhys ap, 14, 15

Tudor, William ap, 14, 15

Tutbury (Staffs.), 25

Twickenham, 97

Ullerston, Master Richard, 26, 37

Umfraville, Sir Gilbert, 35, 140, 173, 193

Usk (Mon.), 24

Usk, Adam of, 14, 15, 16, 26, 193

Valenciennes (Nord), 171

Valmont (Seine-Mar.), 108, 109

Vaurus, Bastard of, 175, 178

Vegetius, 65, 121

Vendôme, Louis, Count of, 61, 90

Verneuil (Eure), 123, 131

Vernon (Eure), 81, 146

Vexin, 147, 149

Veyse, John, 24

Villeneuve-le-Roi (Yonne), 175

Vincennes (Val-de-Marne), 154, 162, 178, 181, 182, 183

Voyenne (Aisne), 84

Wakeryng, John, Bishop of Norwich, 113

Walsingham, shrine of, 168

Walsingham, Thomas, monk and chronicler of St Albans, x, 18, 33, 41, 43, 49, 50, 57, 76, 125, 161, 169, 192

Ware, Master Henry, 79

Warwick, Richard Beauchamp, Earl of, 3, 5, 6, 103, 111, 113, 115, 133, 138, 145, 146, 153, 167, 177, 180, 182

Waterford, 9

Waterton, Robert, 152

Waurin, Jean de, 116, 192

Welshpool (Mont.), 16, 50

Westminster: 10, 12, 13, 36, 39, 40, 42, 43, 47, 56, 58, 93, 98, 109, 113, 120, 167, 168, 183, 184; Abbey, 41, 96, 185, 188, 189; abbot of, 12, 103; palace of, 42, 112, 117, 167

Whittington, Richard, 31

Winchester (Hants): 62, 63, 74; Bishop of, *see* Beaufort, Henry

Windsor (Berks.), 11, 12, 71, 101, 177

Winter, John, 68

Worcester, 16, 24, 107

Worcester, Earl of, *see* Percy, Thomas

Wycliffe, John, 34, 51, 96, 98, 104

Wydeville, Richard, 165

Yolande, Queen of Jerusalem and Sicily, widow of Duke Louis of Anjou, 131

York, 168

York, Archbishop of, *see* Scrope, Richard

York, Edward, Duke of (d. 1415), 3, 36, 62, 90